TOWARDS A POLITICS OF COMPASSION

Socio-Political Dimensions of Christian Responses to Suffering

Emeka Christian Obiezu, OSA

AuthorHouse™
1663 Liberty Drive, Suite 200
Bloomington, IN 47403
www.authorhouse.com
Phone: 1-800-839-8640

© 2008 Emeka Christian Obiezu, OSA. All rights reserved.

No part of this book may be reproduced, stored in a retrieval system, or transmitted by any means without the written permission of the author.

First published by AuthorHouse 8/13/2008

ISBN: 978-1-4343-9965-6 (e)
ISBN: 978-1-4343-9964-9 (sc)
ISBN: 978-1-4343-9966-3 (hc)

Library of Congress Control Number: 2008906039

Printed in the United States of America
Bloomington, Indiana

This book is printed on acid-free paper.

In loving memory of Fathers Clement James Danock OSA, Robert Okey Obiagwu and Francis Ngozi Ajali, my friends and colleagues who died in 2007.

Contents

PREFACE	ix
ACKNOWLEDGEMENTS	xiii
ABBREVIATIONS/ ACRONYMS	xv
INTRODUCTION	xix
CHAPTER ONE: SUFFERING	**1**
Defining Suffering	1
Types of suffering in relation to evil	3
The Effects of Suffering on its Victims	9
Destructive suffering	10
Transformative Suffering	11
Responding to suffering	13
Theoretical theodicy	13
Apathy	15
Practical or pastoral approaches	16
Summary	18
CHAPTER TWO: COMPASSION	**19**
Towards a meaning of compassion	19
Christian Understanding of Compassion in Relation to Socio-moral and Political Concerns and Actions	26
Towards a Politics[153] of Compassion	33
Compassion in Relation to Socio-moral and Political Concerns and Action: A Response to the Critics	39
CHAPTER THREE: SUFFERING AND COMPASSION: A NIGERIAN PERSPECTIVE	**45**
Suffering: A Nigerian Perspective	45
Suffering in Nigeria: A Description	46
Causes of Suffering in Nigeria	57
Compassion: A Nigerian Perspective	70
The Church[297] and its response to socio-economic and political situations in Nigeria	70
Accounting for the disabilities of the Nigerian church in taking up socio-moral and political actions in response to the Nigerian sufferings	75
Summary	80
CHAPTER FOUR: POLITICS OF COMPASSION IN RELA-	

TION TO THE NIGERIAN CONTEXT 83
   The Meaning of a Politics of Compassion 84
   Implications of a Politics of Compassion 85
      Preferential Option for the Poor 86
      Inclusive Community 95
      Solidarity with the Earth: a Christian compassionate response to climate change 98
   Challenges of Politics of Compassion 107
   Dynamics of a Politics of Compassion 117
      Communal Prayer 117
      Forgiveness 120
   Summary 122
CONCLUSION 123
(Notes) 127
SELECT BIBLIOGRAPHY 171
INDEX 193

PREFACE

For the past ten years I have been actively engaged in many activities that have opened my eyes to the untold hardship of various people in many parts of the world. Some of these experiences occurred while serving on the Commission of Justice and Peace both in Nigeria and Canada and others while representing my Augustinian Order in the United Nations and participating in NGO conferences and workshops. There was also the suffering I encountered in my daily parish ministry. Such indelible experiences are the reality of deep and wide gulf between the rich and the poor, between the oppressors and the oppressed, between the advantaged and the disadvantaged. These sufferings are as deep and torturous as those experienced in my very country Nigeria, where injustice and corruption have contributed to the untold hardship of so many of its people. The thought of these various sufferings have kept me up many a night. It is from this backdrop that I seek in this book to provide a critical theological hermeneutic for a fruitful and effective Christian witness within the world of Nigerian economy and politics. It is my conviction that an in-depth critique to these issues will provide some positive movement towards eliminating the suffering of my people.

This book explores critically the contemporary socio-political issues in Nigeria and proposes some specific practical measures to tackle the situation. This will serve as my contribution to the local Church's response to these challenges. The work explores especially the concepts of 'suffering' and 'compassion,' in providing a theological context for the creative development of a 'politics of compassion' that is original, doctrinally sound, and pastorally functional.

Compassion as a response to suffering is a primordial spiritual force that binds us to one another and to the whole of creation. To a Christian, compassion is both a vocation and the basis for redemptive hope. Focusing on the contemporary Nigerian situation, this work argues that the widespread and scandalous forms of suffering, economic deprivation, human rights violations, and ecological destruction demand that one expands the horizon of Christian compassion beyond the traditional focus on individual-personal cases. Drawing upon relevant theology and social theory in critical but creative ways, I identify this orientation in terms of a "politics of compassion," an advocacy inaugurated by Jesus of Nazareth in response to the social and political ills of his time. It challenges Christians to witness to Christ through socio-moral and political concern and action in solidarity with suffering humanity.

The academic research and theological perspective of this work are meant to serve practical pastoral purposes, namely: the theoretical groundwork and specific motivation for Christian participation in the political process and economy of Nigeria. This work is consistent with the tradition and reputation of promoting dialogue on theology and social justice in the developing countries, as well as with the commitment to the cause of the oppressed and exploited. In its analysis and application, this book is targeted to Nigerian Christians, though it might be adapted and applied to situations and places beyond that context.

Chapter One explores the general meaning of suffering and discusses various kinds of suffering and its relationships with dimensions of natural evil, moral evil and structural evil. It considers the effects of evil on the victims, surveys various possible responses to them, and it takes cognizance of the varying viewpoints of select scholars who focus on suffering, especially as it relates to compassion and solidarity.

Chapter Two defines and analyzes the concept of compassion, in reference to current scholarship on the subject. It compares compassion with various concepts that are often confused with it. It explores the concept of compassion within the Christian tradition and demonstrates that, for Jesus Christ, compassion goes beyond interpersonal activity to include socio-moral and political concerns and activities. This politics of compassion is made clear through various illustrations. In response to critics of compassion, I articulate a politics of compassion that provides the foundation for this work.

Chapter Three analyzes the socio-economic and political situation of Nigeria, with a view to identifying various forms and causes of suffering. This chapter also evaluates compassion within the Nigerian context while surveying the various ways the Church has responded to the sufferings therein. Since the application of my proposal varies from place to place and situation to situation, Chapter Four, explores the Nigerian context to survey and discover the meaning, the implications, and indeed the challenges of this new paradigm of compassion. This chapter also engages elements of spirituality that give substance to and enhance our commitment to justice and effective political action, thereby ensuring a healthy link between the spirituality, ethics and liberation initiatives.

The book concludes by calling on Nigerian Christians to seize this moment of compassion and move towards eliminating the incredible suffering of their land.

ACKNOWLEDGEMENTS

I remain indebted in a special way to God Almighty for inspiring and strengthening me to write this book. My innumerable thanks go to my Order of St. Augustine in Nigeria for their moral support. I am eternally indebted to the Canadian Province of the Order for their brotherly love and financial support, especially for shouldering the responsibility of publishing this work. I also owe a great deal of appreciation to my friends Modestus Onuoha OSA, Jude Ossai OSA, Tobechukwu Oluoha OSA, Francis Galvan OSA, Thomas Wallace OSA, Rene Delariarte OSA and Tony Pizzo OSA, as well as to Fathers Emeka Adibe, Titus Egbu, Kevin Ezeoke and Obinna Ifeanyi C.S.Sp. Appreciation is also due to Prudentia Ada Nzeribe, Janis Haverlock, Gertrude Nkechi Ihunze, Rosaline and Guelph May, Linda Nonny Ike, Ifeanyi and Ngozi Eze, Luke and Ifeoma Okafor, Rosaria and Toks Oshinowo, Evelyn Ugbaja, Patricia Ogbiti, Theresa and Pius Okuma. To my home family in Nigeria (the Obiezu family), to parishioners of St. Augustine's Ibusa and Bekaji, Yola, St. John's Mararaba, to members of the Catholic Charismatic groups of St. Bartholomew and Prince of Peace parishes in Toronto, and to members of the Igbo Catholic Community Toronto: I thank all of you for your ceaseless prayers that undoubtedly aided my endeavor.

I am grateful to you, my Nigerian friends and colleagues at the University of Toronto, Fathers Joseph Ogbonnaya, Stan Ilo, Emmanuel Mbam MSP, Joachim Nnanna, Jacob Mado OSA, and Francis Ezenezi, who share with me a sincere dream and a genuine commitment to a better Nigeria. For your friendly suggestions and support that kept me focused throughout the period of writing this work, I want to say thank

Towards a Politics of Compassion

you. I recognize and appreciate the inspiration I have drawn from Henry McErlean OSA, Sr. Elise Corriveau CND and Monica Donovan. I also owe a debt of gratitude to the parishioners and staff of the parishes of St. Brigid and St. Catherine of Siena, Toronto, and Sacred Heart, Delta B.C. I have been greatly helped by the provocative thoughts and steadfast commitment of Brian Dwyer and members of St. Brigid Social Justice and Peace Commission, and the supportive prayers of members of the *Quo vadis* prayer group at St. Brigid parish. I remember also the Prior and friars of Our Lady of Grace Monastery, Marylake, King City, as well as the Augustinian Sisters of Good Counsel. To my confreres on the Augustinian UN/NGO team, and to the Augustinian Friars and staff of St. Nicholas of Tolentine Community, Bronx NY: I gratefully acknowledge your support. I also thank Fathers Tony Bature and Onyedika Otuwulunne, whose hospitality I enjoy each time I visit Brooklyn, New York and New Jersey. For the friendship we share and for the special way your thoughts have enhanced this work, I am indebted to you, Fred Hermesmann.

Furthermore, I am grateful to Larry Clark, OSA for combining parish responsibilities at Christmas season with the task of reading some sections of the manuscript and offering helpful comments and emendations to this book. Words are inadequate to express my profound gratitude to Prof. Michael Stoeber, the director of the thesis which gave birth to this book, for standing by me and bringing out the best in me. I am immensely thankful to Professors Marsha Hewitt and Jack Costello, SJ, who served on my thesis committee. I thank in a special way Professors John Paul Szura OSA, James Chukwuma Okoye C.S.Sp and Bartholomew Chidili OSA, who, out of their tight schedules, took time to proofread the final draft of this work. I am grateful for your kindness and encouraging response. I am also grateful to you, Jesús Guzmán OSA, for your interest in reading this work and spreading the news that whetted many people's interest. I am immensely grateful to the numerous authors whose works I relied upon to produce this book. Finally, to many others whose names are too numerous to mention but whose help and care I enjoyed at the course of this work: May God richly bless and reward you.

Emeka Christian Obiezu, O.S.A.

ABBREVIATIONS/ ACRONYMS

ABN	Association for Better Nigeria
CBCN	Catholic Bishops Conference of Nigeria
CCRM	Catholic Charismatic Renewal Movement
DPI/NGO	Department of Program and Information/Non-Governmental Organizations
EN	*Evangelii Nutiandi* – (Evangelization in the modern world)
EFCC	Economic and Financial Crimes Commission (A Nigerian commission constituted by the present administration to fight corruption especially in the public service)
FCSO	Fellowship for Christian Social Order
FTI	Fast-Track Initiative (A World Bank administered process for identifying the developing country education plans that are considered suitable for donor's support)
GASHRUD	Grassroots Action for Sustainable Health and Rural Development
GDP	Gross Domestic Product
GS	*Gaudiium et Spes*, (Document of Vatican II on the Church in the modern world)
HDR	Human Development Report (an annual publication

	of the United Nations Development Program)
HIV/AIDS	Human Immunodeficiency Virus/Acquired Immune Deficiency Syndrome or Acquired Immunodeficiency Syndrome
ICFTU	International Confederation of Free Trade Unions
ILO	International Labor Organization
IMF	International Monetary Fund
JDPC	Justice, Peace and Development Commission
JM	*Justitia in Mundo* – Justice in the World (the document on the social justice by 1971 synod of Bishops)
MOSOP	Movement for the Survival of the Ogoni People
NDVF	Niger Delta Volunteer Force
NGO	Non-governmental Organization
NEEDS	National Economic Empowerment Development Strategy (a Nigerian IMF inspired development program)
NLC	Nigerian Labor Congress
NPC	National Population Commission (Nigerian)
OPEC	Organization of the Petroleum Exporting Countries
PRS	Poverty Reduction Strategy
SAPs	Structural Adjustment Programs (economic reconstruction policies imposed on nations with

	staggering economy to by the IFIS)
TNCs	Transnational Corporations that make up the WTO
UNEP	United Nations Environmental Program
UNFCCC	United Nations Framework Convention on Climate Change
UN/ISDR	United Nations' International Strategy for Disaster Reduction Organization, (a United Nations department)
WB	World Bank
WTC	World Trade Center
WTO	World Trade Organization (the world body in-charge of the global market)

INTRODUCTION

If evil is structured into a society, its remedy must include social transformation, that is, changing the structures and institutions of society. Christian responsibility, then, must include both *charity,* personal acts of compassion in response to individual suffering, and justice, social and political action aimed at transforming the root causes of evil and suffering. Christians should be found in soup-kitchens, tutoring programs, and inner-city clinics, and on picket lines, in political campaigns and congressional lobbies.[1]

Suffering is a very complex reality, deep rooted in humanity.[2] It surrounds us in various forms. In the context of this work, suffering is defined from the perspective of sentient beings as the experience of emotional and physical pain and for non-sentient life forms it is defined as environmental distortion, destruction or devastation. In this work, the worst forms of suffering are considered to be the exploitation and oppression imposed on innocent people, the near extinction of culture/identity of marginalized groups by their fellow human beings via unjust institutional policies, and reckless destruction of ecology. Nigeria and other developing nations bear a bitter testimony to these types of suffering.

Ancient religious traditions understood suffering as punishment due to sin.[3] Jesus, however, breaks the idea that suffering necessarily has to do with sinfulness, either as a punishment or as a consequence of it (Jn. 9:2ff; Lk.13:1-5).[4] In the way he went healing victims of suffering, Jesus shows that his response to suffering is concerned more about helping than accusing the sufferer. His vocation was to be compassionately with the sufferer. Christians, in the manner of Christ, acknowledge the reality of suffering irrespective of the cause and also they appreciate especially the prospects of the transformative dynamics of many sufferings. Yet, we neither glorify suffering nor deny that some sufferings, as utterly destructive, can indeed crush the human spirit when viewed from the perspective of the victim.[5] Finally, by asking us to love the way he loved, Christ invites us to a compassionate response to those who suffer around us.

Compassion is an important theme in every religious tradition, as well as in most ethical traditions. To a Christian, compassion is not just an important theme or something for which only a few saintly persons have a capacity rather it is a fundamental imperative and basic to the tradition. Oliver Davies argues that compassion ought to be the organizing principle of Christian systematic theology.[6] Stephen Best provides an effective definition of compassion for this work, when he says that "Compassion is a response to the suffering of another sentient being. This occurs through empathetic identification with the other's pain. [It] creates a shared experience and emotional bond that shatters the perception of differences. Compassion thereby enjoins us to action and thus becomes authentic moral agents and political beings."[7] However, compassion is not circumscribed within the realm of human relationship only. Compassion is the primordial force that binds us to one another and to the whole of creation.

Often, we think that compassion subsists primarily in works of charity. But the way and manner Jesus practiced compassion challenges our traditional attitude of being comfortable with compassion of "palliative measures" that does nothing to redress unjust and oppressive situations. From the way Jesus practiced compassion as is evident in the Gospels, we know that for him compassion was not simply a matter of sentiment or only a quality of God and of individual value. Compassion for him was a social paradigm, the core value of life in community. He often challenged the sociopolitical paradigm of his society. He inaugurated what Marcus Borg calls a *politics of compassion*.⁸ For instance in his treatment of the case of the woman caught in adultery (John 8: 1-11), Jesus challenged the unjust system and practice of his people that marginalized women, restores the dignity of women and the disadvantaged of the society. At the same time he equally brought the oppressors to the reality of their own sinfulness.

Following Christ's paradigm, this work argues that in order ***to respond compassionately to the widespread and scandalous form of social suffering and oppression imposed on humanity and to the reckless destruction of ecology, Christians are called to undertake social and political actions aimed at social transformation, actions that are rooted in and driven by the experience of compassion***. In this way, we are imitating Jesus. In order to give this study practical significance, we relate this work to the Nigerian situation.

Various Christian churches have indicated in their various social teachings the social dimensions of this call to compassion by Christ and thus provided the theoretical framework for a politics of compassion. In his apostolic letter, *Evangelii, Nuntiandi,* Pope Paul VI recognized that evangelization – bringing good news to the dispossessed of the earth, is to proclaim the gift of God's liberation and to operate prophetically in each historical situation.⁹ By this understanding, "the church is a sign and instrument of the transformation of society in relation to God as liberator."¹⁰

However, it has been noted with utter dismay that when it comes to prophetic and compassionate confrontation with unjust social structures, when it comes to challenging the evil status quo, the social teaching of the churches does not seem to have "taken flesh" in our societies. Yet compassion lies at the very heart of Christian faith and theologies. The question therefore is, in the face of the social sufferings of injustice, exploitation and oppression, how does one respond compassionately in a socially transformative way to properly reflect witnessing to this new way Christ inaugurated as it is being proposed here? To this end, we make bold to propose the three principal responsibilities a Christian is called to opt, namely:

   (1) Option for the poor: – making the issues and concerns

of the poor a central theme and concern of the church's ministry. It involves not only material relief but also actions that challenge, and propose alternatives to, the structural evils and injustice that increase the poor conditions of the poor. The way to achieve this responsibility, as demonstrated in this study, is to broach opportunities that enhance peoples' engagement and encourage public moral discourse, by creating hospitable spaces for reflection and by bringing diverse people and perspectives into conversation.[11] Above all, we are to make sure that the struggle for a political remedy does not simply shift attention from victims to victimhood or to victimizing the innocent.

(2) Solidarity with the Earth: –this in effect means realizing that compassion needs to extend to the entire universe and all creation. Hence, trees, animals and indeed other created things are included in the biblical compassion.

(3) Inclusive Community: This demands as John Macmurray suggests, that we develop a "'new schema of the self' – a new way of relating which shall transcend both the mechanical and organic schema; and which will enable us to construct, consciously and deliberately a civilization that will be at the service of personal life – a true community, whose meaning and essence is friendship."[12]

Finally, some healthy spiritual exercises are proposed to reinforce the dynamics of the politics of compassion as follows: (1) Communal prayer: that is, seeking together the holiness and justice of God. (2) Forgiveness: that is, providing opportunities for a true reconciliation between the oppressed and the oppressor.

This study undertakes an evaluative, analytical and synthetic approach. In doing so, the concepts of suffering, evil and compassion within various theoretical traditions shall be evaluated. Moreover, an analysis of the Nigerian socio-economic and political situation as well as the various responses the church has made in this regard shall be studied. Finally, an exploration of Nigeria in the light of the earlier developments in connection with the politics of compassion shall be synthesized with a view to comparing it with the new paradigm. This approach is considered significant and original because, it creates an interactive scenario where a genuine dialogue could be created with various disciplines involved with social justice. This demonstrates how socio-moral concerns and politics can be grounded in biblically based compassion. What is being presented here is the connection between faith and justice based on the spirituality of compassion as an important source for an authentic social change. This work therefore, brings the spirituality of compassion and Liberation Theology together with the ethical thought into constructive conversation. Moreover, by situating our study within the Nigerian context, it strikes the balance of geographical concreteness, and solidly grounds theoretical principles in concrete experiences and practices. A work like this is very pertinent now that scholarship is seeking for a spirituality that prides itself on justice. My hope is that this work will stimulate further studies in this regard.

This work is studied under four chapters. Chapter one deals with the concept of suffering. It starts with the general understanding of the meaning of suffering and then zeroes down to structural evil using the current global economics as an example. The major concentration is on the Christian perspective of suffering in relation to the ideas of evil. Chapter two defines compassion and examines its relation to socio-moral and political concerns and action. Attention is given to other emotions and acts which are often confused as compassion and to why compassion is preferred by some scholars and theologians as the most effective and transformative response to suffering. This chapter also explores the Christian understanding of compassion and its relevance to the development of the politics of compassion. At the same time, the chapter presents constructively the response to contrary views of some critics who consider compassion to be incompatible with socio-moral and political concerns and action. Chapter three situates this study within the Nigerian context. It presents in brief the major conditions of Nigeria that have contributed to current socio-political and economic distortions and problems of the country. Furthermore, this chapter treats how and why the church in Nigeria responds to this situation. Chapter four focuses on the kennel of our study which actually is the critical exploration of the politics of compassion as it relates to the Nigerian context. It covers the three implications of the politics of compassion, namely, the option for the poor, the solidarity with the earth and an inclusive community. It also reacts to the challenges this new paradigm presents to the Nigerian church. In fine, two facets of spirituality considered salient to this work were suggested as follows:

communal prayer and forgiveness.

Conclusively, the work maintains that our call as Christians to be compassionate as our Heavenly Father (Luke6:36), imposes on us the unavoidable demand to be socio-politically responsive to the sufferings of our time. This work is intended to be an invitation to reflection and partnership in compassion to responding to the sufferings of our time, in consonance with our Christian calling which is witnessing to God's compassion for his people.

CHAPTER ONE: SUFFERING

There is no way one can talk about compassion as a response to suffering without first understanding what suffering is. Such attempts reveal diversity of opinions concerning its meaning, scope, causes, effects, and various responses. This chapter will attempt to explore the meaning of suffering in general – its various kinds as well as its relation to evil: natural, moral and structural evil. It will consider its effects on victims and survey various ways people can respond to suffering. This attempt will take cognizance of the varying viewpoints of select scholars but will focus more on our subject matter: suffering insofar as it relates to compassion and solidarity.

Defining Suffering and kinds of Suffering, in relation to Evil

<u>Defining Suffering</u>

Suffering and evil are so interchangeably used in discussions that one is often assumed when the other is used. Some people hold that they are one and the same thing. For instance, John Paul II insists that in the Hebrew Bible, "suffering and evil are identified with each other. In fact, the vocabulary did not have a specific word to indicate 'suffering.' Thus it defined as 'evil' everything that was suffering."[13] His observation is based on the fact that there is no Hebrew equivalent of the Greek word *pascho* often translated in English as suffering.[14]

As a matter of fact, the close relationship between evil and suffering is obvious. However, some degree of variation is perceptible in the definition of the two concepts.

First, in the case of evil, many scholars hypothesize that it has no independent existence apart from its relation to good, thus they see evil generally as the privation of good, or *due good,* as Reginald Masterson holds. Not all privation of good is evil, he says. To be an evil, "the lack must be of a good which ought to be present," as he illustrates, "that a man lacks the ability to fly like a bird is not evil."[15] In view of this, Paul Schilling sees "whatever it is that militates against the self-realizations of the human person as evil since it inhibits a person from achieving his or her potentials." The nature of evil, he maintains, is such that it hinders humanity from enjoying its cherished values, causes physical pain or mental anguish, disrupts social relations or thwarts the attainment of worthy ends.[16] Schilling's definition provides for the interpretation of the principle of the common good which "embraces the sum total of those conditions of social living whereby [people] are enabled to achieve their own integral perfection more fully and more easily."[17] In this way, his definition also provides the background for studying structural evil as the privation of the common good as we shall later see in the case of contemporary global free-market economy.

Now concerning suffering, the first statement made of suffering states the relationship between it and evil. Suffering is recognized as a dimension of evil that is connected to and experienced by human beings and other creatures.[18] It is indeed the relation of cause and effect.

Suffering as defined by Michael Stoeber is, "the experience of emotional pain – a mode of consciousness that can arise from sensation of intense physical pain, but which need not at all be associated with it… a painful state of consciousness that we wish we did not have to experience."[19] His definition agrees with those of scholars like John Hick and Eric Cassell in identifying suffering as a deplorable state, an emotional consciousness that one would not ordinarily desire.[20]

The awareness of the enormous anguish of human beings and other species, and of ecological decline and destruction, broadens our spectrum of considering suffering such that our definition has to assume a cosmic tone. There is something inherently wrong with environmental horrors that stimulate in many people their distress and compassion, compassion not for any anthropocentric interest but for the intrinsic value of natural phenomena. In view of this, suffering in the context of this work is defined with respect to sentient life as the experience of a painful state of consciousness. However, when I refer to the 'ecological suffering' of non-sentient life-forms and other natural phenomena, I am indicating the decline or distortion or destruction of the environment.

A definition like this underscores the reality of suffering that surrounds us in various forms, such as financial worries for some; poverty, hunger, and starvation for others; family concerns and personal stress that grows as people work harder and for longer hours; social suffering which follows from racism, misogyny, and inequality; various forms of environmental problems; and heavy blows dealt to the earth by war, violence, and terrorism.[21] It also provides for us the universal terrain upon which we can explicate compassion.

Suffering in these various forms, as we have pointed out, is complex. It has repeatedly driven persons to search for some meaning in the burdens of life. Its complexity can be categorized in terms of various kinds or types of suffering.

Types of suffering in relation to evil

Classification of suffering brings us again to the relation between suffering and evil. Here the fact of their cause and effect relationship and interconnectedness bear heavy thrust in the discussion. In relation to evil, suffering is viewed within the major categories of evil namely: natural or physical evil, moral or human-made evil and societal or structural evil.

Natural evil refers to the undesirable experiences of sentient beings due to events in the physical world not subject to human control. These include disasters such as earthquakes, floods, fire, accidents, lightening, plagues, epidemics, death and other forms of natural tragedies.

These natural evils bring about untold hardship and suffering on many people and indeed creation. For instance, the 2005 report of United Nations Environmental Programme (UNEP) reveals that, for many people, 2005 will be remembered for its disasters. The 26 December 2004 earthquake in the Indian Ocean and subsequent tsunami claimed more than 250,000 lives in 12 countries. The Katrina hurricane that swept through the Gulf Coast of the United States in August took more than 1,000 lives and inflicted billions of dollars worth of damage. According to the same report, in October, "a magnitude 7.6 earthquake shook South Asia, at a cost of more than 70,000 lives, mostly in Pakistan, with millions exposed to harsh winter conditions." There was river flooding in Switzerland, drought in Niger, a chemical spill in China and swarms of locusts in Africa.[22] Nature continues to inflict sufferings of pains, sorrows and loss to humanity and entire creation. In the month of May 2008 alone, nearly half a million lives, human and other species, as well as properties worth trillions of dollars were lost to natural disasters. The Nargis cyclone that swept through the Delta region of Mayanmar, Burma, on 02 May 2008 claimed about 28,000 human lives while about 41,000 people were declared missing. The 7.9 earthquake that hit China's Southwestern province of Sichuan on 12 May 2008, took the lives of over 12,000 human beings. It stands in history as China's most devastating earthquake in three decades.[23]

These natural evils are blamed on God by those who see them as either the excesses, extremes, or defects of God's creation (which was pronounced good by the God of Genesis cf. Gen. 1:10-25) or as God's purposefully created pains for his creatures. The bulk of the arguments centering on this issue are taken up by theodicy which though we are not directly concerned with in this work, is referred to in the next section dealing with responses to suffering.

Langdon Gilkey adds a new voice to the argument by his classification of evil as manageable and unmanageable. He challenges the position of those who blame God or nature for these evils by postulating that with adequate intellectual knowledge of a problem, that problem could be managed and controlled.[24] In this way, Gilkey virtually shifts the blame from God or any other natural agent and squarely places it on human beings. Modern science and later research support Gilkey's position. Some environmental analysts maintain that what we call natural disaster are, in most cases, results of human negligence to timely and adequately response to natural or environmental risks, the damages of which humanity with the help of technology has the potential to avert. These scholars claim that the very negative effect of the last tsunami could have been forestalled if there were enough warning and preventive measures put in place.²⁵ This claim remains contentious today. It divides between those who believe that human beings do not care for the environment enough and those who hold that human beings can more or less do nothing to avert natural calamity. As well, it bothers on the use of natural resources by human beings. This is why I argue later in this work that solidarity with the earth is an integral part of our Christian responsibility imposed upon us by the call to compassion.

Even if human beings are not responsible for natural or physical evil which these scholars claim, it is still obvious from our experience, that a host of other evils prevalent in the world are connected to human cause. These evils are classified as moral evils.

Moral evils designate unwanted experiences referable to human agency. These are caused by direct and voluntary actions of human beings. In other words, they are associated with freewill which was given to humanity by God to choose between good and evil. These are the result of choices made by humans that stand contrary to God's purposes or will; that is, where human beings choose evil instead of good.

Our experiences are replete with widespread evils in our world attributable to human causes. These evils impact not only on the perpetrator(s) who commit the sin(s) but also very devastating to those who are victimized by such immoral actions. Many scholars agree that these evils are the most virulent of all forms of evil.²⁶ C. S. Lewis estimates that human wickedness accounts for four-fifths of human sufferings.²⁷ Also, Matthew Lamb argues that, "anguish has taken an anthropocentric turn to the subject. Never before in human history have so many humans slaughtered their fellow human beings on such a massive scale."²⁸ For instance, according to the *Human Development Report* (HDR 2004), there were 57 major armed conflicts in various parts of the world between 1990 and 2004. An estimated 3.6 million people died in these conflicts. Millions were wounded. Millions more had to flee their homes.²⁹

Nature is also a victim of the raging cruelty of human beings. According to the United Nations Environment Program (UNEP), natural resources are being strained severely subject to human pressure. "Woodland and other vegetations are being exploited for reconstruction, heating, cooking and other energy needs; landslides are occurring on slopes destabilized by seismic activity and by erosion due to grazing, deforestation and other vegetation removal."[30] Various kinds of fish and other sea animals are exterminated in an amazing rate by inordinate dependence and contamination of waters. Many of the technological activities of today have adverse impacts which will be felt by future generations. The threat to the climate by greenhouse emissions increases at an astronomic rate. According to Ian Barbour, "radioactive wastes from today's nuclear power plants will endanger anyone exposed to them 10,000 years from now."[31] Reports like these substantiate the fact that "the terrors of nature have tended to take a back seat to the horrors of history."[32]

A careful observation of life uncovers another kind of moral evil where we cannot locate an individual as solely responsible. This is what is referred to as structural evil. They have a correlation with moral evil because they are both consequences of human choices or sins but they have lives of their own. As Dean Brackley describes, "enterprise or structures of death have no real life apart from personal sin; [yet] the collective enterprise of sin is more than the sum of personal sins."[33] Thus Richard McAfee Brown warns, "we misunderstand injustice if we see it only in individual terms and assume that if we can just change (or get rid of) a few unjust individuals, we will have cleared the path for justice."[34]

John Bennett, American theologian, attempts a distinction of sin (personal) and social evil. He sees sin (personal) as acts deliberately chosen and social evil as systems in which we find ourselves enmeshed. However, more than concerned with an ontological distinction, Bennett lays emphasis on the means necessary for overcoming each. According to him, "Deliberately chosen evil [personal sin] can be overcome by an inner change of persons, by real repentance and moral conversion," but, "evil which is not deliberately chosen…can only be overcome by a variety of means which include knowledge of cause and effect and large scale changes in institutions and in external circumstances by social action."[35]

The concept of sinful or evil structures shows how personal evil can be simultaneously strengthened and disguised by social relationships. According to Valpy Fitzgerald, "a particular system, (a historical system of relations between people) can easily create a series of situations which make necessary – and thus apparently reasonable – that conduct which favors one's own greed or that of one's family at the expense of the life and dignity of many others."[36] These include the systematic violation of human rights and the rights of other sentient beings and creatures evident in structures or institutions of social, economic, political, religious and family relationships. Moreover, structural evil is associated with the deprivation of the common good which has always included "subcategories like mutual accountability, subsidiarity, and participation."[37] Coupled with the underlying characteristics of accumulation, domination and self-interest, sinful structures institute injustice that divides humanity, creation, increases misery and creates unnecessary deaths.

Economic injustice holds a central place in this systematic violation of human and nature's rights as is obvious in contemporary global free-market economy, described by Wendell Berry as, "inherently an enemy to the natural world, to human health and freedom, to good work and good economic practice."[38]

The whole idea of the global free market centers on the optimism that the multiple ills of underdevelopment will vanish if all societies around the world are taken into new, interwoven global free market economy.[39] But with the institutionalization of the policy in the 1980s and 1990s, the system became a "dominant form of capitalism claiming victory and assuming unchallenged hegemony over developing globalization of economic structures and networks."[40] The World Trade Organization (WTO) was created with the mandate of global liberalization to protect the interests of Transnational Corporations (TNCs) by "systemizing critical economic concepts – such as ownership, property rights, and local or national systems of regulatory legislation."[41] Through the "dangerous systemic imbalance at the international level" created by this global governing body in its policies, suffering became increased in our time.

First, its policy absolutizes profit, and thus subordinates human rights, social values, ecological concerns and all the other dimensions of the common well-being of the planetary community to the economic needs and interests of a few but powerful corporate bodies and nations. It is absolutely insensitive to human suffering and ecological deterioration. All that matters is that one meets the market demand and makes profit; the conditions under which people work or goods are produced do not matter. So many workers become poorer as they work for longer hours; many have no job security and welfare, and many are exposed to unbearable working conditions.[42] In some cases, there are cases of unemployment as many companies replace human labor with robots[43] in order to maximize profit.

Second, since the market and policy making are controlled by powerful corporations and influential nations dominated by the West, the system legitimizes cultural imperialism as it approves global governance controlled by economic power and political influence. Therefore, systemization of critical economic principles became a transposition of Western cultures and values that led to what some Third World theologians identify as "anthropological poverty" – "despoiling human beings not only of what they have, but of everything that constitutes their being and essence."[44] "It is important to note," Tissa Balasuriya reminds us, that "the destruction of a culture is often the first step in eliminating a people."[45]

Third, the system promotes global trade policies that serve the interests and maintain the dominance of rich multinational corporations and nations over the poor companies and nations. It created a market system of unequal and unfair competition where the rich gets richer and the poor gets poorer. For instance, how can poor nations that depend practically on foreign aid compete equally and fairly in the same market with countries in Europe and America that can subsidize their farmers to the tune of $350 billion (US Dollar) annually?[46] Obviously, this idea kills the idea of local and subsistent economy and leaves the poor nations that are rich in natural resources as primary producers and primary consumers. They export their natural endowments to the rich nations and depend on them for virtually all their needs.

Similarly, the system often introduces new economic principles and issues that poor nations are not adequately equipped to understand, such as macroeconomics which is alien to the developing nations. These types of policies "structure the economy of the poor nations into permanent economic dependency, undermining any possibility of their designing or implementing home-grown development strategies that are better oriented to their local needs."[47]

Lastly through the institutional reform promoted by its armories, International Financial Institutions (IFIs) such as the World Bank (WB) and the International Monetary Fund (IMF) impose on poor nations Structural Adjustment Programs (SAPs) demanding of them the devaluation of their national currencies, deregulation, the downsizing of bureaucracies and the welfare roll, and privatization. This policy has been described by economist Larry Elliot as, "a cure that is worse than the disease."[48] The consequence is that nations are unable to provide for societal needs – accounting for the deaths of many people, especially children, due to hunger, and epidemics like HIV/AIDS in Africa. We shall return to the effects of these policies later in chapter three.

Contemporary economic structures, as Valpy Fitzgerald says, "form a central part of the sin of the world." As mentioned earlier, "this is not just a matter of specific economic injustices which can be rectified by appropriate public or private action by good Christians." Like all structural evils they are principalities and powers, to borrow Paul's words. To respond adequately and effectively to them we need an approach that goes beyond charity and personal conversion. They demand a compassion that takes into account a socio-economic and political responsibility.

From the foregoing it becomes lucid that there is a plethora of sufferings associated with natural, moral and structural evils. Next we turn to the exploration of the effects of suffering on its victims.

The Effects of Suffering on its Victims

In his study on suffering, Daniel Liderbach notes that one other reason why the enigma of suffering remains complex is that, on one hand it slams its victims against the solid wall of the problem of evil and, on the other hand, human suffering transforms some of its victims into the most beautiful of human persons.[49] By this submission, Liderbach introduces us to the dialectics of suffering. Suffering can at one time be transformative and at another time destructive. What does it mean to say that suffering is either transformative or destructive? How do we determine and differentiate the one from the other?

Destructive suffering

Suffering is termed destructive when it does not ultimately lead to a spiritual and wholistic transformation. The realization that our bearing the burden of suffering comes to naught is "the bitterest pill' to swallow," says Dorothee Soelle.[50] There is no goal, or purpose that can be attached to such suffering. This kind of suffering leaves one with no hope of recovery and much less sharing in the suffering of others. Sharing this understanding, Stoeber writes:

> Much suffering remains utterly destructive, insofar as we can discern its effects. Even if some people grow morally and spiritually in their responses to their own or other people's suffering, and some go on to become special exemplars of the transformative ideal, many people are simply overwhelmed by 'destructive suffering'. Many of them, especially children are not able to grow through their suffering.[51]

Likewise, Soelle admits that "our hopes can die or they can grow in suffering…. Many people are overgrown with dead hopes like land overgrown with ghostlike flowers."[52] Indeed, the victims' hopes can die when they are subjected to untold suffering that they least expected or merited. Human experience has shown us that when trouble comes, it seems to do so only to a selected few and in massive amounts well beyond the capacities of people to endure. Suffering comes indiscriminately and erratically.[53] As it happens in most cases, suffering ends up frustrating the victims rather than giving them a jolt to go out and face life anew.[54] It is even more frustrating to know that many of the victims who suffer are innocent persons. There have been ample instances of destructive suffering in the past and there are still more even in our time.

Examples are the many innocent and defenseless people who die everyday in Iraq and Darfur and other war-torn areas. Also victims of rape, child abuse and all the other instances of unwanted and unwarranted pains serve as further examples of destructive suffering. The problem of destructive suffering calls to question the issue of the justice of God. How loving a father is God?

Nevertheless, while we admit that many sufferings hold no meaning, purpose or goal for the victim, and even destroy many people, we have to admit that some suffering seems to be associated with some hope, goal and purpose. In this case we see those sufferings as transformative.

Transformative Suffering

According to Soelle, there are some positive sides of certain kinds of suffering in that suffering can sometimes teach the victims to love life all the more.[55] Suffering, according to her, makes one more sensitive to the pain in the world.[56] Stoeber agrees with this position that there are definitely some positive sides to certain suffering. He identifies three possible transformative orientations open to one in suffering.

First, through suffering we can realize our full potentials. In his words, "It is through suffering, at least in part, that we activate and realize our hidden strengths and potentials, be they physical, intellectual or aesthetic."[57] Suffering then serves as a teacher that leads us on the path to inner transformation and growth. Through the experience of suffering, we transmute and overcome the situation that causes the suffering we go through, we grow in various aspects: "we gain skill and knowledge, we become more aware of life's gifts and pleasures, we become more resilient in life's conflicts or we acquire a depth of moral character not otherwise possible."[58]

Second, suffering can lead us to spiritual growth. According to him, suffering links us to spiritual growth when the victim breaks with the deepest self-isolating orientation[59] and moves toward a deeper relationship with God and other human beings and the created world.[60] The experience then brings the victim into a closer relationship with other victims who together lift their voices to God in hope and expectation that God would intervene in their plight. From this point of view therefore, suffering provides the connection between the triangle of relationship amongst God, humans and nature.[61] It can lead one to become a more compassionate person.

The kind of spiritual transformation that takes place as a result of our experience of suffering is described succinctly by John Hick thus:

> …spiritual growth is the overcoming of egoity, the transcending of individual self-interest in a common human life in relation to God. To overcome natural egoity so fully that one can value others as one values oneself is the heart of the moral life, as understood by Christianity."[62]

As we will later see, this is an act made possible by compassion. According to Max Scheler, compassion "frees us from a privatized way of feeling and acting." For, it "is based on a keen awareness of the interdependence of all the living beings, we are part of one another and all involved in one another."[63]

Third, Stoeber maintains, that our suffering can lead to the healing of others, in this case, we talk of suffering as being redemptive. It is vicarious in nature. It presupposes the fact that one person takes upon him/herself the sufferings of others in order that those others would be free from their own suffering.

Christ has always been put forward as the perfect example of redemptive suffering. He is portrayed as one sent by God to redeem us after a strained or severed relationship with God, where the consequence of which is the suffering that we go through. To do this he endured suffering and death. The overriding purpose for the passion, death and resurrection is the redemptive experience of suffering.[64] By the suffering of Christ, God basically reveals God-self as a "suffering God"[65] who has come to share in the suffering of his people in order to lead them to a better life.

In the same way, Christ has invited us to enter into the suffering of others by calling us to compassion. As we shall develop later, the central idea of compassion stressed here in the act of identifying with the suffering of others is solidarity with, or 'being with.' It is a call to enter into the vulnerability of others, that by our presence they are healed. We shall concentrate more on this later in the section on compassion.

However, Daniel Simundson suggests that these ideas of redemptive and transformative suffering are hardly a workable proposal as we cannot in good conscience interpret every single act of misfortune as a drastic means to achieve rather modest ends.[66] In another case, Paul Schilling warns that it is not unlikely that in this guise, people might enter into a passive trust that accepts evils as somehow sent by God, without the acceptance of the responsibility for removing or reducing them.[67] This masochistic form of pathological passion, a distortion associated with some Christian practices, according to Stoeber, can lead the empathetic person to wallow narcissistically in his or her suffering.[68]

So far we have explored the meaning of suffering, its various kinds in relation to evil – natural, moral and structural. We observed that while some suffering can be destructive to its victims, certain suffering do lead its victims to some hope and transformation. The other question yet unanswered with which we are concerned next is, "how do people respond to suffering?"

Responding to suffering

When it comes to responding to suffering, discussions have often focused on two different levels, the *intellectual level* as a theological defense in the form of theodicy and *pastoral level* in comforting the victim.[69] Apathy is another way that people can respond to suffering. Our main concern here is particularly to focus on the practical or pastoral approach of responding to suffering. But, as a point of departure, I will still state the main thesis of theoretical theodicy and apathy.

Theoretical theodicy

It is in relation to theodicy that Wayne Ferguson postulates that in scholarship the subject of evil is one of the best points of departure for a fruitful dialogue between Christianity, polytheists, and modern philosophy.[70] Theodicy as its original Greek suggests (*theos* – God, and *dike* – justice), means the vindication or defense of divine providence in view of the existence of evil.[71] This is not a problem for polytheistic religions. Frequently, they reconcile the contradictions posed by the existence of evil by attributing it (existence of evil) to the works of one or another god. It is not either for philosophical schools like the

Manicheans who "believed that both God and the principle of evil were some sort of material substance, neither deriving its existence from the other."[72]

But for the monotheistic religions like Christianity, the problem of evil or theodicy "resides in the apparently unavoidable contradiction between the notion of God as omnipotent and omnibenevolent on the one hand, and the existence of evil (natural and moral), on the other hand."[73] Some suggest that in light of the immense presence of evil in our world, Christian orthodoxy should give up one of its two concepts of God – omnipotence or omnibenevolence.

In his work *De Ordine*, Augustine appreciates without pretence this problem as he says, "those who ponder these matters are seemingly forced to believe that Divine Providence does not reach to these outer limit of things or that surely all evils are committed by the will of God."[74] Recognizing that "both horns of this dilemma are impious, and particularly the latter," Augustine goes on to offer what has survived as classical theodicy.

His responses proffer solutions for the existence of evil conceived either as metaphysical or empirical reality. Augustine defends God by submitting, first, that evil is a privation and cannot be properly said to exist at all; second, that the apparent imperfection of any part of creation disappears in light of the perfection of the whole; and third, that the origin of moral evil, together with that suffering which is construed as punishment for sin, are to be found in the free choice of the will of rational creatures. These solutions have been classified by scholars under the principles of plenitude, aesthetic beauty, and freewill.[75] Augustine continues his elucidation of the concept in his later works, especially in book seven of his confession; sometimes admitting his limitations and at other times, venturing into further inquiries.

Since this is not our area of concentration, suffices to say that this approach has received many criticisms. Such criticisms claim that its approach is more theoretical, speculative and abstract and fails to undo through practical response the web that can strangle those who suffer.[76] Again they hold that, on the whole, the intellectual approach, in its efforts to defend and exonerate God of the suffering of the poor, seems to deny the pains the victims of such unmerited suffering go through,[77] and thus may lead to apathy. The book of Job presents dramatically the frustration of the traditional approach to the problems of suffering based on the deuteronomic theology of retributive justice, which translates to mean that *good comes to those who do good and evil/ suffering to those who do evil.*

However, to give up theodicy entirely does not help matters. In the opinion of Stoeber, theoretical theodicy, "grounds and supports a renewed expression of faith that enables the pastoral theodicist to stand alongside the victims by helping the victim; it justifies one's hope of healing and redemption of the victims of extreme destructive suffering."[78] We would definitely lose such hope if theoretical theodicy is treated as completely irrelevant to religious responses to suffering.[79] Having said this, we now turn to apathy.

Apathy

In between the theoretical and practical response to suffering is located another type of response. In this case the essence is to avoid suffering by all means. We call this response apathy. Derived from its Greek origin, *apatheia*, apathy, literally translates to mean non-suffering, a freedom from suffering, an inability to suffer. It is a "social condition in which people are so dominated by the goal of avoiding suffering that it becomes a goal to avoid relationships and contacts altogether."[80] According to Soelle, "it does not mean that the persons do not suffer or that they are a happy people. It denotes a lack in the awareness of their own suffering and the sensitivity for the suffering of others."[81] They experience suffering, Soelle says, "but they put up with it, it does not move them. They have no language or gestures with which to battle suffering. Nothing is changed; they learn nothing from it." They slip into the type of spiritual state, Robert Lifton, describes as "*psychic numbing* – the state of exclusion, most especially the exclusion from feeling."[82]

According to Soelle, the worst type of apathy is political apathy. "It goes hand in hand with an astonishing forgetfulness, as though previous generations had not existed and as though their experiences were vain." The experiences of our past have no effect on our present. This is the main reason why exploitation, oppression and injustice are tolerated and nothing is done to change the deplorable conditions of suffering that strangulate many societies today.[83]

Many reasons have been advanced by scholars that might lead to this type of response. Some link it with the over intellectualization of the problem of suffering, yet others associate it with a kind of spirituality of sentimentality. We shall return to this later. Whatever the reason may be, its approach does not respond to suffering in a constructive way as a practical and pastoral response would.

The victim needs to be comforted, to be touched and to be made to feel loved and welcomed into the midst of other persons, rather than alienated and unwanted. This is our concern here. The practical and pastoral approach to suffering offers us such opportunity where attention is personal and focused on how to provide support to the victims.

Practical or pastoral approaches

The practical approach calls for more than just philosophizing or theologizing over the sufferings of others. It tries to avoid the presumptions that we can solve the problem of suffering by approving and disapproving of certain modes of behaviors, though this may help. It is simply a call to a more committed life to overcome and eradicate suffering.[84] Through entering the chaos of the other, we extend a helping hand in guiding them through their suffering. They are given the hope that there is something greater than their present sad situation. In this we see the nature of a person's commitment to stand in solidarity with those who are ravaged by suffering. True enough, we may not be able to solve the problem of suffering but the decision to walk with the victims through the path of searching for answers and possible resolution[85] would be of tremendous help in their situation.

Extolling the survival method of response to suffering, Stoeber indicates that in this situation the "theological attention orbits around practical questions of compassion that pertains to the distribution of evil: who suffers, who victimizes and how do we solve the problem?"[86] Essentially, what we are called to in this form of response to suffering is to show compassion to those who suffer. Together with those who experience the agonies and pangs of suffering, we should search for better ways to eliminate this evil; it is to make the world a better place for one and all. This is why compassion is robustly presented as the spirituality, that is, that way of life that does justice to the enormous suffering we know. This is God's own way of responding to the suffering of His people as is evident in the Bible.

Biblical faith, Douglas Hall notes, "does not flinch or cloak in pretty phrases, its assumption is that being human means suffering."[87] In the forthright nature of its language of lament, the Bible – especially the Old Testament – comes right to the point to state the reality of suffering in the life of the people of God.[88] "Whoever therefore, tries to read the Bible without taking serious note of the *calamitous* nature of the history to which it bears witness and whoever makes of it a success story... will have misunderstood the Bible in a truly fundamental way,"[89] Hall, concludes.

Though the Old Testament tradition tends to stress the understanding of suffering as a punishment due to sin,[90] yet, according to Edward Schillebeeckx, God and suffering are "diametrically opposed; where God appears, evil and suffering have to yield. So there is no place for suffering..."[91] Evil is inimical to God and God's presence among people, hence in moments of great suffering and tribulation, the Jews were not afraid to use strong words against God such as the prayers of the Psalmist portray, e.g., "Is God asleep?" (Ps 44:23, 26).

Jesus breaks the idea that suffering necessarily has something to do with sinfulness either as a punishment or a consequence. He was not concerned with a metaphysical speculation about the origin of evil. Jesus illustrates this in his response to the question about the man born blind in John's gospel and the murdered Galileans in Luke (Jn 9:2ff; Lk 13:1-5).[92] What then was his approach to suffering? Jesus shows that his response to suffering is concerned more about helping than accusing the sufferer. By this, Christ changed the traditional approach to the problem of suffering from asking *why* to asking *how*.[93] He went about all the cities and villages curing every disease and every sickness – healing victims of suffering and confronting structures of injustices. Jesus' response to suffering is one that aims at eliminating suffering. For him, this is a vocation. This response brought suffering to him yet he remained faithful to God and his vocation.[94] As pointed out earlier in this chapter, in Jesus' suffering, suffering became a redemptive act, an act of compassion in loving obedience to the will of his Father. By choosing this method, Jesus leaves us an example, calling us to show compassion to those who suffer. Therefore, as we will see in the next section, when we embrace compassion we are choosing to imitate God in his vulnerability which is shown in his compassion for those who suffer; this choice is made visible in our election of a suffering love.[95]

Summary

The foregoing has presented an account and analysis of various kinds of suffering in relation to evil – natural, moral and structural evil, using past and contemporary illustrations. It highlighted the tangling web of structural evil and the banality of it. It acknowledged the pains and horror of suffering and stressed that, while in some cases the effects of suffering can be utterly destructive for its victims, it can in other cases become a transformative dynamic leading to spiritual growth and the realization of one's full potentials and healing of the other. This understanding can help to stimulate one to become a more compassionate person. In fidelity to the main concern of this work, which is, reducing the suffering of people around us, the chapter surveyed various ways in which people can respond to suffering: through theoretical theodicy, apathy and practical pastoral responses. It identified compassion as an effective response to the suffering of others, where we are drawn to their vulnerability in solidarity, as we seek the best and possible means to eradicate their suffering and its sources. Compassion is at the center of the Christian tradition. This is what we are exploring in the next chapter.

CHAPTER TWO: COMPASSION

Chapter one introduced the word 'compassion' as the most effective response to suffering. But while there is a sense of familiarity with the word 'compassion' among people, studies show that the word has suffered an untold corruption within years of its numerous uses. In this chapter two we shall define and analyze the concept of compassion. This will include comparing compassion with various concepts that have often been confused with it. It will also explore its understanding within the Christian tradition and demonstrate that for Christ compassion goes beyond interpersonal activity to include socio-moral and political concern and activity, a politics of compassion which will become clear with illustrations as we go along. Finally, as we respond to critics of compassion, we shall articulate some philosophical thoughts that will provide some foundation for this work.

Towards a meaning of compassion

"Language," Matthew Fox opines, "is the first victim of cover-up and corruption." Applying this statement to compassion, Fox argues that the word has been "abused, used, forgotten, lost, distorted and too rarely practiced."[96] Today compassion has been misguidedly used

Towards a Politics of Compassion

as a synonym for 'pity,' 'mercy,' 'sympathy,' 'empathy,' mere 'sentiment' and private 'charity.' Attempts to define compassion therefore must risk redeeming compassion and giving its practice a new birth. This is why I am choosing, like Matthew Fox, the *via negativa* method in my approach to defining compassion. This is "a cautious separation of true compassion from its numerous imposters, by emphasizing first what compassion is <u>not</u> – an emphasis that gradually leads to a fuller unveiling of what compassion might mean."[97] Fox, to whom the originality of this process belongs, describes it as "retrieving compassion from its lonely exile."

Our first attempt in this process of unveiling the true meaning of compassion considers compassion in relation to empathy and sympathy. According to an annotated bibliography compiled by Jennifer Goetz, Nancy Eisenburg attempts a separation of these feelings: "empathy is considered a mirroring or vicarious experience of another's emotions, whether they are sorrow or joy. Sympathy, on the other hand, is a feeling of sorrow associated specifically with the suffering or need of another… it is fellow-feeling."[98] Compassion has something of both but it is not completely represented by either one or by both of them. Like sympathy, compassion stems from the suffering of another, but compassion includes the need or desire and an action towards alleviating suffering.[99] Like empathy, compassion can include the celebration of joy. While compassion involves a movement to action, the above other words compared with it do not.

Secondly, compassion is not pity. Fox says, "reducing compassion to pity and pitiful feelings is to exile compassion altogether from adult living." Etymologically, the two words come from different sources. The word pity is from the Latin word *pietas*; while the word compassion comes from the Latin, "*cum patior*, meaning, to suffer with, to undergo with, to share solidarity with."[100] From a psychological standpoint, Frederick Perls, a Gestalt therapist, argues that the difference in the meaning of the two words is profoundly significant. "Pity," he holds, "sometimes regards its object as not only suffering, but weak or inferior." And to show pity connotes condescension and involves what Perl calls, "the luxury of sentimental tears which is mostly a masochistic enjoyment of the misery" that might lead to philanthropy.[101] Pity leads one to act in this way because it involves a presumption of ego difference as a basic way of relating to reality.¹⁰² This way of relating captures what John Macmurray describes as mechanical unity pattern of relationship. It is an impersonal type of relationship that depends not on the intrinsic differences, but on the position of individuals that leads to egocentrism and isolationism.¹⁰³

Thirdly, mercy is another feeling often misconstrued as compassion. As defined by the *Canadian Oxford Dictionary*, mercy is "compassion or forbearance shown to a powerless person, especially an offender or one with no claim to kindness."¹⁰⁴ From this definition, we can deduce that, like pity, mercy carries the connotation of superiority and subordination and is often situated in wrong doing. "One is merciful to whom one has the right (or power) to act otherwise," and in the words of James Blake, "mercy wears a human face, and compassion a human heart."¹⁰⁵

From close observation, most scholars attribute the confusion that exists between pity, mercy and compassion to the inadequacy of any single English word to translate the Hebrew word *hesed*. It is translated in the Greek Bible as *eleos* – pity¹⁰⁶ and in the Latin vulgate as *misericodia* – pity, mercy, or sympathy.¹⁰⁷ These are equally limited. "What is lacking in all these translations," Fox observes, "is the dimension of action and deliverance of justice, *mispat* that the Hebrew word implies."¹⁰⁸

Fourthly, in relation to sentiment, while it is true to say that compassion springs from sentiment, yet it cannot be reduced to pure feeling or mere sentiment – "mental, emotional or tender feeling." However, we cannot live in the illusion "that it does not matter what we feel so long as we act in the right ways." As Alan Drengson – Professor Emeritus of Philosophy, University of Victoria British Columbia, Canada, points out, "this is true as far as the law goes. But how we feel determines how we are spiritually and vice versa."¹⁰⁹ Sentiment as it refers to passion is a necessary part of compassion. For instance, from the Jewish understanding of bowel and womb as the true seat of deep emotion, the Old Testament describes the Compassionate God as the <u>Passionate</u> God, as the following expressions reveal. "I do earnestly remember him still: therefore my bowels are troubled for him." "Where is your zeal and your strength, the sounding of your bowels and your compassion" (Jer. 31:20; Is. 63:15).¹¹⁰

The use of the womb and bowel, or the Hebrew *rahamim*[111] in describing the God of Israel goes beyond mere identification of the emotional capability of our God. It rather describes the character of compassion and the quality of our God. As Marcus writes, "In its sense of 'like a womb,' *compassionate* has the nuances of giving life, nourishing, caring, perhaps embracing and encompassing." Therefore, he continues, "To say that God is compassionate is to say that God is 'like a womb,' is 'womblike,' …or is 'wombish.'" With all its implications, the womb, in this sense, a metaphorical and evocative expression, provocatively suggests a number of connotations. "Like the womb, God is the one who gives birth to us – the mother who gives birth to us. As a mother, so God loves us and feels for us, for all of her children."[112] Thus, the biblical God, though passionate, is never associated with mere non-active sentimentalism – "weak emotionalism; excessive indulgence in sentiment,"[113] in either the Old or the New Testament. He could not afford to substitute sentiment for action. As we shall see later, the bible is rich in practical acts of God's compassion.

Sentimentalism, Anne Douglas points out, is a very powerful energy – "a political sense obfuscated or gone rancid….(that) never exists except in tandem with failed political consciousness."[114] Sentimentalism leads to flight from action, a flight from politics and a flight from justice-making. Thus Fox submits that, "Sentimentalism, a rancid political consciousness, blocks authentic spiritual development." Compassion, on the contrary, is about action – relieving the pain of others – which is to say that it goes beyond emotion to include action, including political action.[115]

Lastly, while we claim that compassion involves action towards relieving the suffering of the other, action understood only as private charity does not completely define, nor does it substitute for, compassion. In his book, *The Holy Longing*, Ronald Rolheiser[116] differentiates compassion from private charity. Private charity responds to the immediate needs of the sufferer, e.g. providing shelter for the homeless, medication for the sick and bread for the hungry, but does nothing more. On the other hand, compassion provides the opportunity that not only responds to immediate and material needs of the sufferer but can as well go a step ahead and seeks justice, by asking the question, "why are these there?" and thus challenges the systems that create them.

The point Rolheiser makes here does not disparage nor deny private charity as an act of compassion. As a matter of fact, there are occasions when private charity is the only way one can respond to the suffering of the other. In other words, we cannot afford to absolutize socio-political action in such a way that it is presented as the only valid way of practicing compassion or the only way one can and must participate in the salvific event. In other words, we must acknowledge that every individual Christian has not got the vocation or opportunity for this. For instance, prisoners in a concentration camp, where oppressive conditions mean they can do nothing with regards to the socio-moral conditions that cause there suffering, nevertheless might be committed to giving some material relief to the suffering of each other. Still in some other cases these charitable acts appear only as palliative measure, a direct or indirect substitute for action to challenge unjust structures as we shall later demonstrate with the Nigerian experience.

I use indirect here to refer to the fact that ignorance or inability to ask the necessary questions as to why situations of suffering occur renders our private charity insufficient in the face of some suffering as Rolheiser illustrates with the following example. He tells a story of a town built just beyond the bend of a large river. As the children were playing in the river one day they noticed three human bodies floating in the water. They ran for help and the villagers came, picked the three, buried the dead, put the wounded one in the hospital, and kept the child among them within the care of one of the villagers. It happened that everyday a number of bodies came floating down the river, and everyday the villagers came to the various needs of the victims. It became the order of the day that the community developed a more elaborate system to deal with these cases. However, despite their generosity and effort, nobody thought to go up the river, beyond the bend that hid from their sight what was above them, and find out why, daily, those bodies came floating down the river.[117]

This is the extra step compassion takes, something that private charity may not consider as necessary in as much as it helps in the immediate need. It is in situations such as this that we say compassion cannot be substituted with private charity. Moreover, charity, Kara Newell and others say, like pity, sometimes springs from the feeling of superiority and inferiority.[118] Lastly, while charity, pity and mercy create a distance between subject and object, compassion on the contrary breaches all geographic and psychic distance.

This exercise of 'retrieving compassion from its lonely exile' not only aids our definition of compassion, its significance becomes more apparent as the discussion progresses. It will go a long way in helping us to later deal with what Richard A. McCormick identifies as *socially dormant conscience* – a type of social attitude associated with wrong ideas about compassion held by Christians that contribute to the multiplication and continuation of evil in the society.[119] Now that we have shown how compassion differs from its charlatans, we once again ask, "What is compassion?"

Compassion, as defined by Dr. Steven Best, is a "response to the suffering of another sentient being. This occurs through empathetic identification with the other's pain. Empathy creates a shared experience and emotional bond that shatters the perception of differences. Compassion thereby enjoins us to action and thus [qualifies us as] authentic moral agents and political beings."[120] This definition contains three parts or propositions: empathy prepares for compassion; compassion transcends empathy to include because it involves love; and lastly, such compassionate action may include socio-political and moral dimension. As we press on with Best, we appreciate the interrelation of these principal parts of his definition and the progression associated with compassion. More than empathy, compassion involves love which leads to action. Such action will be effective and appropriate if it arises from or is accompanied by comprehension.[121] Best goes on to identify compassion as the primordial force that binds us to one another. According to him,

> In compassion, we make direct contact with another, unmediated by any prejudice or distinction such as class, race, gender, or species; we expose ourselves and become vulnerable to the other's pain…. Through empathy and action we transcend the limitations of our ego and species perspectives, we grasp the unity and interconnectedness of all life, and we establish larger and richer identifications

that expand our awareness and feeling.¹²²

Best's definition is adopted in this work because of its cosmic character. It liberates compassion from the circumscription of the psychologies and spiritualities of human inter-personalism and expands its boundaries to include responsibility for the whole creation. For him, compassion is universal and trans-species in scope, such that it is senseless for one to say that he or she is a compassionate person while arbitrarily drawing boundaries among sentient beings and the entire creation as to who is a proper object of one's compassion and who is not.¹²³ In other words, compassion is "a way of being at home with the universe, with life and death, with the seen and the unseen."¹²⁴ Concerning compassion as it is understood in this sense, Nouwen and others write:

> [It] asks us to go where it hurts, to enter into places of pain, to share in brokenness, fear, confusion, and anguish. Compassion challenges us to cry out with those in misery, to mourn with those who are lonely, to weep with those in tears. It requires us to be weak with the weak, vulnerable with the vulnerable, and powerless with the powerless. Compassion means full immersion in the condition of being human. It becomes clear that something more is involved, more than kindness or tenderheartedness. It is not masochism, it is not self-flagellation.¹²⁵

In the context of our study, the compassion that strives to bring full relief to the suffering of others will not only be concerned with material and immediate succor in all cases. It must, as often as it is necessary, permeate the corridors of the various causes of suffering, as identified in chapter one. Permeating these areas, compassion, must boldly ask the question "why are all these sufferings here?" It must be consistently committed to actions that not only challenge these causes but point to a better option.

Having identified structural evil as the major cause of the sufferings of our time in this work, we therefore submit that, compassion must include a socio-economic and political dimension with its consequent responsibilities in order to respond effectively to such suffering. In other words, as Richard McCormick says, it is not sufficient for a tycoon to build homes for the homeless with "monies piled up through unjust landlord practices or graft."[126] Hence, the father of Social Gospel, Washington Gladden, would suggest that, "if the golden rule of moral conduct was that one should love one's neighbor as oneself, it followed that employers and employees should practice cooperation, disagreements should be negotiated in a spirit of other-regarding fellowship, and society should be organized to serve human welfare rather than profits."[127]

What McCormick and Gladden are saying is that, "wisdom dictates, [that compassion] must become more involved in the formulation of those social policies, so that it fosters structural change – a matter of justice – and thereby substantially reduce the need for exercising charity."[128] As Augustine says in his commentary on the first letter of John: "You give bread to a hungry person; but it would be better were no one hungry, and you could give it to no one. You clothe a naked person. Would that all were clothed and this necessity did not exist!"[129]

In the knowledge of this overriding responsibility, as we go on, we discover again and again why compassion could not be replaced by any of those pretenders from which we have liberated it. Subsequent chapters of this work will expose the meaning, implications and urgency of this new paradigm of compassion, which are socio-political and economic responsibility. First, let us begin with the Christian understanding of compassion as it relates to socio-moral, political-concerns and actions.

Christian Understanding of Compassion in Relation to Socio-moral and Political Concerns and Actions

In the Judeo-Christian tradition, compassion is an epithet of Yahweh. In the theophany to Moses on Mount Sinai, Yahweh is said to have, "...proclaimed, 'Yahweh, Yahweh, a God of tenderness and compassion, slow to anger and rich in kindness and faithfulness'" (Ex. 34:6). He is addressed as the "Compassionate One" (Ps. 103:11; Deut. 13:17). The Yahwist tradition resisted the sentimentalization of this compassion of Yahweh. As we read in Exodus 2: 23-25, Yahweh's knowing of the suffering of Israelites was the motive of the exodus. During the exodus, Yahweh was immanent with his people in their struggle and journey, in the form of a pillar of cloud by day and a pillar of fire by night. He provided for them when they were in need. "His compassion fails not, being new every morning" (Lam. 3:22). He remained with them, guiding and guarding them until they were settled in the land he had promised them. Time and again God demonstrates compassion. Thus, to say that God is compassionate is to say that "God suffers at the suffering of others."[130] This definition, of co-suffering, calls for God to more things, to which He has always remained faithful, even in our days.

The Jewish call to compassion is primarily linked with the passage in Leviticus where God said to His people, "be holy as your God is holy." Yahweh added a human dimension to this holiness by including among the commandments the injunction to 'love thy neighbor as thyself' (Lev.19:2, 18).[131] The Hebrew Bible avers that love of thy neighbor means and includes action towards others and justice-making. The fourteen traditional Works of Mercy – temporary and spiritual - in the Old Testament allude to the fact that compassion is not mere sentiment but leads to works. Feeding, clothing, sheltering, setting free, giving drink, visiting, burying, educating, counseling, admonishing, bearing wrong, forgiving, comforting, and praying are all works of mercy. Though they come from the heart, they are not limited to sentiment or solely heartfelt emotions.[132]

Christianity inherited the idea of compassion from Judaism and made it the centerpiece of its doctrine. Like the Jews, Christians understood the seriousness of the command to *be holy as your God is holy* and interpreted it to include giving. It is not only a new responsibility; it is also a reminder and an invitation to witness to the reality of God in whose image we are made. For the Christians, God is triune – perfect love characterized by self-gift. Therefore, to be made in His image, Michael and Kenneth Himes say, "is to be capable of self-gift."[133]

The gospels portray love as the central theme of Christ's message which is exposed explicitly in the Sermon on the Mount (Mt 5: 43).[134] Like other Jews, Jesus insists that to love means to have compassion for the suffering of others, which involves action and not mere sentiment, as he demonstrated with the parables of the Good Samaritan, the Good Shepherd and the Lost Coin (Lk. 10:35; Jn 10:1-18; Lk. 15:8-10). He not only taught positive sympathy towards the suffering of others but, as the New Testament bears witness, for Jesus the feeling of compassion always gave rise to an outward act of help.[135] His compassion moved him to heal the blind, cleanse the leper, teach the ignorant, feed the hungry and raise the dead (Matt 15:32; 20:34; Mk. 1:41; 8:2; Lk. 7:13). Thus we can conclude that "compassion as feeling separated from action is inconceivable to Jesus."[136] In the same way, Christ instituted compassion rooted in action as the basis of the last judgment, insisting that to be compassionate to our neighbor is to love God: "'I was hungry'… 'in so far you did this to one of the least, of these, you did it to me.'" (Matt 25:31:46).

Treading the path of their Master, the disciples identified and taught the triangular dimension of love – God, ourselves and our neighbor. They maintained that the love of God and the love of our neighbor committed to action are one and the same. John in his first epistle writes, "'If anyone says, 'I love God,' while he or she hates his or her brother or sister, he or she is a liar" (1Jn. 4:20). Again James says, "If one of you is in need of clothes and has not enough food to live on, and one of you says to them, 'I wish you well; keep yourself warm and eat plenty,' without giving them these necessities of life, then what good is that? Faith is like that: if good works do not go with it, it is quite dead…." (James 2:15, 16, 24, 26).

From the above study, there are some basic and significant elements of compassion as practiced by God and demanded of his people that we ought to consider especially for what they represent in this work. First, from the way and manner God of the Old Testament and Jesus practiced compassion we can deduce that the concept of *being with* was a significant and central theme of their compassion. The exodus experience as cited above remains one such moment where God expressed his love for his people by being physically with them in their struggle. Again, Isaiah in his prophesy, identifies the Messiah as "*Immanuel*" – God-with-us (Isa. 7:14 cp. with Mtt. 1:23; Lk. 1:31). In Rev. 21:3-4, God's relationship with his people is captured thus, "He will pitch his tent among them and they will be his people. God will be with them and wipe every tear from their eyes…" *He pitched his tent among us* is the English equivalent of the Greek expression (Καί ὁ Λόγος σάρξ ἐγένετο καί ἐσκήνωσεν ἐν ἡμίν) of the Incarnation of the Word in John's Gospel (Jn. 1:14). The Incarnation is interpreted by scholars as the significant manifestation of God's compassion for his people. It is this same theme of *being with* that characterizes the Christian theology of compassion, especially in relation to the sufferings of those victimized by unjust structures.

What does it mean to *be with* someone? Nouwen tells us that, "*being with* someone asks us that we share in the other's vulnerability, enter with him/her into the experience of weakness and powerlessness, become part of uncertainty, and give up control and self-determination."[137] Each time this happens we notice a new strength surging and a new hope born; we experience comfort and consolation in and through their actions, and by their presence. We experience solidarity and love from them by how they "willingly enter the dark, uncharted spaces of our lives," bringing us new hope and helping us discover new direction.[138] Nouwen brings out in this description an aspect which will play an important part in our understanding of compassion and its socio-moral and political implications, namely *solidarity*. As an integral aspect of compassion, solidarity is often used interchangeably with *being- with*, though with a higher intensity.

Solidarity, as we are using it here is, according to Jon Sobrino, "another name for the kind of love that moves feet, hands, hearts, material goods, assistance, and sacrifice toward the pain, danger, misfortune, disaster, repression, or death of other persons or other people. The aim is to share with them and help them rise up, become free, claim justice, and rebuild."[139] Put in another way, Sobrino acknowledges, "Solidarity is the Christian way to overcome, in principle, individualism, whether personal or collective, both at the level of our involvement in history and on the level of faith."[140] Solidarity as the basic principle of the Catholic social teaching has come through a considerable amount of formulation and reformulation. However, it translates into the willingness to give oneself for the good of one's neighbor, beyond any individual or particular interest that does not connote any idea of condescension.[141]

Within the context of our definition of solidarity we can see that Christ lived a life of solidarity with broken humanity. Apart from the incarnation, Jesus' baptism in my opinion, becomes another concrete and demonstrative act of Christ's solidarity, with huge significance and impetus for compassion in relation to our discussion. Dean Brackley thinks that the early church universalized Jesus' solidarity with the people of Israel, ritually expressed when he received John's baptism, in order to encompass the whole human story. Furthermore, that solidarity revealed a divine purpose, namely the redemption and transformation of the human world in all its dimensions.[142] Christ had no need of the baptism, Matthew writes, yet, he filed out with his people to receive the baptism. It was more of an act of identifying with his people in their brokenness, than just mere baptism because he felt the weight of their depression caused by the structures of sin. He did not stand aloof in the crowd, but was part of the people wailing, yearning and seeking their God and desiring to cross through the threshold of new life God was offering through the Baptist.[143]

Here Jesus' compassion does not yet bring about a tangible help to a suffering people nor does it seem that he has the solution all worked out. It rather consists in identification, seeking together with the people in their haplessness a way out of their predicament, in this case, by seeking God's face through the ministries of the Baptist. This illustrates the point we made in chapter one: that compassion as an effective response to suffering does not suppose that at all times we have the solution to these problems but that we seek together with the people a way out of their miseries. This is another salient aspect that differentiates compassion from pity, charity and mercy.

Thus, when we identify our God as God-with-us *Immanuel*, we simply say and mean that our God has come to share our lives in solidarity with us. This solidarity consists not in providing all the answers or taking away all our sufferings but rather, in entering with us into our "confusions, problems, and questions." It carries an understanding that God is intimately connected with us, suffers with us, and shares our pains and joys. In this way, he becomes our refuge, our helper, our stronghold. This is what we mean when we say with John the Evangelist, "he lived among us" (Jn 1:14).[144]

In the Pauline hymn in Phil. 2:6-11 we have the summary of the compassionate action of Jesus – *God-with-us* in such a way that vividly captures the whole Christ-event – his actions, passion, death and resurrection, as the template for our Christian compassion.

> Though being divine in nature, he did not claim in fact equality with God, but emptied himself, taking on the nature of a servant, made in human likeness, and in his appearance found as a man. He humbled himself by being obedient to death, death on a cross. That is why God exalted him and gave him the name which outshines all names, so that at the Name of Jesus all knees should bend in heaven, on earth and among the dead, and all tongues proclaim that Christ Jesus is the Lord to the glory of God the Father.

The hymn states some strong and obvious facts about Jesus: He was God, he emptied himself, took flesh like us and accepted the place of a slave; he remained obedient even to death on a cross; but God raised him and glorified him. According to John Paul II, for our action to be compassionate, it must possess three characteristics: it must involve suffering, it must be freely undertaken and we must be innocent.[145] As this hymn demonstrates, we have the three complete in Christ. With the final statement of the hymn, we see that the fullness of God's compassion as revealed in Christ does not end in suffering but in glory.[146] So when he tells us to be compassionate as God is, he assures us that, in emptying ourselves to the suffering of others, we may become reduced to nothing, to powerlessness; yet we remain powerful, transformed, and transforming.

Finally, in the Good Samaritan parable Jesus leaves us a model of all-embracing compassion. As John Paul II holds, the Samaritan does not stop at sympathy and empathy alone.[147] These rather became for him an incentive to actions aimed at bringing help to the injured man. In a way, the *Good Samaritan* has become an expression for one who brings help to others in suffering of whatever nature. However, it is not just about being good or bad, as Jack Nelson-Pallmeyer points out. We must always remember that it is about compassion.[148] Such help takes the whole heart of the helper into the situation; it is about being-with, and does not spare material means as well. It is a new way of bringing relief to the needy, not from a distance as pity, charity and mercy would, but by reaching out to the other in a way that includes personal contact, bridging all distances, geographic and psychic.

It is the giving of my very "I," opening it up to the other person, becoming vulnerable. In other words, it is changing my whole outlook on life and asserting that one cannot fully find himself or herself except through a sincere gift of oneself. This is being self-transcendent, according to John Macmurray.[149] We can thus sum up from this background, that "Christian faith is compassion in action. We are to love God and neighbor with all our heart, soul, strength, and mind (Lk. 10:27)."[150] With the compassion imperative, Nouwen submits, Christians might acquire a *second nature*. And in this new nature, he continues,

> Compassion is no longer a virtue that we must exercise in special circumstance or an attitude we must call upon when other ways of responding have been exhausted, but it is the *natural* way of being in the world. Compassion is no longer seen in moralistic terms, that is, in terms of how we have to behave as good Christians, but a new way of being in the world.[151]

And it is in fidelity to this call that we become a sign of hope in the midst of a despairing world.[152] This very fact anticipates our next two chapters where I will argue that it is only with compassion in its newness that the Nigerian church will prove its worth as sacrament of God's presence in the sufferings of his people of Nigeria.

There is another dimension to Christ's compassion which we did not yet reflect upon. It is obvious from the New Testament accounts that Jesus in his compassionate response to the sufferings of his people discovered that acts of injustice inherent in some of the socio-political, cultural and religious systems of his time were the root causes of the sufferings of many. He knew as well that such systems demanded more than individual contacts with sinners and material relief to the poor. He therefore perceived that compassion included a constructive challenge to those unjust structures; hence he took direct and indirect action in words and deeds that challenged those institutions. This dimension of Christ's compassion is what is referred to here and treated in the next section as *politics of compassion*.

Towards a Politics[153] of Compassion

As Marcus Borg observes in his work, though we can say that Jesus' imitation of the compassionate God was rooted in the Jewish tradition, yet it is also true that it was not in the style of the social class of his time. In his own style, yet rooted in Jewish theology, Jesus overturned the dominant themes of the social class of his time. For Jesus, compassion is not just a matter of personal sentiment or a mode of relation that applied only between individuals: it is a social paradigm, the core value of life in community. In other words, "compassion for Jesus is political."[154] What Borg meant by this expression is brought out vividly by Richard Cassidy. In referring to Jesus' compassion as 'social and political,' he maintains, "we emphasize that Jesus responded not only to the social situation of the poor, the infirm, and the oppressed, but also to the policies and practices of the political leaders of his time."[155] Jesus, as the Gospels show us, in response to the sufferings of his time, repeatedly and directly challenged the socio-political paradigm of his world.[156]

As Borg enables us to see, the socio-political dimension of Jesus' compassion comes out "in the conflict between [the] two *imitatio deis* – between holiness and compassion as qualities of God to be embodied in the community..."[157] For many Jews of the time, especially those with power, to be holy as God is holy (Lev 19:2) meant nothing more than purity – 'a separation from everything unclean.' Purity was not solely an individual thing for them but rather produced a politics upon which their society was structured. As is evident in other cultures, purity systems define, demarcate, and classify people from people.[158] It became a boundary line between the good and the bad; the clean and the unclean, the pure and the impure. As in all structural evils, the system marginalized many people, and supported the comfort of few, not simply because of their good deeds, but because of some privileged positions they found themselves in either by birth, health or social status.

When Jesus appeared on the scene, standing on the pedestal of the Jewish prophets especially the eighth century prophets, he, in his message and activities, set up an alternative to the prevalent social system. He gave a new interpretation to the imitation of God. To be holy as God is holy for him meant compassion – justice-making; hence, his injunction was, "be compassionate as your Father[159] is compassionate." By the way he went about his mission he advocated a community built not on the ethos and politics of purity, but on the ethos and politics of compassion. Emphasizing compassion above purity led Jesus to criticize the systems that upheld tithing high above justice. He called the Pharisees "unmarked graves which people walk over without knowing it." By this he meant that they who seek the extension of purity are sources of impurity themselves. Christ extolled the purity of the heart and not of outside appearances; in other words, purity is about the disposition of the heart and not external boundaries.[160]

What Jesus teaches in this new hermeneutic of the Torah's concern with holiness is succinctly captured by Nicholas Wolterstorff in his article, "Liturgy, Justice and Holiness." Here, Wolterstorff insists that for Jesus,

> The holiness of a community resides centrally in how it treats human beings, both those who are members of the community and those outside, even those outside who are 'enemies.' And specifically, the holiness of a community consists…in the members of the community embracing the broken ones, and working and praying for their healing… We learn from Jesus that a community which shuns the broken ones can never be a whole community – that is, can never be a holy community. The holy community is the merciful community, the just community.[161]

The new paradigm Jesus gave to compassion opens up a new understanding of his deeds of compassion. They are not mere relief brought to people in need. They are symbolic acts showing the extent to which his activities shattered the purity boundaries of his social world. He touched the leper and the hemorrhaging woman. He entered a graveyard inhabited by a man of unclean spirit. He would eat with sinners and be touched by them. For many, these were abominable acts within the theology and politics of purity. Within this context too, the parable of the Good Samaritan is understood as Jesus succinct capturing of all he meant by this new movement – the politics of compassion – an articulation of the critique of a way of life ordered around purity. "Whereas purity divides, and excludes, compassion unites and includes."[162]

He finally and publicly attacked the purity system centered on the temple activities. According to Ched Myers, Jesus' journey to and activities in Jerusalem, which include the attack on temple activities, articulate the climax of Jesus' compassionate response against the socio-political and economic activities of the dominant class of his time. His going to Jerusalem as a pilgrim, Myers opines, was not "in order to demonstrate his allegiance to its temple, but as a popular king ready to mount a nonviolent siege on the ruling classes." His actions in this final pilgrimage portrayed an ever-deepening contrast between two kinds of social 'power:' power of the *so-called leader* – leadership by domination and Jesus' alternative power – leadership by service.[163]

He began the inauguration of this new leadership by way of catechesis. His teaching, according to Richard Cassidy is, that "true greatness is not based on rank or position, but accrues from being able to recognize the worth and importance of those members of society frequently considered to be least important."[164] Using his disciples' struggle for positions as an example, Jesus offers a critique of systems of power: political domination, patriarchy and family. Myers suggests that all three of these systems have everything to do with the subjugation of women by men. Therefore, by attacking these systems of power, Mark argues that Jesus defended the equality of women against all patriarchal ideologies (Mark12: 18ff).[165] Women issue is singled out here because it remains one of the contending evils of our 21st century to which the attention of our compassion must be drawn.

Before continuing on the importance of Jesus' journey to Jerusalem, it is fitting to turn our attention, for a while, to the criticism that has come up in recent times against such claims as Myers,' that Jesus defended the equality of women against all patriarchal ideologies of the traditional Judaism of his time. Some contemporary Jewish scholars such as Judith Plaskow argue that to say that sexism, patriarchy and oppression in Judaism were upturned with the appearance of Jesus is an exaggerated opinion aimed at perpetuating the myth of superiority of Christianity over Judaism and also to distract attention from the many sexual discriminations leading to misogyny inherent in the Christian tradition and practices. Thus she accuses Christianity of projecting onto Judaism the failure of the Christian tradition to renounce sexism. According to her, such accounts of Jesus' Jewish milieu suffer from some serious scholarly errors or oversights which are rooted in biased views of Jesus' Jewish origins. Some of those errors and oversight are: using a later document – the Talmud – to judge an older period of history without proper sifting; using only the aspects of the document that talk about women in the negative without referring to such ambivalence in the Christian document; comparing the word of an itinerant preacher with laws and sayings formulated in the rarefied atmosphere of rabbinic academies. In light of the obvious, Plaskow suggests a revision in the treatment of Jesus' Jewish background based on "honest, balanced and nonpolemical discussion of those texts that are in fact contemporary with Jesus." She re-echoes that the Other, Judaism who is the recipient of these projections is of course the same one receiving any failure Christianity cannot appropriate to itself. She recalls the period of witch-hunting - the Inquisition.[166]

There is no doubt that some Christian people may be guilty of Plaskow's accusation. Unfortunately, it is beyond the scope of this work to offer a detailed response to Plaskow. However, as mentioned earlier, Jesus stood on the pedestal of former Jewish prophets whom he came not to abolish but to fulfill. Also as Borg insists, Jesus' compassion was rooted in the Jewish tradition. These two opinions indicate that the concern is not to blame Jews or Judaism. It does not either pretend about, or intend to deny, the many sexual discriminations leading to misogyny inherent in the Christian tradition and practices as Plaskow argues. The main idea being put forward here is that true compassion condemns structural injustice and evil and as a true prophet, Jesus, in his time undertook this aspect of compassion and thus leaves a standard to measure later Christian compassion and the deficiencies thereof.

Returning to our topic, which is, Jesus' journey to Jerusalem and its socio-political implications, it is vital to note that Luke continues the same theological geography.[167] His presentation in the Acts of the Apostles of the movement of the apostles – the first Christian community, to Rome is full of enormous symbolism. It was a continuation of their master's pattern of witnessing to the compassionate Father by fearlessly engaging with institutions and structures of injustice and oppression wherever they are.

According, to J. Milburn Thompson, "Jesus' call to compassion as a radical challenge to the theology and the politics of the dominant social system of the time, a social structure that placed an oppressive burden on the poor and the marginalized, was not addressed only against the Jewish purity system." It was also addressed to the oppression of the Roman Empire of his time. In these oppressive contexts, Jesus proclaimed the good news that the reign of God was at hand, offering liberation, justice, and compassion. The early church took up this mission with valor. In their understanding of the new politics based on compassion, Paul declares: "There is no longer Jew or Greek, there is no longer slave or free, there is no male or female, for all of you are one in Christ Jesus" (Gal 3:28).[168]

Within this context, the disciples call everyone to conversion. Conversion here does not basically connote proselytism. It means first and foremost, turning from selfishness towards love. As Paul admonishes, "Let each of you look not to your own interests, but to the interests of others. Let the same mind be in you that was in Christ Jesus, who … emptied himself, … and became obedient to the point of death" (Phil 2:4-5, 7,8).[169] The implication of this conversion, Thompson maintains, is that Christians are to be socially subversive, that they must work for the transformation of the world in the mind of their master. This implies also that the Christian is called, not only to change his or her heart, but also to change unjust social, political, economic and cultural structures of human existence. "Conversion," he said, "is not addressed to the heart alone."[170] Therefore Borg writes,

> In the midst of our modern culture, it is important

for those of us who would be faithful to Jesus to think and speak of a politics of compassion not only within the church but as a paradigm for shaping the political order. A politics of compassion as the paradigm for shaping our national life would produce a social system different in many ways from that generated by our recent history.[171]

In their social teachings, various Christian churches have interpreted the social dimension of this call to compassion by Christ and thus provided the theoretical framework for a politics of compassion. In a teaching that summarized all the social teachings before and after it, the 1971 *Justice in the World*, the International Synod of Catholic Bishops teaches that "Action on behalf of justice and participation in the transformation of the world fully appear to us as a constitutive dimension of the preaching of the Gospel, or, in other words, of the church's mission for the redemption of the human race and its liberation from every oppressive situation." Work for justice, they maintain, is not optional but central and essential for a life lived in relationship with God.[172] The World Council of Churches in its Zimbabwe 1998 conference came up with the theme, *Responsible Society*, and clearly indicated that justice demands the transformation of social structures.[173]

The concept of compassion advanced in this chapter, especially from the Christian perspective, argues that the love commandment impels the Christian to undertake an active involvement in solidarity to reduce the sufferings of the other. It also obligates the Christian, both individually and as Church, to bring the precepts of compassion to the corridors of those socio-political structures of our society that may, and in fact, do breed suffering. In other words, compassion means that a Christian cares for the helpless and the indigent, and is also concerned about the conditions which produce the need for charity. As illustrated by A. D. Mattson, "The Good Samaritan performed a Christian service when he came to the man who had fallen among robbers '... and bound up his wounds, pouring on them oil and wine; and he set him on his beast, and brought him to an inn, and took care of him.' The Christian has an added interest in such a situation from the point of view of his social responsibility. The Christian is also concerned about making the road between Jerusalem and Jericho safe, so that men (sic) may travel that road without falling into the hands of robbers. Such manifestation of Christian love may not be as dramatic or sentimental as the former, but it is oftentimes more effective."¹⁷⁴

However, this understanding has received a host of possible objections. Some people do not see how compassion can be compatible with socio-moral and political actions. While some Christians worry about how socio-political action is a constitutive part of compassion and Christian life, some secular socio-political ethicists do not see compassion as an inalienable characteristic of our way of life. The worry of some of these Christians we have taken care of in the preceding sections. We maintained all through that the social dimension of our compassion, a consequence of love's responsibility rests upon two significant facts: First, that the entrance of our neighbor into this love affair (i.e. our love of God and self) automatically leads us into the social arena. Second, the fact that Christianity is a social and historical event lived not in isolation but in the concrete existence of time, space, and culture that we call society, brings social perspective to the Christian life of love.

From a practical perspective, as A. D. Mattson argues, our concept of neighbor continues to expand from a single individual to individuals (plural), not limited to the confines of our ecclesial communities but including the environment, the social dimension of the love imperative becomes more apparent. As existential and social realities come to bear on this relationship, it becomes ever clearer to us that there are some demands of our love of neighbor that cannot be limited to or effectively accounted for on the private, one-on-one level. Thus we concluded that there are aspects of our responsibility for the neighbor which can only be approached with the resources of our socio-political arsenal.¹⁷⁵ Our next concern is the position of the secular socio-political ethicists. This is what we will be addressing in the next section.

Compassion in Relation to Socio-moral and Political Concerns and Action: A Response to the Critics

From the ancient to the contemporary philosophical tradition, compassion has occupied a central position. Among its critics, such as the ancient Stoics, Spinoza, Kant and Nietzsche, compassion is criticized on the basis of the relationship between emotion and reason. These philosophers teach that *reason* and *will* are the most important things in life and that "one can achieve a virtuous reason and will by one's own effort without the aid of external resources."¹⁷⁶ For them, compassion, like all other emotions is irrational: it is a "non-cognitive force that has little to do with thought or reasoning of any kind." Thus they hold that employing compassion in public or socio-political affairs is to base "political judgment upon a force that is affective rather than cognitive, instinctual rather than concerned with judgment and thought" – "one that is likely to mislead or distract us when we are trying to think well about social policy."[177] In this light, they conclude that compassion as moral sentiment is unworthy and insulting to the dignity of both the receiver and the giver who are both rational beings. Such "'soft-handed benevolence,' as they say, should not occur at all among human beings."[178]

In response to these attacks, Martha Nussbaum joins other scholars like Robert C. Roberts and Lawrence Blum to argue that emotions and rationality are correlated to such a degree that reason or rationality is said to derive its worth from its connection with affective responses. John Macmurray makes a similar claim in his argument against traditional modern philosophy which maintains that "*cogito ego sum* – I think therefore I exist." Macmurray contends that knowledge does not primarily come from thinking, rather, from "what one does correctly in relation to other agents."[179] Nussbaum thus opines, "Any rationality deserving the name has to be able to explain the emotive force of judgments in the practical setting, and it must understand the ways in which judgments normatively demand certain sorts of affective responses."[180] In other words, for one to make a judgment, one has to understand what the facts of one's judgments really mean. The emphasis therefore is "on the way a person thinks about what he or she feels. This 'thought process' will also entail commitments to beliefs that can be judged by objective yardsticks of *truth and appropriateness.*"[181] In furtherance of the argument in favor of emotions as constitutive parts of cognitive process, Edward Vacek, a leading Jesuit scholar in Christian Ethics, using Charles Taylor's argument, postulates that, "emotions are in part cognitive; they apprehend objects as either positively or negatively valuable, as good or evil. Through emotions we become attached to those great goods that inspire our lives, and without them we 'become incapable of understanding any moral argument at all.'"[182] These arguments are neatly wrapped up in this axiom of a great man of the modern times, G. K. Chesterton, "the madman is not the man who last lost reason. The madman is one who has lost everything except reason."[183]

From this standpoint, Nussbaum contends that compassion is related to reason because, to experience compassion, she claims, does not only involve feeling. It necessarily involves "rational thought and belief based on standards of truth and appropriateness which allows for critical reflection of and a just response to that suffering."[184] In other words, for one to be compassionate involves not only the feeling or passion aroused by the suffering of another person, but also what one cognitively does with this feeling. From her Aristotelian background, she maintains that compassion has three cognitive elements: "the judgment of *size* (a serious bad event has befallen someone); the judgment of *nondesert* (this person did not bring the suffering on himself or herself); and the *eudaimonistic judgment* (this person, or creature, is a significant element in my scheme of goals and projects, an end whose good is to be promoted)"[185]

Based on this principle of eudaimonistic judgment, Nussbaum further argues for relation between compassion and reason, maintaining that compassion provides a solid basis for reason. This principle she says, acknowledges some sort of commonality between the compassionate one and the sufferer "without which one may react with sublime indifference or mere intellectual curiosity, like an obtuse alien from another world; and one will not care what one does to augment or relieve the suffering."[186] Her understanding of eudaimonstic thought expands beyond the individual to accommodate general human flourishing as an intrinsic concern of compassion. This understanding connects with the idea of the common good and provides for the universality of compassion that is developed in this work.

On ground of this evidence Nussbaum submits that compassion is "not merely impulsive, but involving thought or belief... suffused with thought, and thought that should be held to high standards of truth and experience." It is "a central aspect of reason, providing both a justification and motivational explanation for the creation of civil society."[187] In this understanding Nussbaum would say that if our societies are shaped by the principles of compassion, our political thoughts will attend to human facts that will respond to the conditions of the "worst off" groups in society. Thus she concludes, saying that "compassion is intimately related to justice." It both contains "a powerful, if partial, vision of just distribution and provides imperfect citizens with an essential bridge from self-interest to just conduct."[188]

Finally, Nussbaum admits that though "all compassion is rational in the descriptive sense, not all are in the normative sense." She does advocate that we ought to do some filtering to be able to recover the worth of compassion, especially in the public system.[189] Her suggestion reaffirms our attempt at the beginning of this chapter to liberate compassion from its imposters. As Scheler demonstrates, action – immediate relief and justice-making are the criteria by which we distinguish true compassion from pseudo-compassion.[190]

When this is done, Nussbaum believes, our public education system will begin to promote programs that will enable students to imagine the experience of others and participate in their sufferings.[191] Political leaders will begin to "display abilities involved in compassion that do not show mastery of facts about their societies and their history only, but also to take on in imagination the lives of the various diverse groups who they lead." There will be a shift in focus of economic planning, one that will measure national wealth and income by how much they correlate with the quality of lives of the people.[192] This directly responds to contemporary global economic principles as we mention in chapter one and the Nigerian situation as we shall be seeing in chapter three. Legal rationality would then enable judges to acquire the kind of information that not only collects facts but enters into the lives of others with empathy and sees the human meaning of the issues at stake in them. Lastly, public institutions will be structured in such a way that "we do not need in every case to rely on the perfect compassion of individual actors; to rely on philanthropies, since we can design a just welfare system, and a system of taxation to support it."[193] We could agree with Nussbaum that though this is not an easy task yet it is not impossible.

In this work, Nussbaum provides that seamless integration of ethics, philosophy and spirituality that reinstates the validity of compassion in our discussion. The attempt recovers compassion from the jaws of critics so that we can once again say that compassion remains a rich energy source. It is concerned with the preservation of human dignity and that of the entire creation. Thus, it qualifies as the primary ethical act that cannot be ostracized from public and personal life, as some ancient and contemporary critics propose.

Summary

The phenomenology of compassion, we have come to discover from our discussion in this chapter, as Oliver Davies argues, reveals the dynamics of "consciousness itself, and thus provides a resource for articulating a new language of being."[194] It is a broad concept whose connotations and further possibilities keep reverberating.[195] Liberated from imposters, it remains the effective way of responding to others' suffering in a manner that not only provides answers but constantly seeks better ways in solidarity with those who suffer. We saw also that for the Christian it is a vocation that cannot be frustrated or intimidated by any amount of criticism. Equally, in the way and manner Christ our leader practiced compassion, we have received a new impetus that empowers our compassion with a socio-moral and political responsibility; this we have called a politics of compassion.

In the first two chapters we explored the two major topical concepts of this work: suffering and compassion. At the moment, we are going to apply this theoretical context to practical situations in our next chapter, The chapter will contextualize the concepts within the Nigerian situation in order to substantiate their claims and thus prepare us for further inquiry in chapter four, where we will explore the meaning, implications and dynamics of a politics of compassion.

CHAPTER THREE:

SUFFERING AND COMPASSION: A NIGERIAN PERSPECTIVE

As Robert Schreiter reminds us, "meaning and truth are established through practical social judgment and grounded in the narratives of living communities that sometimes mesh, complement, challenge, or correct each other."[196] In the light of this statement, this chapter undertakes the practical application of the concepts of suffering and compassion we have studied. This undertaking will analyze the socio-economic and political situation of Nigeria with the view to identifying various forms and causes of suffering that dwell therein. This chapter will also evaluate compassion within this context by surveying the various ways the Nigerian church has responded to these sufferings.

Suffering: A Nigerian Perspective

Suffering has been previously defined as the experience of a painful state of consciousness and the decline, distortion or destruction of the environment. In order to situate this understanding of suffering in the Nigerian context, we shall divide this section into two, namely: the description and the causes of suffering in Nigeria.

Suffering in Nigeria: A Description

> Nigeria is an enigma wrapped in a puzzle. It is a nation of such enormous landmass, yet citizens are fighting for land, a nation of such incredible wealth, yet it wears poverty like a breastplate; a nation of seemingly deep religion, yet so steep in much sin; a nation so populated by farmers and farmland, yet hunger stalks the land and the nation cannot feed itself, a nation with so many petrol stations, yet no fuel, a nation with so many politicians, but no political class, a nation with millions of houses, yet no houses, a nation with so much riches, but no wealth, a nation with so many believers in God, but no faith, a nation with so many office holders, but no leaders, a nation struggling to develop, but not growing.[197]

In the above words, Rev. Fr. Matthew H. Kukah presents a true picture of the complexity of suffering in Nigeria. His quote suggests that there is much to be explored on this topic and various angles from which one may view the nature of suffering in Nigeria. For the purpose of this work, we will concentrate on poverty, human rights deprivation and environmental devastation.

Poverty: We are using the term poverty generically and descriptively to include both economic preoccupation that expresses lack of food and other material lacks, and the sum total of other human needs of the average Nigerian. For according to the United Nations Secretary General, Kofi Annan, "Poverty is more than just a lack of income; it is also the lack of health care, education, access to political participation, decent work and security. All these factors are interdependent and must be addressed simultaneously if efforts to reduce poverty are to be effective."[198]

The story of Nigeria's Poverty is entrenched in a heartbreaking contradiction that reveals the destructive nature of suffering for its victims on the one hand and the insensitivity of the rich towards the suffering of the poor on the other hand, as the following accounts reveal.

Nigeria is the sixth largest oil producing nation yet the thirteenth poorest country in the world.[199] The country continues to languish in the bottom quartile of the Human Development Index, with over 90 percent of its population surviving on less than $2 (US) a day.[200] At the same time a decimal of its population swims in affluence and scandalous ostentation.

There is a very high rate of unemployment in Nigeria. According to the International Labor Organization (ILO), unemployment is judged by the "numbers of the economically active population who are without work but are available for and seeking work, including people who have lost their jobs and those who have voluntarily left work."[201] For instance, in a report published in May 2000 by World Bank and Nigerian Institute of Social and Economic Research, over 100,000 applications were received by the Federal Civil Service Commission of Nigeria with only 3301 jobs.[202] In today's Nigeria, the estimate is that over 50 percent of the working class have no job at all and about 60 percent of those employed do not have permanent job; and what is more? many of the fortunate ones who work, work for barely a pittance. The average living wage of the ordinary Nigerian worker is N5,000.00 ($50 US) a month while simultaneously a Nigerian legislator earns a salary of N500,000.00 ($5,000.00) a month. Sometimes the salaries of the ordinary Nigerians are slashed, not paid on time or never paid at all. For lack of job, a teeming number of young college and university graduates roam the streets of Nigeria in search of any means possible to make a living. I see today as never before children and sometimes adults in the cities and suburban areas scavenge through hills of garbage trying to eke out a living. On the contrary, jobs are reserved, waiting for the children and kinsmen and kinswomen of the rich and top government functionaries. At times, some of these so called privileged members of the society earn their salary without working for it.[203]

The mortality rate among the people (especially infants) is on the increase. According to the 46th Independence speech of the president of Nigeria, life expectancy in Nigeria today is 57 years.[204] This is because there are very few functional hospitals and clinics, and there is a lack of drugs and an alarming shortage of medical personnel. It is estimated that there are only 27 physicians available to 100,000 people in Nigeria. Today, Nigeria has over one million AIDS orphans and over four million people infected with HIV out of a total population of about 140 million,[205] and many people die of curable diseases.[206] On the other end, there are some Nigerians who can afford the best of doctors and can fly to clinics abroad for common ailments such as headaches, and worse still there are some who undergo cosmetic surgery on taxpayers' money.[207]

There is no welfare and no medical security for the retirees. Pensioners are not paid and many die in long queues waiting for money that may never come. This occurs in the same country where $500 billion US has been stolen from the nation's coffer and piled away in the Swiss and Western banks by leaders for their descendants yet unborn. In that same country a governor in 2005 spent 53 million Naira to buy cars for traditional rulers.[208]

Housing is another horrible condition in Nigeria. Families with as many as ten members pack themselves in one bedroom apartments, often with poor sanitation and without light and water, while some Nigerians own chains of houses within and without Nigeria.[209] Similar kinds of extremes exist in education. The federal ministry of education in Nigeria said in 2004 that about 12 million Nigerian children are unable to attend school for lack of funds.[210] Many Nigerian children who pass entrance examinations into secondary and post secondary institutions are never admitted because their places have been bought and reserved for the children of top government officials and the rich. Money and social status, not academic qualifications, are the major prerequisites for gaining admission into educational institutions. Again, in a country where schools are regularly shut down and teachers' salaries are not paid because of lack of funds, a state governor could afford to spend 300 million Naira to travel abroad with the state legislators for a purported training course on parliamentary procedure.[211]

As we shall later discuss, these contradictions pose a great question that material relief as a response to suffering cannot answer. As we have seen from this situation, it is true as Kofi Annan says, that "Many ingredients go into making poverty, but factors like discrimination, unequal access to resources, and social and cultural stigmatization have always characterized it. These "factors" have another name: the denial of human rights and human dignity."[212]

Human Rights violation: Nigeria has a bad human rights record. It dates back to the era of military in politics. Democracy has not upturned the ugly situation; instead, the situation goes from bad to worse. There is a widespread use of torture by the police on suspects and sometimes innocent and defenseless citizens. There are numerous cases of innocent civilians maimed, or killed at security posts by the Nigerian police and soldiers, in attempt to extort money illegally from the victims in most cases. Last Christmas, a US-based Nigerian young man was shot dead in his car by soldiers who mounted an illegal road block (security check point) on one of the Nigerian high ways. The victim's offense was that he delayed in responding to the soldiers' need, and for wanting to know why he had to give them money. A similar incident took place in February this year, in Lagos, when another US-based Nigerian businessman was gunned down by a policeman on patrol.[213] Of the many cases of these abuses by law enforcement agents, none has been brought to justice by the government.

As a matter of fact, the government sometimes mandates such atrocities. We have fresh in our memories the Odi military massacre of November 22nd 1999[214] and the Zaki-Biam blood spill of October 2001 both of which claimed not less than 200 lives of defenseless civilians. These were committed by the Nigerian military called upon by the government to protect the interest of the oil companies in Niger Delta and to revenge the killing of some soldiers by militant groups.[215]

The story of Odi massacre is deep-rooted in the justice and equity struggle of Ijaw people of the Niger Delta area of Nigeria. They demand a fair share from the proceeds of the natural resources God has generously deposited in their land. As <u>The Washington Post,</u> of Nov 9, 1998, described, "The curse of natural wealth has fallen heavily around the Niger river delta, Africa's most lucrative oil field. Nearly 40 years of oil production, directed mostly by military governments, has left the delta peoples poorer, sicker, less nourished and less educated than the rest of the country. Oil spills have damaged fishing grounds and farmland."[216]

In this area that harbors about 6 million of the Nigerian population, the people have no electricity, clean water, roads, and other basic amenities. Unemployment is on the increase in this area. Yet, excruciatingly, the people watch "the crude oil tapped from their land, piped hundreds of miles to the north, where it is refined, providing employment and industrial activity to the political dominating group – the 'Hausa-Fulanis.'" It was this insufferable situation that ignited the fire of the struggle for justice, in the hearts of some Niger Delta activists. They insist on not just equity but a redistribution of income from their oil.[217] At some stage in the struggle, as it appeared to them that the Federal Government was not yielding to their demand, the activists included secession threat as a component of their struggle. The first of such threat was in 1965, when the Isaac Adaka Boro-led group called for a Niger Delta Republic. The call was resurrected again in the 1990s by Ken Beeson Saro-Wiwa's Movement for the Survival of the Ogoni People (MOSOP). The government of Gen. Sani Abacha was indeed threatened by this call for Niger Delta Republic. The President saw it as another Biafra saga and thus condemned Saro-Wiwa and his eight men to death by hanging. He saw to it that they were executed, regardless of plea for clemency and justice from Nigerians and international communities.[218]

The death of Saro-Wiwa and his compatriots only provoked more commitment to the struggle to the degree that frightened the Nigerian government. In order to keep the situation under their control, the federal Government embarked on full militarization of the Niger Delta area. The soldiers were charged with dual responsibility of protecting oil companies, and to disarm and to distract the people from commitment to their plight. Instead of being deterred, the people were rather re-energized the more. "In December 1998, 500 men from Ijawland came together to sign what is known today as the Kaiama Declaration of the Ijawland.[219] They asserted their ownership of their land, demanded the withdrawal of what the people identified as military forces of occupation and repression by the Nigeria state. They further threatened that any oil company that employed the services of the armed forces of Nigeria to protect its operations would henceforth be regarded as the enemy of the Ijaw people.[220] They formed their own security outfit – Niger Delta Volunteer Force (NDVF) and vowed to go to war at the violation of any of their mandates.[221]

In order to avert this threat and more so, to demonstrate its power and unflinching sovereignty over all the areas of Nigeria, the federal government deployed more police to that area. A section of the militant youth rejected the deployment and they massacred 12 of the policemen as a show of their anger and to register their protest. In retaliation, on Nov. 22, 1999, the six months old democratic government of the Federal Government of Nigeria led by Gen. Olusegun Obasanjo (rtd) dispatched a military troop to Odi. Their mission was just one, namely to take their pound of flesh. They did exactly that, by "unleashing [of] mindless carnage on the entire people of Odi, an Ijaw community."[222] This incident lives forever, in the memory of Nigerians as Odi military massacre.

Even with all this, condition of living has not improved in any way in that region nor has the struggle ended. The plight for a better condition and a free and united Niger Delta Republic has also continued. Their current leader, Alahaji Mujahid Dokubo-Asari is presently (at the time of this writing) detained in one of the country's clandestine prisons.

It did not take long after the Odi bloodbath for the story of wanton desecration of human life and destruction of properties of defenseless citizens by the Nigerian Army to repeat itself. This time it was in the Middle-belt region of the country. The Tiv and Junkun – two neighboring tribes, have a long history of tribal rivalries and conflicts. Their tribal crisis erupted again in October 2001. Soldiers were called in to quell the disturbances and maintain peace in the area since the police were not up to the task. Some militiamen among the Tiv abducted 19 soldiers and killed them in a most barbaric and gruesome manner. In retaliation, the President of Nigeria in his usual manner commanded that more soldiers be deployed to that area, again, to take their pound of flesh. Again, the soldiers did just that by razing the whole area, rendering it a ghost town. They raped, maimed and killed innocent civilians, and destroyed properties and forced many to an unprepared refugee.

At the end of the ordeal, an independent investigation of the Human Rights Watch, indicted the government in its report saying, "It was a well-planned military operation, carried out in reprisal for the killing of 19 soldiers in the group. Those who died at the hands of military were victims of collective punishment, targeted simply because they belonged to the same ethnic group." President Obasanjo, did not refute the allegation but rather replied, "I dismissed the Human Rights Watch report with the contempt it deserves because it failed to condemn the killing of soldiers who were sent to separate the feuding Junkuns and Tivs." The same President also had earlier said to Financial Times in April 19, 2002, regarding the ordeal, "you do not expect me to fold my hands and do nothing because tomorrow neither soldiers nor policemen will go anywhere I send them.... When you send soldiers, they do not go on a picnic... in human nature, reaction is always more than action."[223]

Apart from these two examples, various governments in Nigeria have been indicted in other cases of the destruction of human lives by armed hoodlums, where corpses are sometimes allowed to rot in the open. There are cases of state-hired security agents organizing the killing of suspects in full view of people, including children. Most disheartening about these killings is the brutality with which they are carried out. Many a time the victims are hacked to death with machetes and set ablaze, as people watch them burn.[224]

According to the 2006 report of the International Confederation of Free Trade Unions' (ICFTU), there is evidence that about 15 million children are engaged in illegal labor, 40 percent of this number are trafficked, and 2 million work more than 15 hours per day. The same report reveals that several child slave camps exist in the western states of the country, where children are used in mining and on rubber plantations. Those who challenge the situation and other labor related issues are jailed and tortured. In 2004, the National Legislature pressured by the President passed a law restricting the rights of the National Labor Congress (NLC). They declared strike actions illegal in Export Processing Zones; contravening the conventions of the International Labor Congress (ILO).[225]

Apart from children, women are the highest victims of human rights abuse in Nigeria. They are discriminated against in politics, economics, family life, and religion too. Surveys show that a wide gap exists between men and women in labor market. Findings by the United Nations Development Funds for Women (UNIFEM) observed that "Nigerian women are under-represented in the paid workforce. In the formal sector, women constitute 30 per cent of professional posts,

17 per cent of administrative/managerial positions, and 30 per cent of clerical positions; 17 per cent are employed in 'other' categories. Women are disproportionately concentrated in low paid jobs, particularly in agriculture and the informal sector."[226] Such is the case because some jobs are still considered men's prerogative. Therefore, women are not adequately trained or not trained at all for such jobs. This is why 67 million Nigerian women are currently represented by only 3 out of the 109 elected senators in parliament.[227]

Finally, to a large extent, women are seen as instruments for the selfish interests of men or as objects of pleasure. Reports indicate that about 15,000 Nigerian women and girls were trafficked to Italy alone for prostitution between 1999 and 2002.[228] A Nigerian woman is still considered her husband's property and in fact it is thought that she derives her dignity and fullness from her husband, as this Igbo saying holds, "*mma nwanyi bu diya*" – "the beauty of a woman is her husband." This is why, according to Luke Mbaefo, "women decide to be second wives in order to escape from the social opprobrium of social status of having no husband." At a time, Mbaefo continues, "the number of wives a man had was taken as index of his wealth and social status."[229]

Focusing on the "bride prize" custom in Igbo culture, Mbaefo goes further to accentuate and vehemently insist on his claim that that a woman is said to be bought by her husband hence she was practically viewed by this culture as a piece of property of her husband. Some African scholars contest this claim and would disagree with this interpretation. They see this as a Eurocentric bias, a derogatory interpretation of the Igbo custom of "bride prize."[230] But Mbaefo would insist otherwise. He further argues that for the fact that a man can send back his wife to her parents and receives his "bride price" back proves that she belongs to him as any property would.[231] In fact, within this tradition, a divorced woman whose bride prize has not been returned to her divorced husband cannot legitimately remarry until she has done so.

On the account of many of these odds, as Stan Ilo notes, some "Nigerian wives live silently with domestic violence, domestic enslavement, marital infidelity, and the drudgery of household work as part of what it means to be a wife."[232] Many of these women are forced into marriage at an early age below eighteen. In many of these cases, these marriages serve the interest of the parents. There were occasions where young girls were given into marriage just to settle a financial debt owed by their parents. These issues of early marriage account for the increase in pregnancy and child birth related deaths. According to the Grassroots Action for Sustainable Health and Rural Development Report (GASHRUD) as quoted in Stan Ilo's work, "one out of every five pregnancies in Nigeria ends in death of the mother." Should their husbands die before them, such widows are subjected to untold inhuman treatment.[233]

This situation of human rights violations especially that of women, presents a disheartening amount of suffering that, as mentioned in the previous chapters, our compassion cannot afford to overlook. It substantiates as well the claim that compassion must surpass charity as material relief, for it to respond effectively to some sufferings. But let us consider another form of suffering in Nigeria.

Ecological destruction: As mentioned in chapter one, nature is a victim of the raging cruelty of human beings. There is something about the wanton destruction of the environment that stimulates in us our distress and compassion. This becomes more evident when we consider the deplorable condition of other species and ecological life in Nigeria. As Akande Adebowale observes, since the discovery of oil in Nigeria in the 1950s, ecological life in Nigeria, especially in the Niger Delta region has suffered various forms of exploitation.[234] Gas flares burn day and night, roaring and polluting the air with thick sooty particles. There are oil spills and fires resulting from rusted pipes of the oil companies. These spills and fires account for the many cases of deforestation and destruction of biodiversity in the country. According to US Energy Information Service, there have been 4,000 oil spills in the Niger Delta since 1960. Almost all the waters in the Niger Delta are polluted and poisoned.[235] Nigerian ecology also suffers destruction because of commercial purposes. For instance, there is an increase in the European and North American demand for wood from Nigeria for which trees are felled indiscriminately without replanting new ones. In the final analysis, the harmful effects of the degradation of the ecosystem are borne dispassionately by the poor, contributing to growing inequalities and disparities across groups of people. Many a time, these factors constitute major causes for poverty and social conflict.[236] The Niger Delta region of Nigeria presents a perfect example of these results.

These attitudes contribute in no little way to the present climate change havoc that threatens the whole humanity. Gas flaring is the greatest contributor to greenhouse emission, maintains a communiqué issued at the end of an environmental parliament to draw attention to issues of global warming by Environmental Rights Action/Friends of the Earth Nigeria (ERA/FoEN). As we have earlier observed, it contributes more than 85% of the greenhouse emissions in Nigeria. "Nigeria flares and wastes more gas than any (other) place in the world because BP and Shell and Agip companies only care about getting the oil and never about what happens to the gas getting burned off in the production process."[237] Leslie Fields (an African American woman who battles for sanity and reason in an insane, unbalanced world) recounts during one of her visits to Ogoni land, "they flare on the ground, they flare it ceiling high, they flare it all over the place; so all these communities have terrible pollution. I've seen pipelines next to health clinics and elementary schools – they just put them everywhere."[238]

Unfortunately, the threat of climate change knows no boundaries, says Haya Rasshed Al-Khalifa, President of the sixty-first session of the United Nations General Assembly. That climate change takes its toll on the Nigerian people and environment is not hearsay. As in many other nations of the world, so in Africa, "deforestation, desertification, soil erosion, biodiversity loss, water pollution and urban solid waste are perhaps the most significant environmental problems experienced in Nigeria."[239] I arrived at this conclusion last summer during my holiday in Nigeria. While some of these are direct or indirect consequences, others are primary or secondary causes of climate change. Knowing the wet season in Nigeria, I have some firsthand experience of the drastic effects of climate change, such as overall less rainfall despite particular instances of heavier rainfall in a single day. Traveling within Nigeria, I personally discovered other effects which had previously come to my attention through the report of the editors of Nigerian Climate Change.[240] On one of my trips to the north, I witnessed the disastrous effects of the increased desert encroachment. The excessive heat there was so unbearable that I had to cut my stay in the north shorter than I had scheduled. Even Jos the capital city of Plateau State, which used to be one of the coolest spots in Nigeria is no longer cool. There was also an unprecedented period of total absence of rainfall, which adversely affected agricultural product and other water-related activities in Nigeria. Not only that many livestock died but that it caused pastoral migration which often results in deadly clashes between the indigenes and the migrants.

When at last rainfall increased, it deluged many places causing greater risk of erosion in the process: to the extent that gullies and river depositions created a lot of hazards' for the masses living alongside waterways. It was a nightmare traveling by road. It was horrible traveling through southeastern and south-southern states. Ogoja and Abakiliki roads were almost impassable.

Though forms of land degradation in Nigeria occur on different scales, no part of the country is safe from it. "Flash floods in the north, gully erosion in the east, deforestation in the south, desertification in the north and rapidly increasing carbon dioxide emissions elsewhere - all wreak enormous havoc on humanity [and biodiversity]."[241] Bassey Nnimmo, executive director, ERA/FoEN, disclosed recently, "rising sea levels from warming temperatures may see the whole of Lagos, Bayelsa and River states go under water, with the inundation also covering up to half of Cross River and Delta states. [Those living or doing business on Muritala Mohammad Way, along the Bar Beach in Lagos would confirm this prediction.] Then in the north, advancing desert climate could render economic activities impossible in vast areas stretching across the region from Kebbi, Sokoto and Zamfara states in the northwest, to Yobe, Borno, Adamawa and Taraba states in the northeast."[242] Everyone knows of the present food shortage and the tension into which it has thrown the whole nation.

Simply put, the climate change phenomenon is as real in Nigeria as it is elsewhere in the world. According to a report on Nigeria under United Nations Framework Convention on Climate change (UNFCCC) released on 1 August 2007, "thirteen million Nigerians are currently at risk due to climate change vulnerability, a report on climate has shown." The same report says that those at risk would have to relocate.[243] This was also confirmed by President Yar'Adua in his presentation to the United Nations General Assembly last fall. In his speech, the President acknowledged that climate change has negatively affected the ability of Nigeria and other countries of Africa to meet the Millennium Development Goals (MDGs) and has also been a contributing factor to some of the conflicts on the continent.[244]

Finally, it is worth mentioning that attempts by activists to bring this unfriendly and inordinate use of ecology to an end have always attracted brutality from the government and resistance from the oil companies. The world still remembers that environmental concern was one of the causes for which the Federal Government of Nigeria hanged Ken Saro-Wiwa and eight other Ogoni environmental campaigners on November 10 1995.[245]

We can see from this description the complexity of suffering and the various forms in which it comes to Nigerians. It is obvious that many sufferings lead their victims to loss of hope and to no positive effect; in other words, they are utterly destructive. There is much physical pain, mental anguish, disruption of social relations, inhibition of persons from achieving their potentials and unqualified destruction of nature. However, in some cases, some suffering has become purposeful and transformative for some Nigerians. For instance, the activists who bear the brunt of suffering on the account of their concern for the conditions of others they oppressed, point to this dynamics of suffering that has given hope and purpose not only to them but to the oppressed.

As we realized in our analysis of suffering in chapter one, understanding the causes of suffering is seminal to a fuller comprehension of the concept and how we respond to it. This proposition applies more to the Nigerian situation than in any other case. This is what we shall be looking at in the following section.

Causes of Suffering in Nigeria

Suffering, we have seen, is classified in relation to kinds of evil, such as: physical, moral and structural. The same methodology is applied here in relation to the causes of suffering in Nigerian.

Unprejudiced study of the Nigerian situation reveals a sheer case of nature taking the back seat in the cause of suffering, as Matthew Lamb would say. In fact, Nigerians claim that God loves them more than any other nation as they count their innumerable natural blessings ranging from rich natural resources, good weather, less environmental hazards, and so on. It is apparent that the sufferings as experienced in Nigeria are human-made and a high percentage linked with structural sin or evil – the systematic violation of human rights and rights of other sentient beings and creatures.

Personal sin or evil such as reckless and shameless greed, unrestrained corruption, and accumulation of wealth amount to the various ways individual Nigerians create and multiply the sufferings of their fellow citizens. These are evident in the various accounts of looting of government treasury and the misappropriation of public funds by various leaders of governments. According to the recent report of Transparency International and the Government's anti-corruption body, Nigeria duly remains in the bottom ten of the corruption perception's index.[246] However, some of these personal evils could not be possible without the cooperation of some systems. These systems, as we mentioned in chapter one, create a social relationship that "simultaneously strengthen and disguise" these personal sins. For the purpose of this study, we have identified three principal structures that are connectedly linked with suffering conditions in Nigeria: contemporary global economics, politics and religio-cultural institutions.

Contemporary Global Economies: We recall, as mentioned in chapter one, that contemporary global economies create and increase suffering in societies through the dangerous systemic imbalance in their policies. Such policies as they apply to the Nigerian situation include: replacement of local economies with global economies, introduction of market and economic principles alien to developing countries, repositioning of absolute power to multinational corporations and the confiscation of government powers, and lastly, imposition of stringent economic measures for institutional reform.

First, scholars are in agreement that suffering in Nigeria began to escalate in the 1970s when Nigerian oil gained global interest. With this development, the oil industry displaced agriculture which until then had accounted for 63.3 percent of the nation's Gross Domestic Product (GDP).[247] Because of the displacement of agriculture, and other local market and subsistence economies by the oil industry – which were controlled by foreign multinational corporations and few privileged Nigerians – many Nigerians had nothing to fall back on and thus lost their jobs.

Second, as Tissa Balasuriya observes, globalization has been responsible for the most ecological devastation and environmental pollution in the Third World. The environment and other life forms in Nigeria, as in other Third World countries, "have been affected adversely by the modern industrial, commercial culture and the lifestyle of the rich which fails to establish a sustainable relationship with the natural world."[248]

Third, the repositioning of absolute power to multinational corporations gave rise to the arrogance of companies like Shell and their insensitivity to the harms their operations inflict on the Nigerian land and people. For instance, the Nigerian government banned gas flaring since 1969 but Shell and others continue even now, as this writing is going on, to flout the law. Recently, the Nigerian Senate ordered Shell to pay compensation of $1.5 billion to Ijaw communities in the Niger Delta for all its ecological damages to the region, but the oil giant never complied claiming that the legislators were acting beyond their powers.[249]

Fourth, with the IFIS' imposition of SAPs[250] on Nigeria in the 1980s and 1990s, suffering in Nigeria took a turn for the worse. With this economic policy, the Nigerian government was rendered unable to care for its citizens. All government subsidies on education, health, and other social amenities and services were withdrawn. The people watched government-owned infrastructures crumble while the government, spending more on debt servicing, helplessly watched its people die on a daily basis. Downsizing of the workforce resulted in mass unemployment and an exodus of Nigerian skilled workers to other countries. For instance, George Ehusani records that, as of 1996, about 21,000 Nigerian medical doctors work outside the country.[251] As Tissa Balasuriya writes, "The pressure to go abroad due to inadequacy of family income and job opportunities, disrupts family life, distorts family values and relationships, leads to the neglect of children, and, in many cases, the harassment and degradation of women and increased violence against them."[252]

With privatization policies, global economies gave economic

power and dominance to a minority, thus leaving many at the mercy of the greedy tyrants to whom the government abdicated its right to care for the citizens. This development, to say the least, has widened the gap between the rich and the poor, and given vent to proliferation and intensification of class conflict, confiscation and unprecedented violence.[253] Finally, the system cloned a political system whose sole interest is to protect the market and the property of the few. This leads us to the next cause of suffering in Nigeria.

Politics: The problem associated with governance in Nigeria continues to increase suffering on the masses. This issue dates back to the colonial era. Having amalgamated into a nation people of about 250[254] different tribes, tongues, politics, cultures, and social and religious systems, the British immediately advanced a political system that best served their interest at the detriment of the masses. They introduced an *indirect rule* system which left the British in charge of the national government that controlled the whole economy; local governance was left in the hands of local leaders (chiefs and emirs as the case may be). The British consolidated much power on these individuals, who became lords and tyrants. To make sure that their place was protected without challenge from the locals, the British employed the *divide and rule*[255] political technique, which set each group against the other.

The nationalists who took over from the British at independence in 1960 continued in the footstep of their masters. That resulted in renewed rancor between the different tribes and the institutionalization of tribalism in Nigerian politics. These lapses in the political system and the cry of marginalization gave rise to the May 30th 1967 secession of Biafra[256] that sparked off Nigeria's civil war and claimed over 3 million lives. Since then, Nigeria has been left with a porous political system that breeds injustice, exploitation and marginalization.

Post-colonial Nigerian politics has been dominated by thirty years of brutal military dictatorship. With the suspension of the constitution, the junta ruled by decrees which they issued at will. Since the economy is so tied to the national government, their rule was sustained by corruption, sometimes resulting in incessant coup d'états, bloodshed, lawlessness, and the violation of human rights and untold hardship so pervasive that Nigeria has become synonymous with bad governance.

The story did not change with democracy. The few times democracy has been tasted, the rule of law has never been operative, and the leaders have become as corrupt, arbitrary and tyrannical as the soldiers. Yet they are protected by the system. Democracy in Nigeria as in most other developing countries is often more nominal than real. As Amy Chua notes, the "great majority of the impoverished electorate do not have a political voice, whether because they lack information or because the wealthy control the political process through lobbying or corruption."[257] It is a thing of the rich and the powerful. Hence, what we have in Nigeria is a recycling of a particular class – military dictators and dynastic families who are often aided by foreign and multinational corporations whose interests are tied with this class.

Since what matters in democracy in most developing countries are numbers, or as the popular slogan holds, "politics is the gain of numbers," the political class does everything to win the required majority. Today, elections have left bitter memories in the minds of many Nigerians. As the former Vice President of the country, Atiku Abubakar told journalists, regarding the 2003 general election, "Most elections are rigged before they occur because candidates are eliminated through various methods, these include subverting party constitution and rules, the use of thugs, corrupting party officials to disqualify or annul the nomination of some candidates and other illegal methods of distorting the wishes of the electorate."[258] John Odey calls it "Democracy through the barrel of guns."[259]

The same story was told everywhere in Nigeria about the 2007 general election. Clifford Ndujihe in his article, "April Polls Already Rigged, says Nwabueze," quotes Prof. Ben Nwabueze (SAN) saying, "Nigerians should realize that rigging has started. Rigging does not start on the election day. It starts from the voters' registration and continues up till the elections. We saw it in the last voters' registration exercise where registration machines were found in private homes and people were registered illegally and such voters would be used for ballot stuffing". In the same article, the chairman of a group of eminent Nigerians called *The Patriots* added: "Now, the next level is disqualification of strong candidates. This is to weed out people that will give them stiff competition. In Anambra State, they have excluded Governor Peter Obi, Dr. Chris Ngige and Nicholas Ukachukwu and left only Andy Uba so that he will walk to the governorship seat unopposed. With Vice President Abubakar out, they are clearing way for Alhaji Umar Musa Yar'Adua".[260]

When in power, the members of the ruling class do everything within their reach to bend the constitution to achieve their selfish interests, as President Obasanjo tried to extend his stay in office beyond the constitutional two terms through a stage-managed constitutional review. Hence, using the words of the same President, politics or governance in Nigeria is characterized by "wanton greed, unbridled corruption, intolerance, injustice and primitive accumulation of wealth." And as the President admits, this is a case of leaders deliberately and indirectly inflicting hardship on people through an institutionalized bad leadership, bad government and misplaced priorities.[261]

Indeed, the way democracy operates in Nigeria has forced many to ask whether democracy is necessarily the most efficient form of government. The evil of this structure is so intense and agonizing because of its deep-rooted hypocrisy. It is called government of the people, by the people and for the people, yet it harbors and allows for an organized manipulation by a few who perpetuate exploitation and increase the suffering of the masses under the cover of the law.

The celebrated economist, George B. N. Ayittey, in his bestseller book, *Africa Unchained: The Blueprint for Africa's Future,* summarizes for us the political scenario of Nigeria espoused by this work. "A leader is supposed to pursue the common interest of the people but in [Nigeria] we have those who pursue only their selfish interest and do not give a damn about us. They oppress us, brutalize us, and steal our money to accumulate a huge personal fortune in Swiss banks."[262]

This is a very painful situation. Like the proverbial guard that has been put in charge of the poultry to prevent the chickens and eggs from being stolen, our leaders like the guard, made away with our chickens and eggs to the chagrin of all and sundry.[263] Ayittey's examples here are simply illuminating. "After only four and half years in power, the late General Sani Abacha ("The Butcher of Abuja") amassed a personal fortune worth more than $5 billion. General Ibrahim Babangida ("The Great Maradona of Nigeria) accumulated more than $7 billion. He walks freely, thumbing his nose at the people."[264] He was campaigning for the presidency in this year's election until he agreed to step down for his kinsmen, Musa Yardua and General Mohammed Buhari.

"As Senate President for about a year and half, late Senator Chuba Okadigbo controlled 24 official vehicles but ordered more at a cost of $290,000. He was also found to have spent $225, 000 on garden furniture for his government house, $340,000 on furniture for the house itself ($120,000 over the authorized budget); bought without authority a massive electricity generator whose price he had inflated to $135,000; and accepted a secret payment of $208,000 from public funds, whose purpose included the purchase of Christmas gifts."[265] "Senator Arthur Nzeribe once declared that General Babangida was the only person good enough to rule Nigeria. When pressed, he confessed: "I was promised prime ministerial appointment. There is no living politician as hungry for power as I was who would not be seduced in the manner I was to invest in the ABN – Association for Better Nigeria, with the possibility and promise of being Executive Prime Minister to a military president."[266]

On September 2, 2004, the then governor Joshua Dariye was arrested by the British Police. He laundered more than £2 million. He jumped bail and returned to Nigeria where again the obnoxious immunity clause provided protection for him. Soon after Dariye's case, another governor, this time from the oil rich Niger Delta, Dieprieye Alamieyeseigha was also arrested on the grounds that he was making attempts to transfer £20 million from his account with the HSBC in London. It was alleged that the Metropolitan Police recovered about £1million and €70,000 from him.[267] The list of instances of corruption is indeed lengthy and we can go on enriching this list with many more examples. In the recent probe going on in Nigeria regarding bogus $16bUS contracts that were awarded by the immediate past president of the country to build up the energy sector, one hears the same old story. Most of these contracts were discovered never to have been awarded or they were awarded to fictitious or incompetent companies which turned out to be in the names of either the president himself or his son or other allies of his such as Gen Abdusalam Abubakar rtd, Nigeria's last military leader that handed over power to him, Obasanjo in 1999.[268]

Seeing this picture one may agree with the Nigerian World-class novelist Professor, Chinua Achebe that:

> The trouble with Nigeria is simply and squarely a failure of leadership there is nothing wrong with the Nigerian character. There is nothing wrong with the Nigerian land or climate or water or air or anything else. The problem is the unwillingness or inability of its leaders to rise to the responsibility, to the challenge of personal example which are the hallmarks of true leadership.... I am saying that Nigeria can change today if she discovers leaders who have the will, the ability and the vision.[269]

However, suffering in Nigeria cannot be linked to contemporary global economy and governance only. Some of it is caused by some religio-cultural institutions in Nigeria.

Religio-Cultural Institutions: Nigerians are so much tied to their religions,[270] ethnicity, culture and traditions. As is noted by Stan Chu Ilo,

> In Nigeria, people identify themselves more by their ethnic origin than by their national identity. One is first a Yoruba, Ogoni, Hausa-Fulani, Igbo, etc., then a Nigerian. The priority of the ethnic identity in Africa over the national identity is ontological as well as historical. People can connect with their ethnic identity in terms of their personal history, their cultural traditions, their language, way of dressing, customs, etc. What is referred to, for instance, as a Nigerian culture is a nebulous concept. It is true of other African countries.[271]

Ethnicity, "or a sense of 'peoplehood,'" according to Naomi Chazan, and co., "has its foundations in combined remembrances of past experience and in common inspirations, values, norms, and expectations."[272] [It] is defined here in line with Fredrick Barth's idea as "a distinct group in society self-consciously united around shared histories, traditions, beliefs, cultures, and values, which mobilizes its membership for common political, economic, and social purposes..."[273]

In Nigeria as well as in other African countries, it is said that "the blood of tribe is thinker than the water of baptism."[274] This idea thus makes politics of indigene and non-indigene a very serious issue in Nigeria. According to the April 2004 report of Human Rights Watch on Nigeria, "Throughout Nigeria, non-indigenes are forced to cope with state and local government policies and practices that exclude them from many of the material benefits of Nigerian citizenship."[275]

Nigerians are also dubbed the most religious inhabitants of the planet by an international opinion poll.[276] In the streets of Nigerian cities churches and mosques are lined up in numbers one would rarely see in any other place in the world. And on Sundays and Fridays, Christians and Muslims attend to their religious businesses in their teeming numbers respectively. It is not unusual to observe that most government offices in Nigeria do not start the day without, first, saying their morning prayers.

Unfortunately, religion has combined with some cultural practices to become oppressive tools that serve and worship the interest of a few while increasing the suffering of majority in Nigeria. Sometimes the policies of these institutions promote very subtle and devastating injustice. It is the unquestioned attachment to these institutions and the manipulation of the systems by the rich, and the ruling class – elders, chiefs and emirs, priests, pastors and other religious leaders as the case may be – that have often given rise to bloody religious and communal crisis and violence in the country, from which Nigeria has lost over 10,000 lives since 1999.[277] Such ethnic and religious sentiments lead to ethnicism, tribalism, fanaticism and bigotry that come up especially when one seeks either employment or admission into schools.[278]

As we observed in the case of the Jewish purity system in Jesus' time, some of the tribal or ethnic purity systems denigrate many people not just to a second class ranking but to nobody at all. The *osu*[279] caste system prevalent among the Igbo of Nigeria defines people on the borderline of free-born and slave. Until recently, the *osu* were subjected to horrible conditions, worse than the outcast of the Jewish time. They never mingled nor intermarried with others and they were not considered nor counted during population census. These practices against the *osu* prevailed among Christian communities. Acts such as these will later occupy our attention as we allude to the inherent contradictions in the church impeding it from adequately challenging unjust structures.

Sometimes too, the laws of these religio-cultural institutions are applied differently to people depending on one's economic class or gender. For instance in the Zamfara state in the northern region of the country where *shar'ia* law is enforced to the letter, anyone caught stealing will have his or her limb amputated. Recently, the state governor approved the amputation of the hand of one Mallam Jangedi accused of stealing a cow. A few months after that, the governor was accused of embezzling the state's money. To date, this *sha'ria* tenet has not applied in his case.[280]

Inter-ethnic and religious strife in Nigeria has made Nigerians suspicious of each other even to the point of death. In 2003/4 the Muslim authorities in Kano state suspended polio vaccination over suspicion that the vaccination has side-effects – suspected as a plot of the Christians to reduce the number of Muslims in the country. Unfortunately, while the children of poor families bore the effect of this decision, the rich Muslims would have had their children inoculated elsewhere.[281]

Again, women are the most affected by the systematic injustice of these institutions. Most Nigerian religio-cultural settings are very patriarchal. The systems encourage misogyny and other ill-treatment of women. There is a high preference of the male-child over the girl-child in many cultures in Nigeria. For this, the people invest more in the training and development of boys than girls. For example, in the Muslim dominated northern Nigeria, school enrolment for girls lags significantly behind that of boys.[282] As mentioned above, some laws are applied differently according to gender or class. It took the intervention of the international community to spare the life of one Alhaja Amina who was condemned to death by stoning for an act of adultery in the above mentioned Zamfara state; but nothing was said of the man with whom she committed the adultery. A woman seen on the street in the same state dressed in pants or trousers will not go without being harassed, punished and stripped naked but there is no dress code for the men.[283]

Marriage institutions of many of the tribes in Nigeria, such as those we have seen above make it difficult for women to protest against domestic violence and mistreatment. While it is lawful and easy for a man to divorce his wife, it is very difficult for a woman to leave a marriage no matter the condition. Polygamous practices still prevalent in some Nigerian societies are very unfair to women who are seen as properties of the men, and they subject these women to many unbearable situations. The woman has no right of inheritance either in her maiden or in her marital home. Again, and very important, some socio-cultural and religious policies make it difficult for women to be gainfully employed without being married. As pointed out earlier in this chapter, when a woman loses her husband, she is subjected to an inhuman widowhood.[284]

Customs concerning widowhood have been described as most maltreating elements of the Igbo culture and practices. The practice varies from locality to locality but as Rose Uchem expresses, widowers do not suffer the same treatment as widows. This is why she sees it as subjugation of women. Luke Mbaefo thinks that this treatment stems from the fact that a woman by marriage is seen as the property of the man without whom she is no person hence when the man dies she goes back to her state of 'no person.'[285] Some of the rituals the widows are expected to go through are: to remain in a ritual confinement for a year, go barefoot, wear tattered wrappers, have their hair shaved, keep indoors in a dark room, sit or lie on the bare floor, prove their innocence of the man's death. In many cases, women are often suspected and accused of being responsible for the death of their partners. In such cases, in some localities, they are administered water used for washing the corpse (their husbands) to drink as a proof of their innocence of the man's death.[286]

As Kwok Pui-lan, a Chinese feminist, holds "many missionaries, both male and female, accused indigenous traditions of being oppressive to women without the slightest recognition of the sexist ideology of Christianity."[287] This is very true even in the Nigerian situation. For instance, P. K. Uchendu notes that the few privileges women enjoyed in the pre-colonial and pre-Christian Nigeria were lost with the advent of Christianity. Among others, Uchendu points out that Igbo women had some voice, and distinct role in the traditional society and its governance through the various women associations allowed within the traditional system, such as *Umuada* – "the daughters of the clan."[288] It was the empowerment that came from these associations that enabled Igbo women to rise up against the British government in Nigeria in 1929 when they instructed that women should pay tax.[289] But when Christianity came and preached total renunciation of one's culture and people, Christian women lost their place and participation in the government of their local communities.

In other instances, Rose Uchem suggests that there is a malicious collaboration between Nigerian cultures and Christianity in perpetuating subordination and subjugation of Nigerian women. She cites an example of this type of relationship with the Igbo cultural denial of women of the right to participate in the blessing and sharing of "kola nut" which is also endorsed by Christian men. She thus relates that practice to the theology of Catholic priesthood. These are referred to as men's prerogative.[290] In her interpretation, the prohibition of women to participate in the kola nut ceremony/ritual is an expression of men's pre-eminence and women's subordination, which is reinforced by the continued exclusion of women from Catholic priesthood.

She observed with dismay that when women rise against these practices in the society and the church, they often meet an "identical reaction in both cases: 'It is our culture! It is our tradition! We cannot change it!' in this case, what women experience as oppressive custom is defended and accorded a permanent and sacred status in both church and society."[291] Uchem notes also that sometimes, Christianity cooperates in the subordination of women by being indifferent to the cultural and structural practices of subordination of women while concentrating on personal sin and co-existing with these social ills.[292] As we shall treat in the next section of this work, this is one of the lapses of the spirituality of dualism – its inability to see the connection between the secular and the sacred or sometimes a deliberate act of bifurcation between the social and the religious that simply maintains the status quo.

Of a very significant concern, as in other structures – global economics and Nigerian politics, the custodians of these religio-cultural institutions command an enormous amount of unchallenged authority which makes it easy for them to do and undo. From the exposition of these three structures, we come to see how structures can cooperate in various ways to increase the sufferings of many people. Again we agree with Dean Brackley as cited in chapter one, that "enterprise or structures of death have no real life apart from personal sin; [yet] the collective enterprise of sin is more than the sum of personal sins."[293] Therefore, re-echoing Richard McAfee's words, "we misunderstand injustice if we see it only in individual terms and assume that if we can just change (or get rid of) a few unjust individuals, we will have cleared the path for justice."[294]

Finally, the Nigerian story as we have just seen, presents to the younger generation, the future hope of the nation, nothing but "distorted human consciences through structured injustices of society into which they were born."[295] As Reuben Abati, *The Guardian* prolific columnist, graphically articulates:

> Young people in Nigeria today face special challenges. They live in a society that is morally disturbed, where values have been turned upside down and there is so much uncertainty. They are bombarded daily by spectacles of failure and dispossession. They are surrounded by compatriots who are involved in a rat race. At an impressionable age in their lives they read about thieving governors, about ministers who have inflated contracts, and collected or given bribes; they hear about Governors who dress like women and jump bail in a foreign land; local government chairmen who go to the Council only at the end of the month to share money, lawmakers in the National Assembly who collect N50 million to mortgage the people's sovereignty…They see all these persons and they are persons who by Nigerian standards are considered successful. Young people in Nigeria today are left at the mercy of dangerous signals…[296]

Having concluded this section on suffering in the Nigerian perspective, the most obvious question that comes to mind is, "what is the response of Nigerians to these sufferings and their causes?" Since our concern in this work is with the Christian responsibility, I have chosen to respond to this question by attempting to contextualize compassion as we have studied within the Nigerian situation. This is the topic we are tackling in the next section.

Compassion: A Nigerian Perspective

As we have articulated in this work, compassion leads us to enter into the vulnerability of others in solidarity that seeks the best possible means – material and otherwise – to eradicate their suffering and its causes. In attempt to relate this understanding and our analysis of compassion to the Nigerian situation, we shall divide this section into two. The first part surveys the responses of the Nigerian church to the Nigerian sufferings as we have outlined above while the second attempts to understand why the church responded the way it did.

<u>The Church[297] and its response to socio-economic and political situations in Nigeria</u>

In their joint pastoral letter on the 1st October 1960 – Nigerian independence day, the Nigerian Catholic hierarchy assured the people of Nigeria that their "efforts will be constant to defend and further the freedom that has been won, to make independence in all aspects real and not something held in name."[298] It is on record that no other document from the Nigerian bishops has been as rich and focused as this 1960 pastoral letter. The document was very detailed and practical in its treatment of Nigerian issues – both as experienced then and anticipated. By its statement in this document, the church in Nigeria pledged a firm commitment to actions that will not only sustain and enhance the nascent independence, but also improve the life of the people, thereby giving its mission a social dimension. In other words, the Nigeria church acknowledges compassion, the readiness to enter into committed actions for the other, as a part and parcel of its mission.

The Bishops remained true to their words as their subsequent pastoral letters and communiqués would always reflect on one Nigerian issue or the other. For instance, their message addressed to leaders and people of Nigeria in November 1966, bemoaned the tragic event of bloody coup d'état that took place that year. They called for fraternal love.[299] At the heat of the Nigerian civil war, their December 1968 letter, apart from expressing the church's distress and embarrassment over the allegation that the church was supporting some sections of the country in the war, appealed to all people "to leave aside bitterness, to give up recrimination, to pray and work earnestly for peace."[300] Of course, the bishops joined the people of Nigeria to celebrate the end of the civil war. In their February and March 1970 letter christened, "Statement, Decisions and Recommendations," the bishops lent their voices to those of other Nigerians in thanking God "for the most longed for blessing of peace."[301]

After the 1960 letter, the February 1972 document became the first letter to take up social justice problem again. The document – "The Church and Nigerian Social Problems," pin-pointed the 'signs of the times,' itemized the issue of social problems in the country, such as unemployment, housing, migration, sanitation, education and the lot of women. The document asserted that "the world to which the church has been sent to is depraved, sick, and divided. This weighs heavily on consciences in modern times. All men (sic), especially church men (sic), have the duty and obligation to cooperate with others to heal the sick world, provide succor to the deprived, foster unity and lessen tensions in the world."[302] The document indeed renewed the promise the hierarchy made in 1960 to the Nigerian people – an unflinching commitment to the cause of justice.

When in the late 1990s the military dictator, Sani Abacha, threw the country into a political impasse with his rapacious intent to succeed himself, the church called the whole country to prayers and fasting and came out with a well worded prayer, christened "prayer for Nigeria in distress:"

> All powerful and merciful Father, you are the God of justice, love and peace. You rule over all the nations of the earth. Power and might are in your hands, and no one can withstand you. We

> present our country Nigeria before you. We praise and thank you for you are the source of all we have and are. We are sorry for all the sins we have committed and for the good deeds we have failed to do. In your loving kindness keep us safe from the punishments we desire. Lord we are weighed down not only by uncertainties, but also by moral, economic and political problems. Listen to the cries of your people who confidently turn to you. God of infinite goodness, our strength in adversity, our health in weakness, our comfort in sorrow. Be merciful to us your people. Spare this nation Nigeria from chaos, anarchy and doom. Bless us with your kingdom of justice, love and peace. We ask this through Jesus Christ our Lord. Amen.[303]

This prayer may remind us of a similar call to prayer by the South African church in the apartheid days.

> We now pray that God will replace the present unjust structures of oppression with ones that are just, and remove from power those who persist in defying his laws, installing in their places leaders who will govern with justice and mercy….we pray that God in his grace may remove from his people the tyrannical structures of oppression and the present rulers in our country who persistently refuse to hear the cry for justice… we pledge ourselves to work for that day.[304]

In the similarity of these prayers one can still notice a very significant difference. While the South African prayer is ended in, "we pledge ourselves to work for that day," the Nigerian's ends with, "through Christ our Lord." The simple implication of the difference in the two endings is, while the South African church would not leave the work to God alone, the Nigerian church does not pledge any commitment to action and instead believes that it is God's work. However, using

Gregory Baum's expression, my criticism of the way Nigerian church ended its prayer does not intend to "present the struggle for liberation as a Promethean project, thus failing to stress God's unmerited grace that empowers people to act on behalf of justice."[305] Instead as St. James would insist, our faith must be matched with action, for faith without deeds is totally dead (James 2:14-26).

Since then, after the Abacha saga, there have been repeated calls to prayer for the Nigerian situation by the church at different occasions. However, like the first, none of the prayers gave any clue that the church is ready to be actively involved in any way. From the tone of these prayers, it would seem that the Nigerian church's understanding of compassion is limited in relation to compassion as understood in this work both in its general concept and in the new paradigm within which our discussion is based. According to the secretary of the Catholic secretariat of Nigeria, George Ehusani, "When it comes to prophetic confrontation with unjust social structures, when it comes to challenging the evil status quo, the social teaching of the church does not seem to have 'taken flesh' in the Nigerian context."[306]

In most cases, the Nigerian church has interpreted and taken compassion to mean providing material relief for the poor, the displaced and the needy only. There are many educational institutions, hospitals, food banks, clean water programs, homes for the destitute, etc, run by the church. There are St. Vincent de Paul societies in almost every church in Nigeria. These and other related groups such as interdenominational relief committees cooperate with local and international NGOs to bring aid to many people.

It is observed too that every diocese in Nigeria has both at the diocesan and parish levels a Justice, Development and Peace Commission (JDPC). The members of this Commission occasionally engage in socio-political actions like the monitoring of elections, providing job opportunities for some people and advocating for the marginalized. Very importantly, the church spearheaded the abolition of the *osu* caste system in most part of Igboland. It is also important to mention that members of Catholic Charismatic Renewal Movement (CCRM) have in many occasions taken up heroic steps to defend women against unjust acts. At this time, the Nanka martyrdom comes to mind. In this particular incident that occurred in the late 1980s, members of this pious group had turned out en masse to support their widow member who at the demise of her husband, refused to be subjected to those inhuman widowhood practices we have seen above. Unfortunately, the group lost two of their members in this episode, as members of the local community later turned the scenario into a deadly fiasco.[307]

However, a general evaluation of these activities of the church classifies them as piecemeal compared to the expectations Nigerians have of their church. Equally, pastors sporadically call the rich from the pulpit to be generous to the poor. A few church leaders occasionally also talk on social issues, but in most cases such talks lack the bite strong enough to challenge the unjust structures. According to Ehusani, "They have remained on passionate appeals, and benign denunciations, but lacking any practical gestures of solidarity."[308] Or as Paul VI puts it in *Octogesima Adveniens* – a letter addressed to Cardinal Maurice Roy, president of the Council of the Laity and of the Pontifical Commission for Justice and Peace, May 1971, "... It is not enough to recall principles, state intentions, point to crimes, injustices, and other prophetic denunciations. These words lack real weight unless they are accompanied for each individual by the lively awareness of personal responsibility and by effective action."[309]

On the whole, though these acts of the Nigerian church made tangible contributions and brought some relief to the needy, yet they do not challenge oppressive systems that continue to increase suffering for people. They are something short of the concept of compassion we have developed in this study – a compassion that not only provides relief materials but would, when demanded, permeate the corridors of causes of suffering – a compassion that not only challenges these causes but points to a better option. The type of compassion Christ demonstrated by his baptism – identifying with the people in their yearning and moving towards the solution to their problems. The type, as Rolheiser suggests in our story in chapter two would "go up the river, beyond the bend and find out why, daily, those bodies came floating down the river." Or as Augustine says, "you give bread to the hungry; but it would be better were no one hungry, and you could give it to no one" – a compassion that works to substantially reduce the needs for exercising charity. The troubling question then is: "But why has the Nigerian church neglected this all-important aspect of compassion in its attempt to respond to the many sufferings of the people of Nigeria?"

Accounting for the disabilities of the Nigerian church in taking up socio-moral and political actions in response to the Nigerian sufferings

Two major reasons have been advanced as to why Nigerian Christians and churches seem unfamiliar with the socio-moral and political dimensions of Christian compassion.

First, the spirituality inherited by the Nigerian church from its missionaries is proposed as a possible reason why the church and Christians have responded in the way they have to the Nigerian problems. This traditional spirituality preached a dichotomy between body and soul based on the belief that the body was evil and the soul good, time was corrupt and eternity pure, that earth was to be shunned and heaven sought, that flesh was the seat of impurity and spirit the seat of blessedness.[310] Therefore, to be saved subsists in disengaging from the evil world. This means that one is to scorn one's body for the sake of the soul, forsake earth for the sake of heaven, and stamp out the flesh for the sake of blessedness.

This spirituality, as Robert McAfee Brown notes is exemplified in the writing of Thomas a Kempis, *The Imitation of Christ and Contempt for All the Vanities of the World*, a treasured spiritual book in Nigeria still. This devotional prayer book taught Christians to look for the things in heaven where Christ is, because the world is not an arena for human fulfillment and Christian living but an arena fraught with temptation, sin and suffering. The spiritualist advises, "he who loves God, despises all other love." This conclusion led him to assert that "love for neighbor, love for one in need, and love for a spouse are all to be spurned so that love may center exclusively on God." Distancing oneself from others and the use of worldly things like food, clothing, and shelter without desire is regarded as saintly, for God looks with favor on those who "for love of virtue withdraw themselves from their acquaintances and their worldly friends."[311]

As we have seen in chapter two, such spirituality encourages sentimentalized compassion, masochism and apathy that avoid action in the face of the suffering of others. It negates Jesus' teaching on love of God and neighbor which, according to Augustine, are our feet. To stand on one, he says, is to be crippled.³¹² Such love as Christ taught and practiced meant compassion demonstrated by action and justice-making. In summary, the problem of this spirituality is not with its insistence on the doctrine of eternal life. Rather, its deficiency lies in the inability of its theology of salvation to see any correlation between this-world and other-world.

The implications of this spirituality are enormous in the socio-political lives of Nigerian Christians. It results in what Richard McCormick describes as *dormant social consciousness,* splitting between *articulated Christianity and lived Christianity,* the components of which are ignorance, inadequacy and apathy. "Such ignorance suffices in separatism or dualism – that continues the belief of discontinuity between this life and the life after, church attendance and domestic virtues." It also gives rise to "individualism that conceives social responsibility in terms of one-on-one relationships." The combination of the two – separatism and individualism, McCormick says, leads to "inadequacy – a sense of hopelessness and powerlessness and ultimate apathy."³¹³

It is this spirituality, still taught today with vigor in some Nigerian churches, which makes the people inert in the face of injustice, oppression, and suffering. They take consolation in the words of St. Paul, "the sufferings of the present time are nothing to be compared to the glory that is laid for us ahead" (Rom. 8:18). As for their unjust oppressors, Paul commands that we should obey constituted authorities, hoping that on the last day the Lord will bring those wretches to a wretched end (cf. Rom. 13:1ff; Luke 16:19-31; Matt. 21:33-46). The political world for them does not belong to the children of God, the children of the kingdom; it is earthly, with no relation to the Christian thing and is guided by its own autonomous dynamics.³¹⁴

For them, as Herbert A. Deane notes, "there is only one true republic in which perfect peace, harmony, justice and satisfaction are assured to all citizens; that society is the *civitas Dei,* which exists eternally in God's heaven and is the goal of God's elects while they sojourn as pilgrims in this sin-ridden, wretched earthly life."³¹⁵ Even though the 1960 pastoral letter of the Catholic Bishops Conference of Nigeria encouraged participation of its laity in secular politics, it was not until in the late 1980s that the church for the first time, in a more concrete form, encouraged its laity to take active participation in political activities. At this time, there were series of lectures, seminars and workshops on the laity and politics organized in Catholic churches across Nigeria. Yet, many people would still be scandalized today when their pastors talk about political things, challenge unjust structures or agitate for a political reformation.

Finally, there is an intrinsic hypocrisy associated with this spirituality. Its idea of sin is much more limited to individual personal sins which are often based on the commandments of the church. In that light, a Christian feels righteous when she or he attends Christian worship and other Christian regulations, contributes to the support of the pastors, gives alms to the poor while he or she is still involved in unjust systems. For them this simply means "giving back to Caesar what belongs to Caesar and to God what belongs to God" (Mk. 12:17).

Secondly, because of contradictions in the life of the church, the Nigerian church has not been able to respond to the socio-economic and political structures of sufferings the way it should. Because of the presence of these contradictions, the Nigerian church lacks the moral credibility and authority to speak out in the face of social evil. For example, there are elements of craving and insatiable hunger for material things and favor in the church which only the rich and influential people in the government and society can quench. For these, the church becomes vulnerable to the baits of politicians, for they say, "he who pays the piper dictates the tune." Hence the church is manipulated by the oppressive authority in the society.[316]

Like a political economy that values human beings only by what they can produce, churches and pastors are sometimes rated by the hierarchy according to how much money they make.[317] Poor parishioners are taxed and the administration of some sacraments depends on the payment of these levies. These practices also encourage bribery, as people seek to maintain their lucrative parishes and ecclesiastical positions, just as politicians do. There are elements of nepotism, tribalism, embezzlement and scandalous displays of affluence among the clergy. There is also sexism, class distinction, lack of accountability and transparency. Clericalism, as is the case in the Nigerian church, appears in all its forms: patriarchy, paternalism, subordination, dominance, accumulation and self-interest. These factors widen the gap between the sheep and their shepherd. The people cannot, as it were, approach their pastors. So when the wolves appear the sheep are left defenseless on their own without their shepherd.

Before, many looked up to the churches, says Reuben Abati, but now the story has changed. In some places of religious worship these days, the principal message is that only the rich can get to heaven. The rich have special seats. They are accorded special recognition. They are often praised as being hardworking and specially blessed by God. The poor, on the other hand, are the only ones who are required to listen to the scriptures.[318] They become doubly marginalized as they are meant to feel that they are the cause of their poverty.

Some religious ministers are no different from the political tyrants and usurpers. According to Toyin David-West in his article "Our Dollar Pastors,"[319] our pastors use the bible to coerce the poor to donate money not just for their (the pastors) upkeep, but mostly to sustain their indescribable luxurious and extravagant life style. The idea is that if you do not give, you will not escape God's wrath, as David-West describes in the following passage. Toyin David-West is one of the many Nigerians who make their living in the United States of America. One day he returns home, Nigeria, on one of his annual visits to his fatherland. While in the city of Port Harcourt, he worshiped in this Pentecostal Church where he experienced what he writes in this article:

I am compelled to write on this subject owing to my recent experience in Nigeria where the term "church planting" has assumed a new meaning. Some of our dearly "beloveth" dollar pastors are on the prowl again and this is very troubling. Church planting has become a mega-business and many families are now dependent on it for daily survival. The world of corporate churching in Nigeria as scandalizing as it is, is gaining more momentum. This trend is a testament to our dwindling moral fortunes as a society, a people and most importantly, as a nation. It's a further testament to the sad fact that the unsavory economic situation has compelled many to venture into areas once considered sacrosanct and inviolable. The pulpit meant for truly anointed men (women) of God now parade sycophants, hypocrites, Pharisees and wolves in sheep's clothing canvassing to be men and (women) of God and at the same time smiling all the way to the bank. My grouse, however, is with the methodology of accomplishing this noble goal.

On this occasion, the pastor, decked in a made-in-heaven three-piece suit of an unimaginable styling and cost, rose to his feet and claimed the attention of all. He read from a portion of the Bible that served as a precursor to his charismatic appeal for funds. When it was time for the rubber to meet the road as they say, the pastor made it clear that those who were holding back risked damnation from God. He stated clearly that even if you do not have, you must give. But how would they give? From what will they give? Can one get water from a rock? There were people in the congregation who were truly poor and destitute and did not even know where their next meal would come from. Later, I learned that the pastor was already living in a six-bedroom mansion located in the very expensive new Government Reserved Area (GRA) of town where a mere 50 by 50 plot goes for upwards of N5 million. It also came to my knowledge that the pastor takes frequent and expensive shopping trips overseas (London in particular) and had in his garage a fleet of expensive cars in the form of Mercedes Benz S-class for himself and a Lexus jeep for his wife and Toyota Land cruiser as spare, all brand new. With all these, it is safe to say that the cost of these cars, the jewelries worn by his wife and his most expensive suit can account for fifty percent of the cost of building the new church.[320]

Worse still, church workers do not receive good remuneration, welfare, medical care, gratuity or provision for their retirement. Like government workers, some church workers do not get their salaries on time, yet various church leaders can afford luxurious meals in five star restaurants, medical care in the best hospitals at home or abroad, paid for by the church collections or levies of their parishioners.

With all this contradictions, the church cannot afford to challenge any unjust structure without being reminded that it is only normal to see the plank in your eye before seeing the speck in your neighbor's eye (Matt. 7: 3-5; Lk. 6: 41-42). There is truth in believing that in order to hide its sins, the church takes up the rational and speculative option in response to the problems of suffering. It always believes that the work of liberation and reformation of the society is God's work, as we noted in the way the church ended the prayer for Nigeria in distress, and other subsequent ones. As James Cone suggests, "instead of emphasizing the biblical insistence on the Divine liberation of the oppressed as its starting point," the Nigerian church offers a "naïve orthodox providential claim that 'all things work together for good to them that love God, to them that are called according to his purpose" (Rom.8: 28).[321]

Finally, the unresolved problem of dualism of the earlier missionary spirituality is once again resurrected. Such dualism situates the resolution of problems of suffering either in the logical structure of the intellect or in sentimentalized compassion. Both alternatives contribute to political conservatism that does not either engage with or suggest what the oppressed must do in order to eliminate the social and political structures that create evil.[322]

Summary

Nigeria, we have seen, is in a state of enormous suffering. The situation in Nigeria, to say the least is in a state of squalor and despair. The evolution of Nigerian politics and economics like most other African nations came with changes in relations and emphasis on class distinction and renewed violence associated with this wide gap between the haves and have-nots.[323] The various institutions and systems ally with some individuals to increase and perpetuate this suffering condition through corruption, injustice and greed. Indeed, the situation is so messy that it is no longer only a national disgrace and an international embarrassment; it is also a scoff at our Christian vocation and a challenge to our whole commitment to the concept of compassion. For as people helplessly look everywhere for a solution to their problems, they turn to Christianity as well to ask "Is the God of Christians impotent in the face of the enormous sufferings we see all about us?"

Indeed, the church has responded to these situations in various ways, such as providing the poor with relief materials and asking the rich to be generous to the poor. But because of inherent contradictions and a spirituality of dualism, the church has not effectively employed a justice-making dimension of compassion in its response. This situation leaves us with the reality of an inherent "contradiction between the historical praxis and liberating praxis" as Gustavo Gutierrez would say.

This contradiction ruptures these previous ways of mediating God's presence among our people, and heightens the urgent need for a change in paradigm.[324] This is what a politics of compassion advocates as we shall be discussing in the next chapter.

CHAPTER FOUR: POLITICS OF COMPASSION IN RELATION TO THE NIGERIAN CONTEXT

We have maintained throughout this study that our chosen style of compassion should be an effective response to the sufferings of our time, especially those caused by unjust structures. The said compassion must necessarily encompass socio-political-action and concern. This dimension of our compassion is called a politics of compassion in consonance with the claims of Ronald Rolheiser when he asserts that, "in the face of unjust systems and corrupt governments, Christians cannot get away with simply practicing private virtue."[325] Since the application of this concept varies from place to place and situation to situation, we adopt the Nigerian situation in this context to explore and synthesize the meaning, implications and challenges of this new paradigm – a politics of compassion. At the same time, we propose and discuss the dynamics of a politics of compassion, which engages some elements of spirituality that may give substance to, as well as enhance our commitment to justice and effective political action thereby ensuring a healthy link between spirituality, ethics and liberation initiatives. We begin this section in earnest by explaining once again the meaning of a politics of compassion. This position enables us to beam further light on our chosen topic.

The Meaning of a Politics of Compassion

A politics of compassion as we discussed in chapter two derives from Christ's paradigm that includes a socio-political concern as constitutive part of compassion. Many of the contemporaries of Jesus understood and practiced compassion as a matter of personal sentiment or a mode of relation that applied only between individuals. For these people, compassion marked the distinction between the spiritual and the temporary, the holy and the unholy. They understood compassion as a solely religious principle with little or no business with the secular. But Jesus perceived a connection between unjust structures and the various sufferings that his people experienced. He would not subscribe to the popular idea that kept compassion out of public life. Instead, he included in his compassionate agenda a social paradigm that repeatedly and directly challenged the unjust structures of the socio-political institutions of his time and thus made compassion a core value of life in community.[326] Such action does not reduce or disregard material and immediate response to suffering, rather it richly complements it. At the same time, it insists that while material relief is valuable and indispensable, it does not suffice in all circumstances, In other words, there are occasions where it can be demeaning both to the giver and receiver, as it pretends to be the only possible option, while it is not.

By this claim on a politics of compassion, we understand a very significant difference between private charity and social justice, between private morality and social morality. Ronald Rolheiser helps us in articulating such differentiation as he writes:

> Private morality is something that I do on my own. Other persons might guide me or inspire me, but, in the end, I am moral and charitable on the basis of my own personal goodness and personal actions. Social justice, on the other hand, has to do with the social system I am part of and participate in. I can be a good person in my private life, churchgoing, prayerful, kind, honest, gentle, and generous in my dealings with others, and still, at the same time,

> be part of a social, economic, political, and even ecclesial system that is unfair in that it works for the benefit of some at the cost of victimizing others. Issues such as war, poverty, violation of the ecology, feminism,… are caused not simply, nor indeed any longer primarily, by individual persons acting in bad conscience and doing bad things, but by huge impersonal systems that are inherently unfair and are, to an extent, beyond the control of the individuals who participate in them.[327]

A politics of compassion therefore, lays upon the Christian and the church the impetus to work for transformation of the world – the challenge to change unjust social, political, economic and cultural structures, as part of their compassionate acts in accord with the mind of their master. As the 1971 *Justice in the World* holds, this "action for justice and participation in the transformation of the world fully appear to us as a constitutive dimension of the preaching of the Gospel."[328]

Translated to the Nigerian perspective, while we recognize the various efforts of the church in responding to the many sufferings of the Nigerian people, analytically we observe that, in some critical situations, such response has not reflected the understanding of compassion that separates private charity from social justice. We observe as well that the deficiency of this response betrays an understanding that still separates compassion from public action – justice-making. Thus the Nigerian church is challenged to a paradigm shift, recognizing that, as Louise Arbour the UN High Commissioner for Human Rights, emphasizes, "Combating poverty, deprivation and exclusion is not a matter of charity, and it does not depend on how rich a country is;"[329] it is a matter of involving change of the social systems by which such sufferings exist.

We come to appreciate the full scope of this new paradigm when we understand its implications, challenges and dynamics.

Implications of a Politics of Compassion

By implication a politics of compassion, means the various ways in which the church and Christians, especially in Nigeria, put into practice the meaning of this new way of being compassionate and indeed being socio-economically and politically responsive. The three areas we are about to discuss here are chosen because they relate and respond to the three types of suffering experiences in Nigeria discussed in chapter three. These areas are the preferential option for the poor, inclusive community and solidarity with the earth.

Preferential Option for the Poor

This term *preferential option for the poor* first introduced by Latin American bishops in Medellin, Colombia, and confirmed in their Puebla, Mexico conference, means solidarity with the poor and their struggle for social justice – a call that demands action and public witness.[330] Since then, the theme often discussed side by side with the theme of structural sin has become a central agenda of the church's social teaching.[331] The Bishops were inspired by the Second Vatican Council's Document on the Church in the Modern World. In this document, the church declares that "the joy and hope, the grief and anguish of men and women of our time, especially of those who are poor or afflicted in any away, are the joy and hope, the grief and anguish of the followers of Christ as well." This implies that, concerning the poor, the church has the responsibility of compassion and solidarity.[332] As Frei Betto says, "There is nothing more sacred than a person, the image and likeness of God. The hunger of a person is an offence to the Creator.... A religion that cares for the supposed sacredness of its objects but turns its back on those who are the real temples of God the Spirit, is worthless."[333]

There are two basic ways by which we can express our preferential option for and solidarity with the poor, namely committed action and reading the signs of the time.

Committed Action: on behalf of the poor finds expression in many biblical passages. Rebecca S. Chopp maintains that it does not simply imply, that "the poor are simply to be helped, assisted along, the chronically 'underprivileged.' But [that they] must be granted their rights to speak, to eat, to work, to think."[334] It is this nuance that is contained in the oracle of prophet Micah, "You have been told, O man, what is good and what Yahweh requires of you: to act justly, love tenderly and work humbly with your God" (Micah 6:8). Robert McAfee Brown explains, "love without justice is sentimental and naïve; we can hardly be said to love victims of economic deprivation if we are not working to create economic structures in which their exploitation will no longer be possible...."[335]

Chuck Gutenson says that committed action for the poor asks the question, "What would God expect of us in these circumstances?" He concludes by saying, while we focus on the immediate solution, we must also ask, "What things ought we do to prevent future recurrences? How can we act preemptively to minimize suffering in the future?" This means, "we must begin to act in ways that meet God's expectations, moving from the current *laissez faire* individualism to a deeper sense of inter-dependency. And that means putting those who are at the margins in first..."[336] It challenges the traditional attitude that when we give alms to the poor and do nothing to change the structures and systems that oppress them, we have done our part.

This is the paradigm shift in our Christian experience, a shift which uses its solidarity with the poor to identify with the whole human subject.[337] Though the poor is its primary concern, its ultimate goal is to provide for general human flourishing. Thus, embarking on socio-political actions that respond to the sufferings of many Nigerians (those who scavenge the heaps of garbage, the many youths roaming the streets without a job, the many workers who toil for hours with little or no pay, the many children deprived of school, the families without a home, medical care or social amenities) does not aim at merely alleviating their suffering or at bringing them up to the same socio-economic and political level as the rich. Rather, it is hoped that challenging and changing the *status quo* will make life better for everyone. This is not a matter of merely generalizing particular situations, or as Mercy would say, of shifting attention "from victims to victimhood." That in itself stifles action for justice.[338] It is rather a response that not only identifies the root causes of suffering but is committed to eradicating them so that, as Augustinians would say, "we may not have to give charity always." "The ultimate principle in any economics of compassion," according to Matthew Fox, "is that it is to the self-interest of all of us and it is to the private and greedy of none."³³⁹ Or as Gandhi puts it, "there exists enough for everyone's needs, but not for everyone's greed."³⁴⁰

The various ways we carry out committed action for the poor may include, participation, speaking out, conscientization and, above all, listening to the victims.³⁴¹

Participation: The language of preferential option for the poor is the language of *being-with*, an important aspect of compassion developed in chapter two. Being with the poor has a transformative power and dynamism, and a revelation of the greatness and weakness that lie hidden in us. As Mary Jo Leddy says, "Being faced by the victims we see Christ the crucified in them, and being close to them (the crucified), enables us to hear their stories, and what their stories are telling us, an opportunity limited to those at the foot of the cross only. We are challenged, inspired and empowered by what we hear and what we see."³⁴² Our argument is that, solidarity with the poor cannot be effective when it is heard only in eloquent sermons from marble pulpits without being seen in the slums, to feel the brunt of the scourging sun, and the drenching rains with those to whom these have become daily blessings.³⁴³ When we make being with them a point of duty out of love, they often appreciate us and all our efforts. Even when weakness invades our bones, and we are not as active as we could be, they still feel that they matter to us. In other words, with and in us, their lives are possibly transformed.³⁴⁴

Participation is an important dimension of being with the poor. The idea of participation, according to the Jesuit scholar, Edward Vacek, had long and often obscured history. In his work, *Love, Human and Divine: The Heart of Christian Ethics,* earlier quoted in this work, Vacek, borrows from John Finnis and Lourencino, to assert that "a technical term in metaphysics, [participation] has been used to explain the relation between this world and its ultimate ground, a relation which we do not experience but rather deduce from principle of causality."³⁴⁵ He goes on to observe that the "biblical idea of participation is concerning less with a metaphysical origin and more with an existential relationship."³⁴⁶ Participation as an act of solidarity and option for the poor derives from this biblical nuance – existential and personal. It means identifying and participating with them in their own struggle for survival – participating in the program which they, not necessarily us, must draw. This understanding challenges, as Elizabeth Lynn and Susan Wisely identify, the traditional model of social reform which takes up the task of speaking for the poor and pleading their cause, in which workers make unilateral decisions "on behalf of" the poor, without much openness to the wisdom or will of the poor.[347]

Participation, Leonardo Boff maintains, requires that our preferential option for the poor does not subsist in "being for the poor," i.e. doing things for the poor, which on many occasions celebrates our ego and make the poor inferior and dependent on us. Rather, the type of participation envisioned here is one that makes the poor feel and know that they are consubstantial with us. It is this understanding that Edward Vacek projects by maintaining that "existential or personal participation is a way of being united with 'another' which does not diminish, but rather enhances, the distinctiveness of those who are united" – a kind of relationship in which persons share life without losing themselves.[348]

This act of participation illustrates another significant difference between compassion and pity, mercy or mere charity. While these latter differentiate, compassion unites as it emphasizes the oneness of the giver and the receiver. Participation means, "'unity-in-difference,' a sharing through which the uniqueness of the parties is enhanced."[349] This finds expression in the understanding of compassion we have insisted on in this work, that is, our reality, our being radically relational. Or as Daniel Day William puts it, in the matter of subjectivity, "the fundamental human craving is to belong, to count in the community of beings, to have one's freedom in and with the response of others, to enjoy God as one who makes us members of our society."[350] When we participate with the poor in their program and activities of their lives we fulfill this ultimate goal of our existence. "When we lose them, we lose ourselves for without them we could not be ourselves and might not be."[351] Hence James Gustafson concludes, "The human venture is participation."[352]

The Nigerian church must discover a way to make this aspect of compassion its project. She must recognize that compassion demands that the church does not withdraw from identifying with the poor in their struggle for fear of damaging her long preserved image. Participation means that the Nigerian church "must march alongside and with the people as they move toward their own complete humanization."[353] For instance, sometime in 2002, a group of Nigerian Catholic women marched to their state government house to protest against the non-payment of workers' salaries (especially those of teachers) and pensions. Had the church hierarchy publicly stood with them, such an action would have spoken volumes both to the victims and the victimizers. Such solidarity as practiced by Christ neither substitutes nor subjugates the poor. It rather empowers them to rise to their potential. Unfortunately the Nigerian church was busy considering how people would interpret its involvement in such action, apparently insinuating that it would be a scandal for the church to engage in such action. But, as a matter of fact, the scandal lay in their inaction and none participation in such a noble act.

As we have seen in chapter two, Christ our model, though sinless, proved his integrity by making the radical option of identifying and participating with his people in their search for the solution of their problem. He did this even in the most risky moments when people would misconstrue his sinlessness (consider those acts of Jesus we enumerated in chapter two: his baptism, his eating with sinners, being in the company of women, going to the graveyard to deliver a demoniac, touching the leper, etc.). In these ways that Christ physically participated with his people (not those that make history but those who suffer history); he made participation in peoples' own program a strategic action that speaks more eloquently than any voice. To his critics, Christ offered a response that suggested that his sinlessness can only be understood in relation to his commitment to the purpose of his incarnation – an act of solidarity and participation with the poor. He always insists that it is for this that he came (Matt. 9: 9-13; Mk. 2: 13; Lk. 5:27). It was for this that he called the first community of believers and I believe it is for the same reason that he has called the Nigerian church and every individual Christian in Nigeria.

Conscientization is another aspect of the preferential option we make for the poor that translates to and gives a socio-political dimension to our compassion. The concept – '*conscientization*' was first introduced in the circle of liberation theology in Latin America by Paulo Freire.

He used this to refer to "a basic education in literacy linked with a heightening of critical awareness of the situation in which people find themselves." In summary, Freire teaches that conscientization "involves a critical and active grappling with reality understood in the light of a form of social analysis which interprets the situation in terms of oppression and calls for the overthrow of all oppressive structures." It encourages the oppressed to "'name their world,' to confront the facts, to free themselves from the culture of silence and the ideology of oppression."[354]

Often times, on hearing about the contributions of social analysis to social justice, some people have come to idealize and mythicize the concept as "a wonder tool," implying that as soon as one gets hold of it, transformation of the society becomes almost automatic. We cannot limit the adequacy of social analysis as a tool of social justice and society transformation. Indeed, we need some degree of social analysis to undertake a challenge of unjust structures. It helps us to understand the nature and dynamics of such structures. Yet we believe that there is still some sense of naivety in seeing social analysis in itself as a society transformation or as its magical tool. Such naivety is obviously based on a misunderstanding of the real value of social analysis as tool of social justice. Within the context of social justice, engaging in social analysis is not merely for providing new information that was unknown to people in the past. Rather it is aimed at helping the "oppressed come to an understanding of who is exploiting them and how; and to have their consciousness transformed through this process of discovery."[355] This is why it is usually associated with conscientization, as Freire provides.

Conscientization requires unmasking the more or less deliberate lies that suffuse everyday discourse and cloud people's minds. The church now stands in a better position to do this, but also owes this to the poor as a grave responsibility. For instance, the present privatization of government establishments and the deregulation of petroleum products are presented by the government to the Nigerians as the best thing that could happen to the nation for economic vibrancy, welfare and human development. It belongs to those who know the truth to unmask what is behind these economic policies, their implications and consequences for the poor, and how they serve as an arsenal of the rich that maintains and widens the gap between the rich and the poor. Again, as the Nigerian government records the provision of mobile telecommunication as one of its achievements in recent times, conscientization means that we expose the hidden irresponsibility of the government for failing to put the land phone system in place. It will also analyze the economic advantage the mobile phone industry serves for the rich and its effects on the poor Nigerians whose meager income goes into servicing these phones. As Dean Brackley says, the key questions conscientization asks are: "Who suffers? Why? Who profits? Who controls? To whom are they accountable? How do these policies and institutions affect the weak?"[356]

Speaking out: Finally, to be actively committed in solidarity with the poor, means, being their voice; it means speaking for them against all that oppresses them. This can be done in various ways: Writing can be one such way. As Ngugi Wa Thiong'o, writes, "our pen should be used to increase the anxieties of the oppressive regimes. At the very least, the pen should be used to murder their sleep by constantly reminding them of their crimes against the people and making them know that they are being seen. The pen might not always be mightier than the sword; but used in the service of the truth, it can be a mighty force."[357] Yet this has to be appropriate to the situation and time and must not replace practical speaking out and confrontation against all that hatches sin and suffering. Nigerians have very poor reading habits and the church knows this. Therefore, the church must not be content with doling out communiqués which Archbishop John Onayikan, former president of the Catholic Bishops' Conference of Nigeria, once acknowledged that even they (the bishops) forget as soon as they leave their meetings.[358]

To speak out involves memory, because "justice without memory," says Elie Wiesel, "is an incomplete justice, false and unjust. To forget would be the enemy's final triumph." Therefore, he concludes, "Forgetfulness is damnation and memory is redemption."[359] Remembering a people's story is in a way witnessing to compassion and hope, for as Miroslav Volf says, to "erase memories of the atrocities is to tempt future perpetrators with immunity. And to remember is to create a barrier against future misdeeds."[360] Accordingly, Rosa Luxembourg holds that "the most revolutionary deed is and always will remain to say out loud what is the case."[361] In Nigeria, we pretend to forget the past so easily and no one makes reference to it. We often say that "it is Christian to forgive and forget," and for this, every evil comes and takes its turn on the poor and goes unchallenged.

However, it is important that we should be mindful of what we do with our memories because salvation does not lie simply in memory but in what we do with our memory.[362] We do not recall memories in order to incite hatred and violence. A compassionate remembrance of our past differs from the way others might remember, because we remember with love, not hate, hence we seek reconciliation, not revenge. Gregory Baum maintains that, "…love also affects the manner Christian activists look upon the elite that defends the existing order. They will refuse to demonize these men (sic), but instead look upon them as human beings and, hence, bearers of human rights. They will shun the use of violence, and, because they believe in the power of forgiveness, they will be ready for a social compromise and unwilling to destroy the elite altogether."[363] We shall return to this in the next section on the dynamics of politics of compassion.

We are not oblivious to the dangers associated with speaking out in the manner we are suggesting or as our act of compassion demands. It could be life-threatening, as it has been the case in Nigeria. Almost every Nigerian remembers Dele Giwa, a fearless and prolific journalist and editor who died by assassination through a letter bomb in the late 1980s.[364] "When you say some things you know are the case too loudly you may lose not only a friend or a job, but even your life."[365] But the church in Nigeria should not forget that this was the distinguishing mark of the prophets. They saw what should not be the case, and they said in public what others dared only to whisper in secret places. As long as the oppressors use secrecy to shield themselves and their power and make the poor accept the lies they feed them on and so accept their suffering as normal, or use intimidation to force victims to accept the responsibility of their situation, we cannot afford to keep quiet and not force them to recount their evil deeds. It is on such occasions as this that the prophets resisted being drawn into the war of dissimulation, and instead offered their own "counter-truth" as weapons in a battle. They dared to see what was behind the veil of deception and had the courage to speak out loud the truth about the oppressors.[366]

Moreover, we should remember that it was for this that Christ lived and died. Before his death he said, "Unless the grain of wheat falls to the earth and dies, it remains alone; but if it dies, it produces much fruit." "Whoever loves his life will destroy it, and whoever despises his life in this world keeps it for everlasting life" (Jn. 12: 20-27). As we know, the Nigerian church has the privilege to see and hear these things – the evils that go on in the society - and the church is often respected as moral influence and listened to if it speaks. "This gives the church the opportunity to speak out, to assume leadership in the public forum for the eradication of injustice and in the [Nigerian] community."[367] But it is only an insignificant few who have the courage to speak. Many are still afraid of death. But the truth is that not until the Nigerian church is able to say like Archbishop Oscar Romero of Salvador, "If they kill me I shall rise. The bishop will die but the church, which is the people of God, will live," we have not yet come to terms with the implications of our existence on the Nigerian soil and at this particular time in history.

Reading the signs of time: Closely connected with conscientization and speaking out is *reading the signs of time*. In this lies the challenge that the church and the Christian be aware of the world in which they live, the starting point in the work of social justice. Brackley believes that we cannot change a world we do not understand. In paragraph four of *Gaudium et Spes*, the Second Vatican Council identifies the reading of the signs of time in the light of the Gospel as a grave responsibility of the church in order for the church to intelligibly answer people's ever-recurring questions about the meaning of this present life and of the life to come, and how one is related to the other. "We must be aware of and understand the aspirations, the yearnings, and the often dramatic features of the world in which we live."[368]

Reading the signs of our time is about knowing where we stand, to whom we listen, and then how we respond. This involves, as Dean Brackley recommends, that we observe, read, remember, question, interpret, think and dialogue, and reason.[369] This is what Karl Barth means when he suggests that, the Christian must have the "bible in one hand and the newspaper in the other."[370] Unfortunately, many Nigerian Christians, most especially the hierarchy, have not found the wisdom in reading or listening to news. That is why most often we do not hear things when they happen but only discuss them extensively when they are stale.

The difference between a Christian reading signs of the time – a compassionate approach - and that of a political or social or economic analysis is that the Christian is called to go beyond mere socio-economic and political analysis and engage in discernment which is based on discovering the moments of either sin or grace in the particular situation. This is where the signs of the time are interpreted in the light of the Gospel. To do this well presupposes that the Christian understands the scriptures and the Christian faith. The Nigerian Church needs to take up this seriously in order that Christians do not end up being either mere socio-economic and political analysts or compromising their stand and their faith in the face of a serious challenge or enticement from the authorities (as has often been the case).[371]

While we have used the term *preferential option for the poor* to respond to the material poverty of the Nigerian populace, we intend in the following section to use the concept of inclusive community to respond to Nigerian suffering associated with the violation of human rights.

Inclusive Community

The call for inclusive community in our society and church today has its root in open table fellowship, a part of Jesus' paradigm against the politics of purity of his Jewish community, says Marcus Borg. By eating with sinners, having women at table with him, allowing his disciples to eat without washing their hands up to the elbow, Christ negated the boundaries of the purity system. These were not mere table fellowships but a sharp attack on the system that was exclusive in its androcentrism, patriarchy, and elitism. The action points to the radical social reality of Jesus' movement; subversion of the world social order and proffering of an alternative vision, "a discipleship of equals," embodying "the egalitarian praxis" of his vision.[372] His disciples, the early church, continued the inclusiveness of his movement, as it is evident in the teachings and practices of the early church. We cited in chapter two Paul's letter to the Galatians: "[In Christ there is no east or west no south or north]; no Jew nor Gentile, slave nor free, male nor female" (Gal 3:28).[373]

In the Nigerian churches and society today, there is evidence of spoken and unspoken struggles between groups that emphasize "holiness and purity" in the very manner that some Jewish social systems of Christ's time did. They draw their own social boundaries between the righteous and sinners, and by this act create a system that marginalizes many people. We have boundaries between male and female, priests and laity, "the church" and other churches, "the faith" and other faiths, the rich and the poor, and the indigenous and foreigners.

The call towards compassion demands first, that we change the structures within the church that treat others as second class – change our whole orientation towards the roles of each member of the church, and create opportunities that encourage mutuality, freedom and equal participation of members. For as long as some people are still treated with contempt or neglect, our responsibility towards them remains greater. The type of participation we advocate for includes our decision-making process of the church. It should reflect the communitarian decision-making partner of the New Testament Church in Acts 6: 1ff. In this passage, the Apostles, or rather the community, settled the charge raised by the Hellenists against the Palestinian Christians because their widows were being neglected in the sharing of food. Their decision-making reflected both partnership and service involving the entire community in the resolution of the problem. As James F. Cobbles Jr. interprets, "although this should not be construed as democracy, it does point to the importance of the shared life and mission of the church in decision making and problem solving."[374]

Furthermore, this call to compassion includes also a mandate for a true ecumenism built on the freedom, equality and mutuality of all the churches. The imperative laid on us leaves us with no option, for Christ's mission, to which we are called to be witnesses, is an inclusive universalism of love and peace, structured around compassion which seeks to remove every barrier that excludes people.[375]

We would therefore suggest that the Nigerian church discover and practice the wisdom in what Martin Marty calls *public church*. This is an idea of a communion of churches involving, according to Johannes Althusius, a 'dynamics of symbiosis' in which the churches pledge to each other, "by *explicit or tacit agreement,* mutual communication of whatever is useful and necessary for the harmonious exercise of social life."[376] We shall return later to this first demand in the section where we shall discuss the challenges this paradigm presents to the Nigerian church.

Secondly, the demand of compassion means that the church fights tirelessly against all forms of segregation – tribalism, class distinction, nepotism and sexism - that hitherto divides Nigerians. However, this does not mean seeking an inclusion that is built on the delusion that equality requires us to be the same, an inclusion that understands universality as uniformity. As we can appreciate, this is at the core of the Nigerian problems – a denial of our multiculturalism by a federalism that thinks that what works for culture and people in state 'A' must work for culture and people in state 'B.' We have to acknowledge that our differences are real and should be appreciated but not exploited.

What we propose here, in accordance with the thoughts of John Macmurray, is that our problems in Nigeria would be half solved if every Nigerian is recognized and related to as a *person,*[377] without distinguishing whether he or she is rich or poor, literate or illiterate, man or woman, from whatever region or tribe. In other words, like Macmurray, while we admit that it is difficult to maintain friendship with everyone, we believe that we can advance a collective sense of mission, partnership, and commitment growing out of friendship[378] that extends beyond any category and boundary in a manner that does not subsume our individuality and uniqueness. This means, as Macmurray maintains, that we overcome "the unity-pattern that mark the mechanical and organic periods of Modern history"[379] to which the individual is either an atomistic and isolated – mutually repellent particles or a mere function of his or her work, allegiances, etc.[380] What Macmurray means here is translated significantly by the Catholic social teaching's principle of solidarity and subsidiarity.

Both of these principles appeal to the fundamental principles of natural law that define every human being first as a person endowed with universal and inviolable rights that cannot be surrendered in any way. And second, every human person by nature is a social being oriented to civic friendship with right to share from, and obligation to promote and protect the common good. Based on the Latin, *subsidium,* 'support' or 'assistance,' subsidiarity, holds that "one should not withdraw from individuals and commit to the community what they can accomplish by their own enterprise and industry."[381] This principle maintains that on one hand, "high-level institutions should not usurp all social power and responsibility, and it maintains that higher-level institutions need to support and encourage lower-level institutions"[382] on the other hand. In other words, it suggests that the primary and intermediary associations must help each other and contribute to the common good, each in its own capacity and degree. This provides and ensures a kind of dialogical relationship between the periphery and the center.

In the same vein, solidarity advocates for a "firm and persevering determination to commit oneself to the common good, the good of all and of each individual in a way that respects every human person, respect true values and cultures of others."[383] By this, we see the "'other' – whether that other is a person, people, or nation [or state in our own case] – not just as an object to be exploited but as neighbor and helper called with us to share in the banquet of life to which all are invited equally by God."[384] We are able to achieve this vision only when, as the principle insists, we "look beyond ourselves in order to understand and support the good of other, to contribute to our own resources in social mutuality for the development and growth that come from equality and justice."[385] "The virtue of solidarity offers an alternative to the assumption of therapeutic individualism that happiness resides simply in self-gratification, liberation from guilt, and relationships within one's 'lifestyle enclave.'"[386]

Summarily, we find in Stephen J. Pope a wonderful expression that illustrates how aptly these Catholic social teaching principles, solidarity and subsidiarity describe the humanism we have developed in this work, particularly in this section. He writes, "If the person is inherently social, genuine flourishing resides in living for others rather than only for oneself, in contributing to one's small circle of reciprocal concern. The right to participate in the life of one's own community should not be eclipsed by the 'right to be left alone.'"[387] Above all, as we have maintained in this work, the whole creation must be included in this, our compassionate call to solidarity and subsidiarity.

<u>Solidarity with the Earth: a Christian compassionate response to</u>

climate change

In chapter two, we linked the banality of the ill-treatment of our environment with the Nigerian experience. It goes without saying that being Christian does not make us either lesser or greater Nigerians; neither does our Christianity grant us any privileged immunity from the effects of climate change. Are we not drinking the same water and eating the same food as other Nigerians? Isn't it the same air that we all breathe? Do we not live on the same streets and ply the same roads with the rest of Nigerians? This we take for granted. Our concern in this section is to explore how our faith might have directly and indirectly encouraged activities that contribute to climate change. We also want to examine how it could be possible for that same faith to help us participate in various activities for overcoming climate change.

Today there is a growing awareness among theologians that in the past we have not related compassionately enough with non-human life forms and the natural world; in other words, the environment around us. This poor relationship has given rise to environmental crises of our time, such as global warming, species-extinction, deforestation and the rapid depletion and exhaustion of other natural resources. Some critics have attributed this type of unhealthy treatment to what he calls arrogant superiority and callousness that follow from the creation myth of Genesis and other Biblical texts. Genesis says that humanity is created in the image and likeness of God and called to be fruitful, multiply and fill the earth, subdue it and have dominion over the earth, with all the other animals and plants to serve the needs of humanity (Gen 1:28).[388]

Despite its richness and call for a balanced relationship between faith and the world, spiritual and temporal, the Second Vatican Council continued this apparent *arrogant superiority and dominion* theme. *Gaudium et Spes,* for instance, reduces solidarity to an anthropocentric, personalist frame of understanding that excludes any ecological concern. The document says that "human need and use are the 'universal purpose for which created goods are meant'" (*GS:* 69). It also maintains that the human "is the only creature on earth which God willed for itself" (*GS:* 24). With this type of human-centered theological anthropology, the document concludes that "all things on earth should be related to man as their center and crown" (GS 12).³⁸⁹ This poor relationship has, to some extent, contributed to disrespect for the earth and other species. It pays little or no attention to the environmental crises of our time, such as global warming, species-extinction, deforestation and the rapid depletion and exhaustion of other natural resources. Larry Rasmussen cites another example with John Paul II's encyclical, *The Gospel of Life*. The Pope maintains that "everything in creation is ordered to man and everything is made subject to him…" The Pontiff also affirms in this work that human beings have primacy over things.³⁹⁰

The Nigerian experience exemplifies this Judeo-Christian *arrogant superiority and callousness* toward the earth. Before the advent of Christianity, many Nigerian tribes took time to preserve some forests, lands and species. It was a taboo for one to hunt such designated species, to fell certain trees for any purpose whatsoever, or to cultivate designated lands. These were seen either as repositories of divine power or as special links with the community. The earth, land and biosphere are sacred because they are links between the present generation and its ancestors and gods. It is through the land and the whole of creation that a god nourishes, sustains and protects his people. Thus, in traditional and authentic African anthropology, the human person is not treated in isolation from the world in which he/she lives. In fact, the human person is considered as one among many spirits that inhabit the earth. In the words of Prof. Emefie Ikenga-Metuh: "For the African, man [sic] is a force in the midst of and in union with other forces in the universe actively interacting with them."³⁹¹

With the coming of Christianity such taboos and sense of the sacred were abolished. The early Christian missionaries uncritically misread African nature-solidarity and connection with their world as idolatry from which they must repent if they were to attain heaven.³⁹² This is because the ancient Christian spirituality we inherited preached a dichotomy between this world and the other, taught us to shun the earth and to seek heaven. Sometimes, in order to exhibit their personal power and superiority and that of their God over the power of the locals and their gods, the missionaries supervised the burning of sacred forests and the killing of some of those protected species.

This attitude that manifests this belief in the ancient *theology of dominion* which says that the earth exists just for us, or that everything earthly is evil, has persisted into our own time. Today, many Nigerian

Christians have not only lost the sacredness of the life of other creatures but have joined in treating nature as a beast of burden. In several cruel cases, some Nigerian Christian exorcists organize the destruction of these forests, lands and other species, alleging that evil spirits repose in them and that they are sources of misfortune in the community. No church leader rises to condemn these acts or to caution their ministers, thereby suggesting that they regard these acts as normal. It is hardly surprising that issues about climate change are not raised in the Sunday sermons of Christian churches in Nigeria, nor are they taught in our Christian schools. As a matter of fact, disciplines such as eco-justice, eco-spirituality or eco-theology are seen as new trends in theology that must be received with serious caution. Those who champion the cause for the earth are thus despised as activists who want to return us to the dreaded paganism. However, now that everywhere else Christianity has come to a full realization that the moral imperative to care for this earth and to guard against climate change has been placed in its trust, "is it not proper that Christians in Nigeria should in worry ask, 'where do we stand, from where do we start?'"

As church people, we are more often silent than vocal in this cause. Today, the violence we have caused and continue to cause to the earth through careless disregard of the gifts of creation stares us in the face. All believe that Christianity has to change and become more earth-loving, just, egalitarian, inclusive and caring. To accomplish this requires that we Nigerian Christians first undertake a change in our own attitude towards the earth. Whatever approach we are going to adopt, must take cognizance of and attempt to bridge the gap between the two extremes often associated with the politics of climate change in both the local and international levels. This concerns the struggle between the belief that the earth is there for us to exploit and the belief that the earth is good in itself but is irredeemably threatened by humanity. This demands that on one hand, we appreciate that human beings are not simply dependent upon the world but are capable of changing it and as a matter of fact "the world is increasingly a world arranged and engineered by human beings."[393] This means that we deal with every form of romanticism, secular or theological, that yearns for, and seeks to take us back to a pure and numinous nature, to its pristine beauty and fruitfulness and a world free from modern technology.[394]

This emphasis exists in tension with the fact that the world as we experience it "is a creation of God to which we are intrinsically related and as that from which we come and in which we remain."[395] Thus we must guard against any idea, secular or theological, that suggests that earth is mere raw material for human dynamism. In this vein, I believe that the first task confronting Christianity in Nigeria in this campaign entails a rediscovery and appreciation of the rich spirituality of our African heritage – a culture to which the dichotomy between soul and body, religious and secular, temporal and spiritual, is alien. This is as well a true Christian position about our relationship with the world. Christian anthropology abhors any sense of dualism between matter and spirit, spiritual and temporal. For the earlier Christian missionaries to have taught otherwise was rather a disservice to authentic Christian teaching and a dishonest witness to the faith. Thus, any approach that tries to reposition Christianity in a healthy and collaborative relation with the world must be both orthodox and radical. That means that it must be committed to "credal Christianity and the exemplarity of its patristic matrix" on one hand, and on the other, rethinks tradition in a way that challenges the earlier weaknesses.[396] Such is the approach of politics of compassion as developed in this work.

With the grace of this rediscovery, Christianity in Nigerian should develop a theology that accommodates concern for the earth as an integral part of African way of doing theology. Such a theology should emphasize the connection between spiritual commitment and ecological practice. Here, as we saw in chapter two, the divine command we have received – to be compassionate as our God is compassionate – enables us to develop this new theology, a theology of solidarity with the earth. This calls for a complete change of attitude, one that refrains from describing the relationship between humanity and the rest of creation as subject-object relationship, to subject-subject relationship. In other words, we see the whole creation as a community. It is a call that expands a theology of justice and compassion to include all creation because we have become more aware of the interrelatedness of all creation. Francis of Assisi preached to birds and to a wolf. He named the sun "brother" and the Earth "Sister" and "Mother."[397] For Augustine of Hippo, love of nature and the return to nature have deep dimensions. First, nature is the great book that speaks to us of God. Second, nature is a visible sign of the Trinity and the unity that dwells therein. To assault nature is to destroy unity. "The word 'universe,'" says Augustine, "is derived from the word 'unity,'... We must therefore contemplate it in its totality if we are to see its beauty and unity. The case is similar to that of a beautiful discourse, which is beautiful not by reason of each individual word but of all taken together"[398]

It is important to note, that as William French suggests, "An ecological frame entails no need for a loss of emphasis on human dignity. It does not guarantee a 'renuminization' of nature by uncritically identifying the earth with *God's body*,[399] as we tend to do nowadays. The way human beings relate to God is and remains significantly different from the way other creatures are that we can say without contradicting ourselves, that the world of nature is not sacred in the strict sense of the word. But it does require an end to "purchasing a celebration of human dignity by a sustained undercutting of any sense of the continuities between humanity and the other animal species, or by loss of a sense of kinship with the Earth, or by an assumption that nonhuman natural world is somehow lacking in its own distinct modes of dignity."[400] This means that we cannot continue to teach, as Karl Rahner taught, that humanity holds a special place in the order of creation, as created in the "likeness" of God (and thus the only hope of nature – the whole creation, reaching its own radical depths and its final and definitive validity)[401] but pay no attention to affirmations, like those of Thomas Aquinas, "that all creatures are created in the 'likeness' of God,"[402] albeit in varied degrees.

We recall again Stephen Best's idea of compassion mentioned in chapter two. Compassion within this perspective is universal and trans-species in scope, so that it is senseless for one to say that he or she is a compassionate person while arbitrarily drawing boundaries between sentient and non-sentient beings as to which is a proper object of one's compassion and which is not.[403] It is a recognition that there is no aspect of creation that does not have a place in the scheme of things and that is not entitled to a measure of respect for its unique otherness, its interdependence and, more simply, its divine lineage.[404] We have to also become more aware that non-sentient beings, our environment and other species are part of all creation, which St. Paul describes as groaning and yearning for redemption (Rom. 8: 19-22).

This theology of solidarity with the earth enables us to appreciate

Gen 2:15 in its context, the call to "cultivate the earth and care for it," as asking humanity to relate to other creatures with compassion. It is within this context that our responsibility as stewards of the earth bears meaning; our movement towards God would then imply movement also towards God's beloved world.[405] Thus, in solidarity and compassion, justice demands that we refrain from all environmental unfriendly and exploitative acts; and that we identify with all actions towards the promotion of earth justice.

In view of this, realizing the transformative dynamism of liturgy, efforts should be made by all Nigerian Christian leaders and theologians to integrate this theology of solidarity with the earth into their liturgies. One such attempt would be for Christian preachers to see that concerns for the earth, the reality and effects of climate change, are heard often in churches through sermons and homilies, as well as catechesis. For instance, if we think that the Earth is important and yearns as well for salvation, we should see it as equally important to pray for the Earth community. Thus using the words of Jesuit Jim Profit, "I yearn for the day when our prayers of the faithful include a prayer for the species that are lost, or for some issues in ecology, for an awareness of the Earth issues."[406] Also Christian authorities should, on a regular basis, monitor the activities of their exorcists in order to guard against abuses of a new trend of exorcism that is abusive to the earth. Christian churches should promote the campaign for clean and friendly environment by organizing lectures, retreats, seminars, workshops and symposia on this topic. Christian schools should look at education targeting youth to change "inbred, selfish attitudes towards consumption and exploitation of natural resources." Collaboration with UNESCO's culture of peace program, and Association of Schools Program Network (ASPnet) could be of immense help here. Also Christian communities could demonstrate ability and interest in sponsoring environmental programs in church and state (local and national) media.

Apart from drawing the awareness to the havoc of climate change, these environmentally based outreaches should teach people some practical methods that individuals can do on their own to avoid climate change. Since action speaks louder than words, churches should, on a practical level, take the lead in some of these environmental friendly simple activities, such as proper and healthy refuse management, acquisition of solar sources of energy, taking their cars frequently for emission tests, turning off electric lights in churches and rectories when not needed, tree planting and greening of church premises, etc. It will be of great value to this campaign and theology, if those responsible for the training of future church leaders (lay and clergy) include these elements in their curriculum.

Another reason why Christianity, especially in Nigeria, must assume responsibility for climate change is because the majority of those affected by climate change are the poor and the disadvantaged, especially children and women. Memories of some of the natural disasters reveal a huge number of poor (children, women and elderly) victims, together with an often infinitesimal percentage of the wealthy. The rich have the means and resources to escape the site of these disasters before they happen; the poor have no such opportunity. Therefore the climate change project enables us to explore the socio-political dimensions of our Christian compassion. This we do by demonstrating our preferential option for the poor and our solidarity with the suffering, allowing our voices to speak for the voiceless with whom we are united in the *mystical body of Christ*. To neglect this would simply be inimical to our Christian vocation, a scandal and a challenge to our concept of compassion.

It is in this concept of the mystical body of Christ, which joins us with both the suffering of today and the people of the future, that we find the reasons why we must take action, materially and otherwise, to mitigate and cushion the effects of climate change. Regarding our future, Ritsuya Kishida, a fourteen year old Japanese junior board member of the Children's World Summit for the Environment 2005 says, "We cannot forget biodiversity when thinking of the future. If coming generations blame us for making creatures extinct, we have no excuse we can give them. It isn't fair that they will not be able to see what we have seen because we failed to take action. We cannot revive species, as some movies have done for dinosaurs, and even if we could, it would not be wise without knowing their habits."[407]

On a final note, we want to reiterate in a loud and clear voice, "climate change is real!" Its effect is hazardous for people today and tomorrow. The threat is no respecter of nationality, race or border, though it is borne more heavily in the countries that are less culpable.

Each one of us has a responsibility towards this phenomenon, for we have all contributed to it, albeit in different degrees. It is an integral constituent of our Christian call to compassion that we cannot afford to neglect. We cannot afford to be silent, for to do nothing or to continue with business as usual is suicidal.

Moreover, it is important to state unequivocally that, after all is said and done, there is an irreversible fact we should not forget, namely, that all creation, including humanity, was created to serve specific needs. To serve these needs is to fulfill their purpose for being. For instance, from our biological knowledge of food web and food chains, we know that human beings depend on some animals and plants to live, just as other animals and plants depend on each other and on humanity. Nevertheless, our compassion towards all creation might help us to distinguish between legitimacy and abuse, and to guard against inordinate use of creation. We must overcome the dualistic thinking that "nonhuman life has *no intrinsic value*, but only *instrumental value* – value only in relation to human purposes and needs."[408] All life has *intrinsic value,* and as such, human dignity must be promoted, yet not at the expense of the dignity of other created things; the reverse also holds true.

Like all other Nigerians and more so as people called to be compassionate in the manner of our heavenly father, we Christians are called to embrace the urgency of the issue of climate change. Undoubtedly this demands that we first put our own house in order. We have to rediscover that our faith is well placed to take a long-term action against climate change based on our view of the whole world as God's creation, intrinsically interrelated. It is interesting to note that, in a country such as ours, where faith too often divides people into warring camps and makes a mockery of the belief in a single creator, the cause of climate change provides a common meeting place for dialogue and ecumenical engagement among Christian denominations and other faith communities.

The full realization of these implications of a politics of compassion is contingent upon one condition – that those reasons for the Nigerian church's inability to rise up to the socio-political dimensions of its response to Nigerian suffering (as discussed in chapter three) are tackled. This condition, which will be discussed in the following section, is what we refer to as the challenges of a politics of compassion.

Challenges of Politics of Compassion

The politics of compassion asks a set of questions which the church and individual Christians must struggle with at all times, as they attempt to respond to the sufferings of their people in this new dispensation. It wants to know "how the church understands its social and political role. How is the church related to society? What internal dynamics are operative in the church and how do these affect the church's public role?"[409] In relation to the Nigerian situation, this paradigm directs its challenges to those reasons mentioned in chapter three that have incapacitated the Nigerian church and Christians from responding appropriately to socio-political, economic and cultural causes of suffering in their land. That is to say, in order for the Nigerian church to undertake socio-political action or concern in response to the many sufferings of its people, it has first and foremost to attempt to overcome its prevalent "political and theological distinction between the spiritual and the temporary planes."[410] Also it has to engage in a radical conversion that will deal with the inherent contradictions within the church.

First, the Nigerian church has to change its inherited idea that "the state was an essential instrument for repressing the consequences of sin and that it was not the vehicle by which men (sic) could attain to true justice, true virtue, or true happiness." This attitude views the state and its functions as being primarily negative, repressive with no positive value for the Christian, thus encouraging Christians to be indifferent to worldly concerns, including politics.[411] With this new paradigm, the church and the Christian must remember often that the world is not only God's creation but was declared good by God (cf. Gen. 1ff). Also, when God sent his only begotten Son into the world, he did not send him to condemn or judge the world but rather to save it (Jn. 3: 16, 17).[412] In other words, they should see the world as St. Augustine saw it, "a current state of creation, which is loved by God or it would not exist at all, redeemed by the sending of the Son, in which the Spirit is at work transforming all things into what they are called to be."[413] With this, the church understands that,

> A faith that is separated from history becomes spiritless and powerless because it remains at the level of immanent progress. Those who attempt to separate secular realities from the sacred dimension simply impoverish humanity and overshadow the role of religion on public life. The connection between secular and sacred dimension affirms the process of incarnation. The link between sacred and secular dimension does not involve any contradiction. The human soul that is truly seeking to save itself is fully social.[414]

In a very particular way, this is for the Nigerian church a rediscovery of the rich spirituality of our culture (our African heritage) – a culture to which the dichotomy between the soul and the body, the religious and the secular, the temporary and the spiritual is alien. We recall Prof. Emefie Ikenga-Metuh words earlier cited in this chapter, "For the African, man [sic] is a force in the midst and in union with other forces in the universe actively interacting with them."[415] This appreciation of the world paves the way for a compassion that recognizes and emphasizes the presence of the divine spark in all things, as Hasidic tradition teaches, reminding us that "there is no place devoid of God." This compassion overcomes the sense of dualism in reminding us that "we are all parts of and connected to sparks found in all of creation, and it is our duty to connect with them and to try to raise them up."[416]

In view of this, "*vita Christiana,* the Christian life," as Jurgen Multmann concludes using the words of Dietrich Bonhoeffer, "no longer consists in fleeing the world and in the spiritual resignation from it, but is engaged in an attack upon the world and a calling in the world."[417] Or, as Archbishop Oscar Romero said shortly before he was shot for interfering with life "in the midst of the city," "[I have been learning] a beautiful and harsh truth, that the Christian faith does not separate us from the world but immerses us in it; that the church, therefore, is not a fortress set apart from the city, but a follower of the Jesus who loved, worked, struggled, and died in the midst of the city."[418] Importantly, this learning will be possible and effective only when the church looks at and learns from the world from the perspective of the victims, not the successors of power. In this perspective, Arturo Paoli writes, "[human being] is the subject and not money or things."[419] It is from this standpoint that it recognizes the dark side of our modern times, dark side that can only be overcome by a conversion to universal solidarity,[420] to which Jesus remains our archetype and savior.

Equally, it is this understanding of the interconnectedness of the world and our personal spiritual lives that Richard Roberts and members of Fellowship for a Christian Social Order (FCSO)[421] suggest, enables us interpret the redemptive work of Christ in a new way – to mean an integration of the spiritual and the material, the personal and the social. Thus, salvation necessarily entails a view of sin, repentance, and holy living as both personal and social.[422] This new awareness which John Line, identifies as *radical Christianity* enables the church realize, more than ever, the serious bond that exists between our individual sins and structures of sin. It also reposes on the church the responsibility of a reinterpretation of its doctrine of sin. Line thus posits:

> Radical Christianity will have a doctrine of sin that is no less emphatic, and its diagnosis of man's predicament will be in terms of sin. But it will reclassify human acts...both by inclusion and exclusion in what it categorizes as sinful. It will include whatever in disposition or conduct is unbrotherly, whatever sunders men (sic) or is contrary to love and loyalty. It will judge sinful all acts and processes that yield affluence, or even sufficiency, to some while impoverishing others, or that cause power to be used in unreciprocal ways the will and freedom of others... Cognate to the doctrine of sin will be the call to repent and to bring forth fruits meet for repentance... It will lay on men their responsibility for the acts of a society of which they are a part, and it will bid them repent of all acts and conditions by which society sins against any of its members. The fruit of repentance will be the will to transform these conditions.[423]

In this dispensation, sin, according to Katie G. Cannon, becomes "anything that fragments, prohibits, or interrupts the progress from outward life to inward life and to outward life in a justice-making world."[424] With this realization, the church compassionately affirms with Gustavo Gutierrez, "Therefore, if our own personal sin embodies itself in unjust and enslaving structures – and it does – if Christ is the Liberator Supreme – and he is – if the Church is the continuance of his liberating presence – and it is – then, clearly, the Church's main task is liberation; and this means from all enslavements, both the roots in sin and the appearance in unjust structures."[425]

Then, as Richard McCormick states, it becomes obvious both to the church and to the individual Christian that "contemporary Samaritanism is not content to pour oil on the wounds of the suffering. It wants to prevent that suffering and get at the causes."[426] It then means that, the Christian landlord will no longer feel spiritually contented that s/he gives alms to the poor, pays her or his church levies, performs her or his Easter duties, while her or his greed and activities in unjust structures continue to inflict and perpetuate the sufferings of those for whom he exercises his corporal works of mercy. The church will then be determined to challenge and chide those governors and government officials, especially the Christians among them, who loot, squander and misappropriate public funds, yet who come to occupy the front pews in the church without qualms, simply because they have kept their church records clean.

Additionally, this new paradigm challenges the church to an urgent change of attitude regarding the way it enters into dialogue with the state. s notes that many a time, we are taught to believe that the world poses the question and the Christian faith provides the answer therefore presenting the case of a question-and-answer situation. This is unproductive, he suggests, because it poses the danger of triumphalism and naivety – church superior and supervisor of the state mentality.[427] Quoting David Tracy, he maintains that an authentic conversation is one in which the partners move past self-consciousness and self-aggrandizement into joint reflection upon the subject matter of the conversation. This works on the ability of the parties to listen, to reflect, to correct, to speak to the point and to allow the question take over.

In every conversation it is the question under discussion that governs and not any of the participants; this is why the conclusion cannot be predetermined. The church should remember that it does not only teach but learns from the world.[428] Humility is an ingredient of such conversation. Nigerian church needs to cultivate this virtue.

Lastly, this new spirituality enables the church to see itself as in a mirror and acknowledges as never before the areas where it resembles the state; that it can and has in some instances been enslaving, just like the state. This means that Christians will begin to realize with Augustine that the church can be both "city of God and city of man at the same time." For the "city of God," Gregory Baum, observes in interpreting, Augustine, "becomes present wherever people love and serve one another, but it gives way to the city of man, the proud city, when people become self-centered, pursue their own advantage, betray their friends and abandon social solidarity."[429] With this mirror, the church sees how its image has been marred by the symptoms and traits of clericalism – dominance, intolerance of pluralism, conformism, fear of risk, secretive use of power, anxiety, joyless security, rejection of oppositions and ultimate apathy.[430] This realization leads us to the second challenge of a politics of compassion – a call to an internal radical conversion.

Sometimes people think that our personal lives have nothing to do with our commitment to social justice. But this idea has long been disproved. As this Chinese proverb indicates, "What you are speaks so loud that I do not hear what you are saying." Or, as Dean Brackley says, "Life is a moral drama; understanding it…depends, in the end, on the kind of people we are."[431] This too was acknowledged in the 1971 synodal statement: "While the Church is bound to give witness to justice, she recognizes that anyone who ventures to speak to people about justice must first be just in their eyes" (*Justitia in Mundo* [JM] 3). As a matter of fact, the Catholic bishops conference of Nigeria, in its 1999 declaration on the state of corruption in the country acknowledged that, "even the church and other religious organizations are themselves not completely free from corruption."[432] In the parlance of the politics of compassion, the critical role of the church as the artisan of a new humanity in the Nigerian world means that the church should rise above the wholesome values of the society. Barnabas Okolo writes: "The church should never be so affected by these values that its power and freedom to act are neutralized and rendered ineffective. If this happens it gradually becomes the slave of the system rather than its transformer. For it cannot whole-heartedly nor effectively oppose the society if it shares exactly the same mentality and values as the society."[433] "Hence we must undertake an examination of the modes of acting and of the possessions and life style found within the Church itself" (*JM* 3). The document highlights some important aspects of justice that must be safeguarded in the church for it to speak convincingly to the society of justice. These include the rights of women, the rights of workers to a living wage, and the rights to suitable freedom of expression and thought. Also it seeks that the use of material goods in the church and the lifestyle of all of its members should bear witness to the Gospel, in solidarity with the poor.

As we observed in chapter three, the church in Nigeria is plagued by three distorted dynamics – self-centeredness, self-preoccupation and self-preservation - that haunt many people and groups, and inhibit efforts at social justice.[434] These are present in the way power is abused in the church, the way people are treated in the church and the way the church deals with the society. In order to have the moral impetus to respond adequately to unjust structures and the sufferings they cause, the church and individual Christians must undergo a conversion that will liberate the church from these contradictions. This conversion makes a list of demands of the Nigerian church in this perspective.

First, this conversion should be modeled on the oracle of Jewish prophets against their religious system. It should take the way and manner that Christ critiqued the purity system and temple practices that oppressed and marginalized many people, challenging and reevaluating the focus of the church – challenging what comes first in the mind and agenda of the church. In its order of cult, the worship of God, and administration, a true human love and concern should be at the heart and center of the church's mission, thus replacing what Hans Kung suggests is "legalism, institutionalism, juridicism, ritualism, liturgicism, sacramentalism."[435]

For the Nigerian church to be a "microcosm which can serve as the concrete model of what a fully inclusive community might look like and as catalyst, within the conditions of current political and economic realities, for actions intended to bring that community into existence,"[436] it must adopt our new way of being a Christian suggested by this work. In the terms of political justice, the authority of the Nigerian church should shun arbitrary use of power and recognize that, though authority deserves respect, it does not undermine autonomy but rather fosters it.[437] The present sole-administrator system of leadership operational in the church, a replica of the military and dictatorial system of the Nigerian government, should be strongly condemned as inimical to the identity and image of the church. The Nigerian bishops should learn from their confreres in other places how to share and decentralize power, especially by appointing auxiliary bishops and using other members of the church.

In most case, when one advocates for fairness and leadership based on the communitarian model of the first century Christianity, one often hears the slogan, "the Church is not a democracy." Yet as Richard R. Gaillardetz observes, one does not hear "its necessary ecclesiological correlate, 'the church is not also an oligarchy.'"[438] The model of leadership that resonates with the aspect of compassion presented here, agreeing with Gaillardetz, does not compare the church to any single political model. It does not identify the church with oligarchy nor any form of liberal democratic polity with the idea of "majoritarianism." The decisions in church must not be made based simply on the aggregate majority of private opinions on a given matter. The church is always a spiritual communion, constituted and guided by the Holy Spirit. In view of this unique nature, decision making in the church must reflect the character of its constitution. It ought to be "an ecclesial discernment process [of the will of God,] acknowledging the indispensable role of ordained church leadership as guardian of the apostolic faith while also remaining open to the prophetic voice so often emerges outside of established institutional structures." [439] As we can see from the Nigerian context, it is very difficult to discern any significant progress in terms of the participation of the laity in decision-making. Therefore our call to compassion challenges the undue emphasis of the restriction of the laity to participate in decision-making in the church.

Of equally importance, this new paradigm advocates that the principle of subsidiarity be applied to the life of the church. This requires that "we transpose the sociopolitical principle into the ecclesiological framework determined by the integrity of the local church 'in and out of which' the universal church is manifested."[440] In other words, the bishop must not do what the parish priest can and should do, the priests should not do what the local church leader can and should do in his or her local community. "It is only when these issues appear insoluble at the various local [or small] levels and/or threaten the faith and unity of the church universal should one expect the intervention of 'higher authority.'"[441] Part of what is demanded by this principle is that the laity should be adequately trained and allowed to take up their responsibility in the transformation of the Nigerian society. The urgency of this demand had been highlighted by John Paul II in his question and challenge to the African church in article 54 of the *Post-synodal Apostolic Exhortation: Ecclesia in Africa*.

> A last question must be asked: Has the Church in Africa sufficiently formed the lay faithful, enabling them to assume competently their civic responsibilities and to consider socio-political problems in the light of the Gospel and of faith in God? This is certainly a task belonging to Christians: to bring to bear upon the social fabric an influence aimed at changing not only ways of thinking but also the very structures of society, so that they will better reflect God's plan for the human family. Consequently I have called for a thorough formation of the lay faithful, a formation which will help them to lead a fully integrated life. Faith, hope and charity must influence the actions of the true follower of Christ in every activity, situation and responsibility. Since "evangelizing means bringing the Good News into all strata of humanity, and through its influence transforming humanity from within and making it new," Christians must be formed to live the social implications of the Gospel in such a way that their witness will become a prophetic challenge to whatever hinders the true good of men and

women of Africa and of every other continent.⁴⁴²

Concerning economic justice, the church must be accountable and transparent in all it does. For example, the church cannot promote good working conditions, just wages and regular payment of workers' salaries, without first treating its own employees with this love and justice. It cannot insist on a government policy that makes adequate provision for the poor without the poor and their concerns occupying a prominent place in the programme of the church. The church should as often as the need be review the working condition of its staff, ensure that they are offered a kind of basic contractual protection. Sometimes it appears that the church finds it difficult to identify with the labor union cause. The problem might not be connected with the fact that the church does not allow the unionization of its workers. It frequently discourages them from forming one, by asking them to see "their work as a 'vocation' or 'ministry' that therefore cannot be compared to correlative positions in the secular business world."⁴⁴³

Likewise, the church cannot fight the subordination and subjugation of women in the Nigerian socio-political economy without first recognizing and granting women equal opportunities according to their potential to creatively and freely participate in the life and administration of the church. This will involve creating equal training and opportunity in church administration for men and women, priests, religious and laity alike.⁴⁴⁴ Good thoughts and teachings in this regard must be matched with practical actions and bold steps that redress past unjust policies and negligence, and also provide care for the affected ones. The church all over the world is drawn to the condition of communities of professed religious women who have for decades served the church for slave wages. "Now they find themselves with an aging population and greatly diminished sources of income while facing soaring health care costs."⁴⁴⁵ Some bishops' conferences in the world have taken up conscientious actions that compassionately relate to the needs of these daughters and handmaids of the Lord. For instance, the U.S. bishops' conference has instituted annual collection for professed religious women's communities.⁴⁴⁶ One wonders when the conditions of this indispensable part of the body of Christ will be a concern for the Nigerian church! Will the hearts of the Nigerian bishops and priests ever be moved by the deplorable conditions most of our women religious in Nigeria find themselves just because they serve the church? Politics of compassion demands that the Nigerian bishops' conference should time and again include in its agenda the welfare, fair treatments of the women religious, and most importantly, the nature of contracts dioceses sign with them.

How can the church fight corruption, tribalism and favoritism in the Nigerian society while its appointments to key positions in offices or parishes are still based on ethnic affiliation or personal bond with authorities? It is impossible for the church to advocate inter-religious mutuality while it is still skeptical of ecumenical programs. Ironically, the "secular powers," John Macmurray notes, are attempting a League of Nations, while Christians, specifically called 'to be one, [Jn. 17: 21] seem unable or unwilling to do so." For the church to be the sacrament of community, unity which it is called to be, Macmurray suggests, "the churches have to overcome their denominational differences and cozy separateness. They have to make concrete moves towards becoming genuinely ecumenical."[447]

Lastly, the lifestyles of church leaders have to change to reflect the simplicity that their call demands, so that the church can remain a sacrament of evangelical poverty and a challenge to the scandalous affluence that describes Nigerian leaders. Evangelical poverty or 'voluntary poverty,' as Aloysius Pieris refers to, "does not mean leading the life of an ascetic but leading a life based on simplicity, sufficiency, and respect for both human beings and the ecological order."[448] "Its hermeneutical underpinning" according to R. S. Sugirtharajah, "is provided by the biblical notion of God's active opposition to Mammon – organized consumerism and greed."[449]

Politics of compassion does not, as Gregory Baum notes in the case of critical theology, "create the impression that all we need is the transformation of institutions, forgetting that we also need the conversion of heart."[450] "More than we need to convert bad systems," Ronald Rolheiser says, "we need to convert ourselves."[451] The radical conversion called for by a politics of compassion is equally directed to each individual Nigerian Christian as a person, realizing that there is an undeniable connection between our personal sins and structural sins. Thus the Nigerian Christians must confront those vices that have held us captive, such as greed, jealousy, and the lack of forgiveness, compromise and respect for others.

"With conversion comes cognitive liberation," Dean Brackley maintains. When we have undertaken this radical exercise and undergone an overhauling of our priorities, "we open up to the world, awakening to new things and seeing old things in a new light."[452] Conversion bestows power and freedom to act and also raises one up as a model to others. With this conversion and a new spirituality the Nigerian church will then be ready in freedom and credibility to undertake the implications of a politics of compassion as explored in the preceding section.

Having concluded this discussion on the meaning, implications and challenges of a politics of compassion, it is important that we reiterate that, above all, what "ultimately grounds our commitment to justice is Jesus and not any liberal ideology."[453] In that sense, commitment to justice as an act of compassion demands more than merely having a just cause and doing effective political action. It is an act rooted in love – loving the way Christ loved. In view of this, we shall discuss in the next section, some elements of Christian spirituality that can substantiate our commitment to justice as rooted in Jesus. These we refer to as the dynamics of compassion.

Dynamics of a Politics of Compassion

The claim we are making here is, as John W. de Gruchy states, "Christian piety at its best, can make a significant contribution to the social transformation of the world."[454] We shall illustrate this claim by exploring the following areas: communal prayer and forgiveness. We shall not be doing a comprehensive study of these areas. Our aim is to show how valuable these can be when they accompany our commitment to justice.

Communal Prayer

A good number of scholars agree that prayer can be an empowering response to suffering. According to Karl Barth, "To clasp hands in prayer is the beginning of an uprising against the disorder of the world."[455] Prayer, as defined here by John Baptist Metz is,

> a cry of lament from the depths of the spirit. But this is in no sense a vague, rambling moan. It calls out loudly and insistently. Nor is it merely a wish or a desire, no matter how fervent. It is supplication. The language of prayer finds its purpose and justification in the silently concealed face of God. Hence, lament, supplication, crying and protest contained in prayer, as also the silent accusation of wordless cry, can never simply be translated and dissolved into discourse.[456]

Metz's description captures the way Africans in general would see and relate to prayer. In prayer we sing songs, moan, lament, and pledge our fidelity to God and promise to avoid what brings suffering to others. Prayer, from an African perspective has a very strong community character – a sense of social responsibility and solidarity. It brings together families, relatives, friends and neighbors in a way that dissolves any class distinction, thus providing a social forum for support. When we identify with the sufferers in prayer, we draw them close to our heart and they feel the touch and support of our presence. Many a time, it is within prayer that the poor are blessed and reconciled with their oppressors. In this community environment that prayer provides, the poor and the marginalized feel a sense of belonging and protection. Prayer is one of the means a suffering community lets God know what they want him to know and do about their lives, and also make a personal and communal commitment to work for the transformation of their community.[457]

Judeo-Christian tradition also witnesses to this dynamism of communal prayer. In the Old Testament, we have repeated records of the Israelites praying as a community. They groaned in their slavery and cried out, and their cry for help went up to God. God heard their cry, remembered his covenant, was concerned for them, and came down to rescue them *(Ex 2:23-24; 3:8)*. Christ, in the New Testament, tells us of the power in two or three gathered in prayer in his name. They will have the gift of his presence and also answers to their prayers *(Matt. 18:19-20; Mk. 11:24; Jn. 16:15)*.

In relation to our commitment to justice, Dirkie Smit tells us that "Christian worship is one of the social locations, perhaps one of the most important places where Christians learn how to see things from a totally different perspective, that is, the perspective of God's gracious reign over the whole of reality." "It is primarily in the worship service," he continues, "where we listen to and hear God's Word, which then helps us to see properly."[458] Douglas John Hall, maintains, "Christian worship is about 'thinking our way into God's world."[459]

Because Christian worship is all about remembrance - *anamnesia*, hope, and experience, it dynamically "liberates its worshippers from the 'givenness' of everyday reality and brings them into a creative tension between past, future, and the present, so that they learn to look [and act] in the right direction."[460] Within this understanding, the Nigerian church and Christian can draw a great inspiration as they struggle to overcome the dualism, the dichotomy between prayer and action, holiness and justice. As Nicholas Wolsterstorff says, "The preoccupation of the liturgy does not separate liturgy from justice. On the contrary, holiness binds liturgy and justice together. God's justice is a manifestation of his holiness; our justice is a reflection of God's holiness. In liturgy we voice our acknowledgement of God's holiness. In struggle for justice we embody that acknowledgement." In conclusion he maintains, "The authenticity of the liturgy is conditioned by the quality of the ethical life of those who participate," for liturgy without justice, we know from the Old Testament, is repugnant to God (cf. Isa.58: 1-15, "this people honor me with lip service" but here is the type of sacrifice that pleases God; cf also, Lk. 12: 35-58, "not those who call me Lord, Lord, but those who know and do the will of my father").[461]

What this work is demonstrating here is that there is such a strong tie between our Christian liturgies and our commitment to justice that we cannot afford to neglect and dismiss religious worship as anti-justice-making. We will come to realize this connection when we understand our Christian worship as basically fulfilling three things: gathering together the people around the Word of God and the sacraments in worship and praise. This worship leads the people to a self-surrender that begins to appreciate the inextricable bond that unites each person to the other and to move to accept mutual responsibility for each other in their physical and spiritual needs. Lastly, within this mutual responsibility for each other, the people begin to discover the dangerous systemic imbalance in society responsible for most sufferings. Upon achieving this consciousness, the people are motivated to include a socio-political dimension in their compassionate action towards the sufferings of each other.[462]

Presently, as I can observe, the Catholic Charismatic Movement in Nigeria (CCM) bears a strong witness to this type of dynamism of prayer motivating social action. Unfortunately, the group seems not to be welcomed in some dioceses and parishes in Nigeria because of their strong relationship with other Pentecostal movements outside the Catholic Church.

Forgiveness is the other element of our Christian piety that we want to discuss here because of its link with commitment to justice.

Forgiveness

According to David Edwards, working with victims of oppression sometimes turns activists into "dissident irate bunches, keen to stick to facts and political discussions yet unwilling to look closely at their own motivation. Indeed, they are notoriously angry and full of hatred for those they deem responsible for the woes of the masses. Feelings of anger and hatred do not bring peace in relationships, not even in the family circle; they prevent even dedicated people from forming cohesive movements for social change."[463] Without forgiveness the oppressed easily turn into the oppressor. Forgiveness is simply understood here as "the process that involves a change in emotion and attitude regarding an offender that results in decreased motivation to retaliate or maintain estrangement from an offender despite their actions, and requires letting go of negative emotions towards the offender."[464]

Forgiveness is at the heart of the gospel of Jesus yet it cannot be prescribed as a dutiful or legal obligation nor can it be demanded from a victim/survivor of oppression. It is a free offer of grace rooted in the truth of the victim. As a dynamic of the politics of compassion, forgiveness is that which can liberate the victim/survivor from the destruction and bitterness as well as from the feelings of being debased, dishonored and disrespected or shamed. It can also deal with self-loathing and self-blame. At the same time the act of forgiveness is an act of judgment. It is saying that the act of violence was wrong, that an immoral wrong was done.

For forgiveness to achieve its dynamic aim of compassion, the victims must recognize that it is a very transformative power they possess and have the freedom and readiness to offer. On the part of the oppressors, it calls for acknowledgment and remorse for the violence done, a change of life orientation and direction, and restitution as a concrete, practical component to the process of forgiveness.[465] In other words, forgiveness asks of the offender the moral response of repentance. For John W. De Gruchy, it is injustice for the oppressor to get away free, yet if their punishment is not redemptive, it deepens the divisions in society, increases enmity and resentment, prevents reconciliation and encourages vengeance. Forgiveness thus rules out that malicious and vindictive vengeance that perpetuates the cycle of violence.[466]

In the political realm, warring parties usually regard forgiveness as a sign of weakness rather than strength;[467] yet forgiveness does not mean political naiveté, though it might appear childlike, and even foolish. It is a worthwhile risk taken for a greater good. In the light of this, Gruchy insists that it is on the message of divine forgiveness buttressed on the crucifixion of Jesus that the ethics of forgiveness is rooted; or else it will be "oscillating between legalism and sentimentality," in the words of Paul Tillich.[468] When we forgive and get others to forgive, we are suing for peace and responding to the suffering of those around us compassionately as our God in Christ did on the cross.

South Africa remains a model here. The Nigerian government in 2000 and 2001 tried this call for reconciliation but, like many other Nigerian issues, it ended up as a mere caricature. The rich and the famous, the influential and the infamous goal getters saw the process as humiliating and condescending to the level of the poor – the 'nobodies' and thus many of the influential people avoided the process. To date, the report of that commission has never been made public. Nonetheless, it is still recommendable that the Nigerian church should discover the power and grace in this spirituality of forgiveness. As its contribution to the rebuilding of the nation, the church should encourage and create an environment where the oppressed and the oppressors would mutually seek healing from the evils committed against the poor within and without the Nigerian church. As we maintain since the beginning of this section, our concern here is to demonstrate that Christian piety has and can still significantly contribute to our commitment to making justice happen to the poor and the marginalized even in our own time.

Summary

This last chapter detailed discussion on the aspect of compassion – the politics of compassion, practiced and taught by Christ, which we often seem oblivious to. Using the Nigerian situation as a test-ground, we explored the implications and challenges of this paradigm. Above all, we insisted on the response to the type of suffering we experience today particularly, suffering resulting from the activities and policies of unjust systems. The chapter explicated that no amount of material relief can replace the need for active participation in socio-political actions and concerns that challenge and attempt to transform these systems. In order to be sure that our commitment to justice is always grounded in Jesus and not in some liberal ideology, we constructed a bridge linking our Christian spirituality and our socio-liberational-transformative activities suggested in the work. It is our hope that the readers of this piece will find it informative and useful.

CONCLUSION

Theology today is particularly aware that it has a responsibility for discerning and responding to the 'signs of the time.' During the time of apartheid the South African church defined the crisis of apartheid as *kairos* – a moment of truth. It declared: "A crisis is a judgment that brings out the best in some people and the worst in others. A crisis is a moment of truth that shows us up for what we really are. There will be no place to hide and no way of pretending to be what we are not in fact. At this moment in South Africa the church is about to be shown up for what it really is and no cover up will be possible."[469] In order to understand the statement South African church is making, it very helpful to note as well that crisis, as Ida Urso writes, does not really "indicate failure and disaster; rather, [it] presents opportunities of growth and fresh effort and when surmounted, provides a sense of gain and freedom."[470] This idea is expressed in the Chinese ideogram for crisis, *wei-chi*, which includes the dual concept of "breakdown" as well as "breakthrough."[471] In other words, the greater challenge facing us, either as individuals or as a church, in time of crisis, is how do we understand and respond to the moment? Posterity bears witness that the South African church showed up for what it really was in responding to the circumstance of apartheid.

Suffering in the various ways it comes to people today presents yet another *kairos* – another moment of truth and opportunities of growth and fresh effort for the church, especially the church in Nigeria, to show who it truly is. As Duncan Forrester notes, the problems of our times do not just evoke theological insights, but especially action: "it is the favorable time in which God issues a challenge to decisive action."[472]

The Nigerian church should see this moment as a moment of grace and opportunity. Drawing from Jesus' method or way of being compassionate, we have in this work presented compassion as a Christian option in this moment that might show us up for who we are. This aspect of Christ's compassion, which we identified as a politics of compassion, provides us with a paradigm for considering and responding to the problems of evil and suffering in our time. It shifts the theological methodology and epistemology from the prevalent and traditional approach which rationalizes evil and often remains inert in the face of suffering, and has even been accused of supporting the status quo that increases suffering. This politics of compassion also criticizes and challenges the comfort of the traditional attitude that sees compassion as merely private charity. Above all, it is an attempt to liberate compassion from its exile by identifying and responding effectively to suffering in the way and manner of the God of the Bible – action that consists in both material relief and justice-making.

Thus we maintain that, in order ***to respond compassionately to the widespread and scandalous form of social suffering and oppression imposed on humanity and to the reckless destruction of ecology, Christians are called to undertake social and political actions aimed at social transformation, actions that are rooted in and driven by the experience of compassion***. How does this work? Other scholars might have many other ways of tackling this problem but as far as this work is concerned our contention is keyed on compassion via socio-political analysis, spirituality and action.

Moreover, we bring this discussion to a final conclusion with an African proverb which says that, "when spider webs unite, they can tie up a lion"—meaning that when people collaborate, they can perform wonders. It is our considered opinion that collaborating with other stakeholders in justice-making we shall immensely enhance the church's effort and commitment to justice. "Self-sufficiency," Dean Brackley says, "sabotages social agendas, abandons society to its own inertia, in practice, its most powerful and least scrupulous members."[473] In our compassionate work for justice we search with others. "We don't start from scratch but rather draw from the wealth of wisdom creatively and critically." We reach out to others for advice and experience.[474] This should include learning from the experience of the churches in other nations, such as Latin America and South Africa, and other civil stakeholders such as various Non-Governmental Organizations committed to justice-making and also from our traditional African religions.

(Notes)

Introduction

[1] Milburn J. Thompson, *Justice and Peace: A Christian Primer*, (Maryknoll: Orbis Books, 2003), 198.

[2] John Paul II, *Salvific Doloris: On the Christian Meaning of Human Suffering*, (Boston: Pauline Books and Media, 1984), 8.

[3] John Bowker, *Problems of Suffering in Religions of the World*, (Cambridge, UK: Cambridge University Press, 1970), 24.

[4] Ibid.

[5] See Michael Stoeber, *Reclaiming Theodicy: Reflections on Suffering, Compassion and Spiritual Transformation*, (New York: Palgrave Macmillan, 2005), 61; William Placher, *Narratives of a Vulnerable God*, (Louisville, Ky.: Westminster, 1994), 18-19 in James Keenan, "Suffering and the Christian Tradition," in *Moral Wisdom: Lessons and Texts from the Catholic Tradition*, (Lanham: Rowman & Littlefield Publishers, 2004), 72.

[6] Oliver Davies, *A Theology of Compassion: Metaphysics of Difference and the Renewal of Tradition*, (Grand Rapids, MI: Eerdmans, 2003).

[7] Steven Best, DR., "Compassion and Action," 4, lecture series in drstevenbest,org/Lectures/CompassionAndActions.php.

[8] Marcus Borg, *Meeting Jesus Again for the First Time*, (New York: HarperCollins Publishers, 1995), 49.

[9] See, Paul VI, *Envangelii Nuntiandi*, quoted in Comblin, *Church and National Security*, 214-24, and in Rebecca S. Chopp, *The Praxis of Suffering: An Interpretation of Liberation and Politics*, (Maryknoll, New York, Orbis Books, 1992), 25.

[10] See, Ronaldo Munoz, "Ecclesiology in Latin America," in ibid.

[11] Elizabeth Lynn and Susan Wisely, "Towards a Fourth Philanthropic Response: American Philanthropy and its Public," 2.

[12] See John Macmurray, "Unity of Modern Problems," *Journal of Philosophical Studies*, Vol. 4 (1929), 179, quoted in Frank Kirkpatrick, *Community: A Trinity of Models*, (Washington D. C., Georgetown University Press, 1988), 158.

Chapter One

[13] John Paul II, 9. In his note on this, John Paul II gave the etymology of the words evil and suffering within Hebrew vocabulary. In this regard he writes, "it is useful to remember that the Hebrew root *r"* designates in a comprehensive way what is evil, as opposed to what is good (*tob*), without distinguishing between the physical, psychological and ethical senses. The root is found in the substantive form *ra'* and *ra a* indicating indifferently either evil in itself, or the evil action, or the individual who does it. In the verbal form, besides the simple one (*qal*) variously designating 'being evil,' there are the reflexive passive form (*niphal*) 'to endure evil,' 'to be afflicted by evil' and the causative form (*hiphil*) 'to do evil,' 'to inflict evil' on someone. Since the Hebrew lacks a true equivalent to the Greek pascho = 'I suffer,' this verb too occurs rarely in the Septuagint translation.

[14] Ibid.

[15] See Reginald Masterson, O.P., *Evil*, in *The Catholic Encyclopedia for School and Home*, (Toronto: McGraw-Hill Books Co., 1965), 165-166. Masterson remarks here that privation has to be qualified because not all lacks of good is evil.

[16] Paul Schilling, *God and Human Anguish*, (Nashville: Pathernon Press, 1977), 14. None of these descriptions of evil says anything about the suffering of other beings and of the entire creation. Their anthropocentrism is very obvious. This is why my definition of suffering includes th entire creation.

[17] Gaudium et spes, 9; see also, Lisa Sowel Cahill, "Globalization and the Common Good," in John A. Coleman and William F. Ryan, eds., *Globalization and Catholic Social Thought: Present Crisis, Future Hope*, (Maryknoll, New York: Orbis Books, 2005), 47.

[18] According to Donald R. Griffin, as paraphrased by Barbour, "in evolutionary history, increased capacity for pain was apparently a concomitant of increased sentience and was selected for its adaptive value in providing warning of danger and bodily harm. The behavior of animals gives evidence that they suffer intensely." See Donald R. Griffin, *Animal Minds: Beyond Cognition to Consciousness*, (Chicago: University of Chicago Press, 2001), in Ian Barbour, *Nature, Human Nature, and God*, (London: SPCK, 2002), 105.

[19] Michael Stoeber, *Reclaiming Theodicy: Reflections on Suffering, Compassion and Spiritual Transformation*, (New York: Palgrave Macmillan, 2005), 20.

[20] In Christ's prayer in the garden of Gethsemane, "my father, if it is possible, let this cup pass from me," (Mt. 26:39), we see the point these scholars are expressing,

namely, "suffering is the undergoing of evil before which man [sic] shudders" see John Paul II 27; Eric Cassell, *Nature of Suffering*, (New York: Oxford University Press, 1991), 31; John Hick, *Evil and the God of Love*, (San Francisco: Harper and Row Publishers, 1966), 292, 318.

[21] Geshe Lhundub Sopa, "The Buddhist Understanding of Suffering," in Donald W. Mitchell and James Wiseman, O.S.B., *Transforming Suffering: Reflections on Finding Peace in Troubled Times*, (Toronto: Doubleday, 2003), 1.

[22] *UNEP 2005 Annual Report*, (Produced by UNEP Division of Communication and Public Information, January, 2006), 8.

[23] See www.nationalpost.com/news/story.html?id=496689. This might not represent the accurate result of death tolls and other casualties in these two events. Later reports reveal that the numbers continue to increase as rescue works labor through the ruins and debris of the earthquake and cyclone.

[24] However, Langdon Gilkey like others will concede that there are other forms of evil that scientific and technological knowledge cannot possibly ameliorate for example death. See Langdon Gilkey, *Maker of Heaven and Earth: The Christian Doctrine of Creation in the Light of Modern Knowledge*, (New York: Anchor Books, Doubleday Co., 1965), 242.

[25] Some environmental analysts insist that there is a deficiency in language and insincerity in the way we describe events as natural disasters. There is nothing as such as natural disaster, they claim. There is, of course, natural or environmental risk or hazard. But when these risks/hazards add up with social vulnerability and human negligence then we experience disaster. They will claim that disaster is more a result of human negligence. For such environmentalist like Salvano Briceno, the negative effects of the 2005 tsunami and other disasters could have been avoided if there was enough warning and other preventive measures on the part of experts. (Salvano Briceno is the director of the Secretariat of the International strategy for Disaster Reduction, UN/ISDR. This was his submission to the 59th Annual DPI/NGO conference at the United Nations Headquarters, New York, 6-8 September, 2006). Michael Stoeber makes the same claim, as he maintains in the following words, "The horror is accentuated by the fact we now possess the technological knowledge and skill to reduce significantly through preventive measures the heavy loss of human life associated with this kind of natural disaster. In this case, the affected areas of the tsunami did not have the warning devices that are already in place in areas of the Pacific Ocean. Indeed, we now have the economic, agricultural, medical and technical resources to eliminate a tremendous amount of the suffering that arises worldwide in the context of various 'natural' evil. Yet often we lack the socio-cooperative will to do so." Stoeber, 12.

[26] Ibid.

²⁷ C.S. Lewis, *The Problem of Pain*, (New York: Macmillan & Co., 1994), 77.

²⁸ Matthew Lamb, *Solidarity with Victims: Towards a Theology of Social Transformation*, (New York: Crossroad Publishing Co., 1982), 3, as cited in Rebecca S. Chopp, *The Praxis of Suffering: An Interpretation of Liberation and Political Theologies*, (Maryknoll, New York: Orbis Books, 1992), 1. Lamb adds a nuance to the discussion indicating that the anguish is not just caused by humanity in a generic sense but specifically by male-dominated history. This issue will be returned to in the course of discussion in this work.

²⁹ See 2004 edition of the *Human Development Report* (HDR 2004), an annual publication of the United Nations Development Programme. Another account holds that about six million Jews and seventy-seven million soldiers and civilians died in the holocaust and World War II. In 1994, Hutus killed eight hundred thousand Tutsis over a period of three months, typically hacking them to death with machetes. As of March 11, 2005, three hundred and eighty thousand have died in Darfur genocide; they die at the rate of fifteen thousand per month. Thirty-four Jewish children between the ages of six and eight died in Israel in 1981 suicide bombings. Approximately, three thousand people died in the September 11, 2001 suicide attack on the World Trade Center (WTC). See Amy Chua, *World on Fire: How Exporting Free Market Democracy Breeds Ethnic Hatred and Global Instability*, (New York: Anchor Books, 2004), 5-6. Also the report of the survey of casualties in Iraq conducted by Johns Hopkins Bloomberg School of Public Health published in Star wire service,("655,000 Iraqi Deaths: Study," *Toronto Star*, Thursday, October 12, 2006, A7) put the breakdown of casualty in Iraq to 16,000 deaths per month in 40 months. This totals, 655,000 deaths since March 2003 through July 2006, representing the period of the USA Army's occupation of Iraqi.

³⁰ *UNEP 2005*, 10.

³¹ Ian Barbour, *Nature, Human Nature, and God*, 132.

³² Lamb, *Solidarity with Victims: Towards a Theology of Social Transformation*, (1982), 3.

³³ Dean Brackley, *Divine Revolution: Salvation and Liberation in Catholic Thought*, (Maryknoll, New York: Orbis Books, 1996), 118-119. See also John Paul II, *Sollicitudo rei Socialis*, 35-37.

³⁴ Richard McAfee, Brown, "Toward a Just and Compassionate Society: A Christian View," in *Cross Current*, summer (1995), 166.

³⁵ John Bennett, *Social Salvation: A Religious Approach to the Problems of Social*

Change, (New York: Scribners's, 1935), 9, cited in Michael Bourgeois, "Historical anticipations of Critical Theology: Why Social Theory Matters for Theology," in Don Schweitzer and Derek Simon, *Intersecting Voices: Critical Theologies in a Land of Diversity,* (Ottawa: Novalis, 2004), 43.

[36] Valpy Fitzgerald, "The Economics of Liberation Theology," in Christopher Rowland, ed., *The Cambridge Companion to Liberation Theology,* (Cambridge, UK: Cambridge University Press, 1999, reprinted copy, 2002), 224. According to Fitzgerald, "as a personal sinner, an individual is seen as both responsible for and as a victim of these oppressive social structures." Often the sinners do not come to know immediately the consequences of these actions to the poor because the effect is felt in the remote and rural areas.

[37] Cahill, in *Globalization and Catholic Social Thoughts,* 44.

[38] Wendell, "The Idea of Local Economy." *Orion Magazine,* (Nov/Dec 2004): 1-11.

[39] John Ralston Saul, *The Collapse of Globalism And The Reinvention of the World,* (Toronto: Penguin, 2005), 3.

[40] James E. Hug, "Economic Justice and Globalization," in *Globalization and Catholic Social Thought,* 56.

[41] Ibid, 60.

[42] In the 2005 International Labor Organization's (ILO) report, "at least 12.3 million people worldwide are victims of forced labor. About one-fifth of all laborers around the world are trafficked. In both transition and industrialized regions, forced labor for commercial sexual exploitation predominates." Thomas Netter, ed., *Forced Labour Today, World of Work,* no, 54, (Geneva: Department of Communication and Public Information of the ILO, August, 2005), 4-7.

[43] We agree that, in some sense, robotization, by itself, is a progress in scientific and socio-economic development. As a matter of fact it does, irrespective of how insignificant, provide employment at least for those who produce, operate and service these machines. It eases the pains of manual and hard labor involved in mass production of goods to meet the teaming and ever-growing world population. However, our argument here is that, this cannot be a conceited effort to maximize profit at the expense of human participation in production, as is the case with many multi-national corporations. This is consistent with the Catholic social teaching on labor and the human right to work. Since many people are not thought how to operate these robots and since it takes only but a few persons to operate them, robotization limits the opportunities for many people to express their right to work, and as such creates mass unemployment. On the other hand too, it widens the gap

between the skilled and unskilled, advantaged and disadvantaged in the society.

[44] See Engelbert Mveng, "Third World Theology – What Theology? What Third World?: Evaluation by an African Delegate," in Virginia Febella, and S. Torres, eds. *Irruption of Third World: Challenges to Theology*, (Maryknoll, New York: Orbis Books, 1983), 217. Explaining Mveng's concept of *anthropological poverty*, R.S. Sugirtharajah notes that this act of robbing the people of their own way of living and cultural heritage, and the resulting low self-esteem has caused the people to internalize the values and models of their oppressors. See R. S. Sugirtharajah, "Poverty," in Virginia Febella and R. S. Sugirtharajah, eds., *Dictionary of Third World Theologies*, (Maryknoll, New York: Orbis Books, 2000), 171.

[45] See Tissa Balasuriya, OMI, "Globalization," *Dictionary of Third World Theologies*, 93.

[46] Stephen Lewis, *Race Against Time*, (Toronto: House of Anansi Press Inc., 2005), 17. According to Stephen Lewis, "at present, the European Union and the United States together subsidize their farmers to the tune of $350 billion (US Dollar)."

[47] Hug, (2005), 61.

[48] Larry Elliot, "A Cure that is Worse than the Disease," in *Guardian Weekly*, Jan 24-30 (2002), 14.

[49] Daniel Liderbach, *Why do we Suffer? New ways of Understanding*, (New York: Paulist Press, 1992), 3.

[50] Dorothee Soelle, *Suffering*, tran. Everette R, Kalin, (Philadelphia: Fortress Press, 1984), 125.

[51] Stoeber, 60-1. Continuing further, Stoeber says, "So there is distinction here between destructive suffering, which diminishes and hinders the person in some way or another and for which there is no transformative impetus or response in the person...."

[52] Soelle, 125.

[53] Ibid, 41.

[54] Hick, 333.

[55] Soelle, 125.

[56] Ibid.

[57] Stoeber, 20.

[58] Ibid.

[59] Ibid.

[60] Ibid., 20-21.

[61] Ibid 21.

[62] Hick, 382-3.

[63] Max Scheler, *The Nature of Sympathy*, (Hamden, Ct. Shoestring Press, Inc., 1973), 136-138.

[64] Stoeber, 45.

[65] Dermot Lane *Keeping Hope Alive: Stirrings in Christian Theology*, (New York: Paulist Press, 1996) as quoted by Stoeber, 49.

[66] Daniel Simundson, *Faith Under Fire*, (Minneapolis: Augsburg Publishing House, 1980), 55.

[67] Schilling argues that people who are really "content to take whatever his gracious will….had sent" can hardly be expected to work actively to oppose evil by striving to undo the damage it has wrought. Paul Schilling, *God and Human Anguish*, 70-1. Barry L. Whitney argues that suffering does inhabit growth in faith and hope. For this reason it would be unrealistic to ask anyone to accept suffering in faith. Barry L. Whitney *What are they saying about God and Evil?* 11.

[68] Stoeber, 45.

[69] James F. Keenan, S.J., observes with resentment that the intellectual level of discussion is the most common and familiar level of discussion. James F. Keenan, S.J., *Moral Wisdom: Lessons from the Catholic Tradition*, (New York: Rowan and Littlefield Publishers, Inc, 2004), 67.

[70] Wayne Ferguson, "Beyond the Problem of Evil," in http://ccat.sas.upenn.edu/jod/agustine/ferg.htm.

⁷¹ Katherine Barber, ed.., *Canadian Oxford Dictionary,* 2ⁿᵈ Edition, (Toronto: Oxford University Press, 2004), 1613.

⁷² Ferguson, Ibid.

⁷³ See Ferguson, "Beyond the Problem of Evil."

⁷⁴ Augustine, *Dei Ordine,* 1.1.1, in Ludwig Schopp, ed., *The Fathers of the Church,* Vol. 5, (New York: CIMA Publishing Co., 1948), 226-232, as cited in ibid.

⁷⁵ See Ferguson, ibid.

⁷⁶ Liderbach, 34. Stanley Hauerwas calls theoretical theodicy a "theological mistake. Stanley Hauerwas *God ,Medicine, and Suffering,* (Michigan: William B. Eerdmans Publishing Co., 1992), ix.

⁷⁷ Terence Tiley argues that the move in theodicy to reconcile the harsh experiences of suffering with conceptions of a theistic divine callously efface the evil that it is. These moves in theodicy create a reality in which truly evil is not evil, insofar as they tend toward rationalizing and thereby justifying the horror that the person has endured. They also tend to inhibit imperatives to overcome suffering. Why, for example, if suffering is justified as conducive to spiritual transformation, ought another person act to remove the evil source of suffering? See Terence Tiley in Stoeber, 63.

⁷⁸ Stoeber, 67.

⁷⁹ Ibid, 68.

⁸⁰ Soelle, (1975), 35.

⁸¹ Ibid, 36.

⁸² See Robert Lifton and Richard Falk, *Indefensible Weapons: The Political and Psychological Case Against Nuclearism,* (Toronto: CBC Publication, 1984), 103, in Douglas John Hall, *God and Human Suffering: An Exercise in the Theology of the Cross,* (Minneapolis: Augsberg Publishing House, 1986), 43.

⁸³ Soelle, Ibid. 46.

⁸⁴ Keenan, 73. Keenan illustrates this point graphically with the story of the four religious women, Maura Clarke, Ita Forde, Dorothy Kazel and Jean Donovan whose

choice to remain in El Salvador to share with the suffering poor their travails rather than escape to a much better life in America, when they had the opportunity to do so. Because they chose to stay, they paid the ultimate price for this decision with their lives and provided hope for the people.

[85] Ibid., 73.

[86] Stoeber, 64.

[87] Douglas Hall, *God and Human,* 32.

[88] Ibid.

[89] Ibid.

[90] Keenan does not subscribe to the opinion that Israel believed that suffering was a punishment from God for sin. He argues that Israel rather saw it as a natural consequence of sin. His argument is that by "sin one departs from the providential way of the Lord God, one will in all likelihood get lost, run into trouble and eventually experience hardship." He is here quoting Bruce Vawter in his article "Missing the Mark" in Ronald Hamel and Kenneth Himes, eds., *Introduction to Christian Ethics,* (New York: Paulist Press, 1989), 199-205. See Keenan, Ibid.

[91] Edward Schillebeeckx, *Christ,* (New York: Seabury Press, 1980), 694-700 cited in Keenan, 2004, 70

[92] Keenan, 71.

[93] Stephen Mitchell, writes "Question, the harrowing question of someone who has only heard of God, is "Why me?" There is no answer, because it is the wrong question." A better way of asking the question is "where are you God?" In the where are you, the "why me" gets its answer. Sometimes the answer might be shocking as it dissolves and contradicts former ideas and opinions we held." In this process we become Spiritually transformed. See Stephen Mitchell, *The Book of Job,* (New York: Harper Prennial Books, 1992), xv.

[94] Overberg, Op. Cit. See also Mt 5:45.

[95] Ibid., 72.

Chapter Two

[96] Matthew Fox, *A Spirituality Named Compassion: Uniting Mystical Awareness with Social Justice,* (Rochester, Vermont: Inner Traditions Intl., 1999), xvii.

[97] Ibid, 2.

[98] Nancy. Eisenburg (2002), Empathy-related emotional responses, altruism, and their socialization. In R. J. Davidson & A. Harrington (Eds.), *Visions of compassion: Western scientists and Tibetan Buddhists examine human nature* (London: Oxford University Press),131-164, quoted in Jennifer Goetz, "Compassion and Empathy: Annotated Bibliography," in http://peacecenter.berkley.edu/research_compassion_goetz1.html.

[99] Ibid.

[100] Fox, (1999), 3. Some scholars, like Martha Nussbaum, do not consider this differentiation of much importance. For her the "emotional phenomenology of pity is indistinguishable from compassion at least from the emotional content experienced by the pitier." Even though she agrees that there are subtle differences in the understanding and experience of these emotions, she advises against a different naming of what appears as a single emotion. For her this is a mere distraction. I do not agree with Nussbaum here especially in the light of the results of further scholarships which take into account the person's belief structure that provides a cognitive background operating in the various ways one may interpret the moral consequences of such emotions. This is exemplified later in this work in the various ways pitying actions are interpreted by the pitier and the pitied in relation to the social and structural evils of our day. See Martha Nussbaum, "Compassion: The Basic Social Emotion," in *Social Philosophy and Policy Foundation,* Vol. 13, No. 1, (1996), 29; also Steven R. Smith "Keeping Our Distance in Compassion-Based Social Relations," *Journal of Moral Philosophy,* Vol. 2, No. 1, (2005), 72.

[101] See Frederick Perls in Fox, (1999), 3.

[102] Ibid.

[103] John Macmurray, *Persons in Relation,* (New York: Humanity Books, 1999), 137.

[104] Katherine Barber, ed., *Canadian Oxford Dictionary* 2nd edition, (Toronto: Oxford University Press Canada, 2004), 970.

[105] Marcus Borg, *Meeting Jesus Again for the First Time*, (New York: HarperCollins Press, 1995), 48.

[106] See Georg Autenrieth, *Homeric Dictionary*, tran. Robert Keep, (London: Gerald Duckworth & Co. Ltd., 2002), 106.

[107] *Misericodia* is also translated as compassion in here. John C. Traupman, *The New College Latin and English Dictionary*, (New York: Bantam Books, 1995), 262.

[108] Fox, 11.

[109] See Alan Drengson, "Compassion and Transcendence of Duty and Inclination," *Philosophy Today*, 25(Spring 1981), 39, Edward Vacek, *Love, Human and Divine: The Heart of Christian Ethics*, (Washington D.C.: Georgetown University Press, 1994), 6.

[110] See Kazoh Kitamori, *Theology of the Pain of God*, (Vancouver: John Knox Press, 1965), 98 in Ibid, 20; see also Marcus Borg, *Meeting Jesus Again for the First Time*, 47.

[111] *Rahamim, rahum,* comes from the root *rhm* used for womb.

[112] Borg, *Meeting Jesus Again for the First Time*, 48.

[113] Stuart Berg Flexner, ed., *Random House Unabridged Dictionary*, 2nd edition, (Toronto: Random House Inc., 1983), 1746.

[114] Anne Douglas, *The Feminization of American Culture*, (New York: Knopf, 1977), 254, in Fox, 6.

[115] Ibid.

[116] Ronald Rolheiser, *The Holy Longing*, (Toronto: Doubleday, 2000), 167-191.

[117] Ibid, 168.

[118] Kara Newell, and Judith Dueck, *Conrad Grebel Reviews*, Vol. 13 (3), (1995), 233-241.

[119] Richard A. McCormick, S.J., "The Social Responsibility of the Christian," *Blueprint for Social Justice,* Vol. LII, No. 3, (November, 1998), 1.

[120] Steven Best, Dr., "Compassion and Action," lecture series in drstevenbest,org/Lectures/CompassionAndActions.php.

[121] Stoeber, *Reclaiming Theodicy: Reflections on Suffering, Compassion and Spiritual Transformation,* (New York: Palgrave Macmillan, 2005), 38.

[122] Best, *Op. Cit.*

[123] Ibid. Jennifer Goetz while agreeing with Bests point out that, "we expect, however, that there are specific conditions in which people will be more likely to feel compassion, that there are differences in individual propensities to feel compassion, and that many people and cultures may view compassion as a basic human value." See Goetz *Op. Cit.*

[124] Fox, (1999), 20.

[125] Nouwen, 3-4.

[126] Richard A. McCormick, S.J., "The Social Responsibility of the Christian," 2.

[127] Washington Gladden goes further to advocate for profit sharing as an alternative economic policy which represents this golden rule imperative because according to him: "it rewards productivity and cooperative action; it channels virtues of self-regard and self-sacrifice; it socializes the profit motive and abolishes wage system; it promotes mutuality, equality, and community." See Washington Gladden, *Applied Christianity: Moral aspects of Social questions,* (Boston: Houghton Mifflin, 1889), 8-32; Gladden, *Recollections,* (Boston: Houghton Mifflin, 1909), 300-304, in Gary Dorrien, "Social Salvation: The Social Gospel as Theology and Economic," in Christopher H. Evans, ed., *Social Gospel Today,* (Louisville, Kentucky: Westminster John Knox Press, 2001), 101-113. *Washington Gladden, an evangelical preacher born in 1836 is named the father of social gospel because according to Gary Dorrien's aacount, "social gospel began in the mid 1870s as Gladden's gloss on the golden rule" – expressing his theologically liberal and mildly social approach to Christianity" 102.

[128] *Document and Decisions of the Ordinary General Chapter 2001 of the Order of St. Augustine,* (Roma: Pubblicationi Agostiniane, 2001), 17-18

[129] See Augustine, *Homily on 1st John,* 8,5, in ibid.

[130] Fox, 19.

[131] Joel Federman, "The Politics of Universal Compassion," in *The Search for Common Value.* http://www.topia.net/common_undeerstanding.html. Recent Jewish scholars argue against the predominate theology of some Christian thought that 'Holiness was understood by the Jews as a matter of purity and mere spiritual sentiment. These scholars insist that the Jews understood Holiness to mean and include act of justice-making, work of mercy. See Fox, 19.

[132] Fox, 8.

[133] Michael Himes and Kenneth Himes, OFM, *Fullness of Faith: The Public Significance of Theology*, (New Jersey: Paulist Press, 1993), 61.

[134] Joel Federman, *Op. Cit.*

[135] Jose Miranda, *Being and the Messiah*,(Maryknoll, New York: 1974), 61 in Fox, 10.

[136] Fox, 10.

[137] Henri J. M. Nouwen, Donald P. McNeill, and Douglas A. Morrison, *Compassion: A Reflection on the Christian Life*, (New York: Doubleday, 1983), 12.

[138] Ibid.

[139] Jon Sobrino and Juan Hernandez Pico, *Theology of Christian Solidarity*, (Maryknoll: Orbis Books, 1985), vii.

[140] Ibid, 5.

[141] Pontifical Council for Justice and Peace, *Compendium of the Social Doctrine of the Church*, (Canada: Catholic Conference of Catholic Bishops, 2005), 86.

[142] Dean Brackley, *Divine Revolution: Salvation and Liberation in Catholic Thought*, (Maryknoll: Orbis Books, 1996).

[143] William Reiser, *Jesus in Solidarity with His People: a Theologian Looks at Mark*, (Collegeville, Minnesota: The Liturgical Press, 2000), 53.

[144] Ibid, 15.

[145] John Paul II, *Savifici Doloris: On the Christian meaning of Human suffering*,

(Boston: Pauline Books and Media, 1984), 26.

¹⁴⁶ The last part of the Pauline hymn expresses the fact that our suffering as a compassionate response to others' suffering has a transformative effect both for us and the victims. It is this final statement, that our suffering does not end in emptiness, which empowers us in our participation in the suffering of others. See Nouwen, 31 and also Victor Frankl, *Man's Search for Meaning*, (New York: Pocket Books, 1983).

¹⁴⁷ John Paul II, *Savifici Doloris*, 26.

¹⁴⁸ Jack Nelson-Pallmeyer, *The Politics of Compassion*, (Maryknoll, New York: Orbis Books, 1986), 11. Nelson-Pallmeyer suggests that a reading of the parable of the Good Samaritan that is based on being good or bad sometimes makes one interpret the meaning form the perspective of one of the characters. "The problem with that interpretation is that we individualize and personalize the meaning of the parable and therefore lose much of what it is saying. We either bask in the false glory of self-righteous behavior or we sink deeper into guilt, which reinforces our sense of our own worthlessness. The truth is that we are all of the characters in the story: lawyer, priest, Levite, Samaritan, and roadside victim. Each of us is capable of denying or giving birth to compassion. If we affirm that each of us has the capacity to be either compassionate or hardhearted when confronted with difficult personal or social problems, then many new possibilities emerge. Grace can free us for involvement rather than pacify our guilt."

¹⁴⁹ See John Macmurray in Frank Kirkpatrick, *Community: A Trinity of Models*, (Washington, D.C., Georgetown University Press, 1986), 188.

¹⁵⁰ Jack Nelson-Pallmeyer, 10.

¹⁵¹ Nouwen et. al., *Compassion*, 27-28.

¹⁵² According to John Paul II, the parable of Good Samaritan belongs in an organic way to the gospel of suffering. It defines who our neighbor is; what we are to do in the face of others' suffering. It challenges us not to pass by on the other side of a victim of suffering. It demands us to stop not for curiosity but for availability. It makes us sensitive and opens up our heart to an interior disposition from which comes compassion; an expression of love and solidarity with the sufferer. John Paul II, 43, 48, 49.

¹⁵³ In its original usage, the word *politics* comes from citizen and is about our being and our acting and being acted upon. Today, many people confuse politics with politicians so that it appears to be one more game at assuring individuals their

security in their compulsive and competitive climb up the political ladder. Politics is used here "in a broad sense to mean concern with the shape and shaping of *city* and, by extension, concern with the shape and shaping of any human community" – the activities of citizenship. See Borg, 49, Fox, 221, 222.

[154] Marcus Borg, *Meeting Jesus Again for the First Time*, 49-68.

[155] Richard J. Cassidy, *Jesus, Politics and Society: A Study of Luke's Gospel*, (Maryknoll, New York: Orbis Books, 1978), 20.

[156] Borg, *Meeting Jesus again for the First Time*, 49.

[157] Ibid.

[158] Ibid, 52.

[159] This is one of the four times Jesus used Father to refer to his disciples' God. In those four times he has used it in the context of prayer. However, L. John Topel, suggests, "Thus with this one word *pater*, used only once in the sermon, in the climactic place of the love commandment section, Jesus makes clear that his ethic is not about obedience, but about personal love. Thus the climactic motive for the whole of the love commandment is *imitatio Dei*. L. John Topel, SJ, *Children of a Compassionate God: A Theological Exegesis of Luke 6:20-49*, (Collegeville, Minnesota: The Liturgical Press, 2001), 177.

[160] Borg, *op. cit.*

[161] See Nicholas Wolterstorff, "Liturgy, Justice, and Holiness," in *The Reformed Journal,* (December 1989), 20, in in Dirkie Smit, "Seeing Things Differently: On Prayer and Politics," in Lyn Holness and Ralf K. Wustenberg, eds., *Theology in Dialogue: The Impact of the Arts, Humanities, and Science on Contemporary Religious Thought – Essays in Honor of John W. de Gruchy*, (Grand Rapids, Michigan: William B. Eerdmans Publishing Co., 2002), 279.

[162] Borg *op. cit.*, 54, 55, 58.

[163] Ched Myers, *Binding the Strong Man: A Political Reading of Mark's Story of Jesus*, (Maryknoll, New York: Orbis Books, 2005, '15th printing), 277-291. According to Richard Cassidy, "humility and service are Luke's Jesus' presuppositions for criticizing political relationships of domination and oppression." See Richard Cassidy, *Jesus, Politics and Society,* 39.

[164] See Cassidy, *Jesus, Politics and Society*, 38.

165 Myers holds that within the context of Jesus' new leadership paradigm based on service, Mark makes a strong case for women's equality with men. According to him, women were portrayed in Mark as the only ones who fulfilled the vocation of service from the beginning to the end of Jesus' life and mission. "Whereas the men desert Jesus the very point at which their following becomes politically risky, the women stay with him to the cross and after." Therefore, as against the patriarchal dominated socio-cultural order, women alone are fit to act as servant-leaders. Ibid.

166 Judith Plaskow, *The Coming of Lilith: Essays on Feminism, Judaism, and Sexual Ethics, 1972-2003,* (Boston: Beacon Press, 2005), 89-95.

167 John Szura, OSA, "Theological interpretation of the new Augustinian Venture at the United Nations (UN)," a workshop on Justice and OSA UN/NGO and Formation, (Racine: September 18th-22nd 2006).

168 Thompson, *Justice and Peace: a Christian Primer,* (Maryknoll, New York: Orbis Books, 2003), 188-191. However, one does not deny that there are other passages of the scriptures particularly from Paul which are not quite generous to women e.g. his marriage code in Eph. 5:21-33; Col. 3:18-24; and his women's dressing code in 1Cor. 11:1-16. According Rosemary R. Ruether this "Pauline legacy laid the basis for dualism that has haunted subsequent Christianity to the present day: namely, a bifurcation between a creational theology of subordination and an eschatological theology of equivalence." See Rosemary R. Ruether, "Christianity," in Arvind Sharma, ed., *Women in World Religions,* (New York: State University of New York Press, 1987), 213-214.

169 Ibid, 193.

170 Ibid, 194.

171 Borg, 60; see also Stoeber, 39.

172 See International Synod of Bishops 1971 in ibid, 195.

173 See World Council of Churches Harare, Zimbabwe 1998 in Ibid.

174 A. D. Mattson, *The Social Responsibility of Christians,* (Philadelphia: Muhlenberg Press, 1960), 14.

175 Ibid, 17, 20.

[176] Nussbaum, "Compassion," 41, 42.

[177] Ibid, 28.

[178] Ibid.

[179] John Macmurray, *Interpreting the Universe,* (London: Faber and Faber, 1933), 16, 21, also quoted in Frank Kirkpatrick, *Community: A Trinity of Models,* (Washington D.C., Georgetown University Press, 1986), 147.

[180] See also Nussbaum in Elisa A. Hurley and Matthew Burstein, "Blunted Affect: The Flattening of Emotion in Nussbaum's Upheavals of Thought," in http://philosophy.georgetown.edu/news_events/grad_papers/HurleyBurstein10.7.doc. Also, Robert C. Robert, "What an Emotion Is: A Sketch," in *Philosophical Review,* XCVII, No. 2, (April 1988), 183-209; Lawrence Blum, *Friendship, Altruism, and Morality,* (London: Routledge and Kegan Paul, 1980), 133ff, in Dana Radcliffe, "Compassion and Commanded Love," in *Faith and Philosophy,* Vol. 11, No. 1, (January 1994), 50-71.

[181] Steven R. Smith, "Keeping Our Distance in Compassion-Based Social Relations," in *Journal of Moral Philosophy,* Vol. 2, No. 1, (2005), 71.

[182] See Charles Taylor, *Sources of the Self,* (San Francisco: Harper, 1991), 95 in Edward Vacek, *Love, Human and Divine,* 6.

[183] See G. K Chesterton, *Orthodoxy,* (Westport, CT.: Greenwood Press, 1974), 32 in Vacek, ibid.

[184] Martha Nussbaum in Steven R. Smith, 72.

[185] See, Nussbaum, *Upheavals of thought,* 321 in Elisa A. Hurley, "Blunted Affect." Nussbaum appreciates the limitations inherent in some of these principles, especially with determining the seriousness of suffering. Since it is the compassionate one that makes this determination, the apparent question to be asked, "From whose point of view does the pitier make the assessment of 'size?'" Even if it will be made from the sufferer's point of view and by the sufferer himself or herself, the nature of suffering is most often so much more brutalizing than ennobling or educative that it becomes difficult for one to make judgment especially concerning the size of the suffering. Again, she notes that it is not uncommon that in determining the innocence of a sufferer, that people will blame or reproach the sufferer rather than pity him or her. Nussbaum, "Compassion," 31-33.

[186] Ibid, 35.

[187] Nussbaum, Compassion, 31; also Nussbaum in Steven R. Smith, 71.

[188] Nussbaum, "Compassion," 37, 57.

[189] Ibid 29.

[190] Scheler in Fox, 34.

[191] Ibid, 51.

[192] Ibid, 52.

[193] Ibid, 53-57.

[194] See Oliver Davies, *A Theology of Compassion: Metaphysics of Difference and the Renewal of Tradition,* (Grand Rapids, MI: Eerdmans, 2003), 20 in Michael Stoeber, a review of Oliver Davies, *A Theology of Compassion,* in *Toronto Journal of Theology,* Vol. 22, No. 1, (2006).

[195] Monika K. Hellwig, *Jesus, The Compassion of God ; New Perspectives on the Tradition of Christianity,* (Collegeville, Minnesota: The Liturgical Press, 1983), 121.

Chapter Three

[196] See, Robert Schreiter, *The New Catholicity: Theology between the Global and the Local,* (Maryknoll, New York: Orbis Books, 1997), 43, as quoted by Lisa Sowle Cahill, "Globalization and the Common Good," in *Globalization and Catholic Social Thought: Present Crisis, Future Hope,* (Maryknoll, New York: Orbis Books, 2005), 48.

[197] Matthew H. Kuka, Rev. Fr., cited in Efeturi Ojakaminor, *Nigeria's Ghana-Must-Go Republic Happenings,* (Iperu-Remo, Nigeria: Ambassador Publication, 2004), 11.

[198] Kofi Annan, "Eradication of poverty and other development issues: implementation of the first United Nations Decade for the Eradication of Poverty (1997-2006) Observance of the International Day for the Eradication," (United Nations A/61/308, General Assembly, 5 September 20), 8.

[199] Fuel shortages are common in Nigeria. Often, people jam service stations for days and nights especially during festivities like Christmas in search of fuel which many may never get. Yet as Bode Kuforji laments, "boats leave Nigeria for America every day filled with oil." In situations like this and also because of poverty, many people will risk their lives for anything that will give them fuel or place food on their tables. For this reason, tapping of the pipelines for gasoline has become common in Nigeria. This has brought frequent accidents. In 2006 alone, there have been two pipeline explosions caused by illegal tapping in Nigeria in which a total of 419 lives were lost. In 1998, another pipeline fire killed 1,500 people in Nigeria. See, Katherine Houreld, Associated Press, "269 Dead After Nigerian Pipeline Explodes while Scavengers were collecting Fuel," in *Toronto Star,* (Wednesday, December 27, 2006), A7. In this irony, we see one of those effects of contemporary global economics which encourages the production of what is sold to the rich countries but not the necessities of the local people. Nigerian crude oil, as Kuforji observes, leaves Nigerian shores in barrels on a daily basis for the US and other Western countries while Nigerians beg for refined fuel.

[200] Akande Adebowale, "Nigeria Latest," in *One World. Net,* 12, Nov., (2006), 2, http://uk.oneworld.net/guides/nigeria/development.

[201] Mike I. Obadan and Ayodele F. Odusola, "Productivity and Unemployment in Nigeria," www.cenbank.org/publications/occasionalpapers/rd *2nd/abe-00-10-pdf,* 2.

[202] See Nkechi Nweke, "Open Letter to the President of Nigeria," in *Youth Action*

Net: Connecting Youths to Create Change, June (2005) 1. http://youthactionnet.org/resources/essaycontest/employability/nkechi.cfm.

[203] John Odey, *The Parable of a Wasted Generation*, (Enugu, Nigeria: Snaap Press, 2000), 35.

[204] President Olusegun Obasanjo, "Time to reject pseudo leaders" 46th Independent Speech, in *Nigeria Guardian,* Online edition, Sunday, October 1, (2006), 15.

[205] This is the recent figure (140,0003,542) published by the National Population Commission (NPC) on Friday December 29th 2006. See Martins Oloja, "Nigeria Population now 140 Million," in *The Guardian,* Saturday, December 30, 2006, 1.

[206] Akande Adowale, "Nigeria Latest," 3.

[207] In October 2005, Mrs. Stella Obasanjo, the first Lady of Nigeria died in a hospital in Spain. She died of complications from cosmetic surgery (and not a life threatening one) to remove fat and enhance her looks as she prepared to celebrate her 60th birthday which was to be on the 14th of November that same year. She could afford liposuction on taxpayers' money while millions of Nigeria could not afford a full square meal. Like others in her class, she could afford medical treatment in the best hospital abroad even for something as vain as just to enhance her looks, while 130 million of her fellow Nigerians had no reliable clinic to attend at home. See Toye David-West, "Death of Nigeria's First Lady, Stella Obasanjo: A Lesson for Life and Death," in *This Day online,* (Wednesday, October 26 2005), 23.

[208] Also, another governor spent 120 million Naira to purchase cars distributed to 38 legislators for their private use. See Wale Akin, "Faculty of Political Practice in Nigeria," in Tell, (July, 17th 2006), 16. The country spent N650 million ($5.2m US) to host 143rd extra ordinary meeting of the Organization of Petroleum Exporting Countries (OPEC) 11th -17th Dec. 2006, see Yakubu Lawal, deputy energy ed., "Nigeria Spent N650million to host OPEC," in *The Guardian,* Dec. 20, (2006), 1. According to the report of the chairman of the Economic and Financial Crimes Commission, Mallam Ribadu Nuhu, $500 billion (US) was looted from the Nigerian coffers between 1960 and 1999. The World Bank states that 80% of Nigeria's oil and natural gas revenue accrues to 1% population of the nation. See David Blair, "Nigeria's dictators squandered $500Billion," in *Nigeria Post,* (Sat. June 25, 2004), 6 and http//www.eia.doc.gov/emeu/cabs/Nigeria.html. quoted by Joseph Ogbonnaya, *The Contemporary Nigerian Church and the Search for Social Justice in Nigeria,* (TST, THM Thesis,2005), 75.

[209] Ruben Abati, *What Young People are Going Through,* in *The Guardian,* (Sunday, October, 8, 2006), 7.

[210] Chris Garba, "12 Million Nigerian Children out of School, says Report," in Guardian Newspaper Wed. Oct., 27 2004, cf. http//www.guardiannewsngr.com/news/article, cited in Joseph Ogbonnaya, *The Contemporary Nigerian Church and the Search for Social Justice in Nigeria*, 76.

[211] Wale Akin, "Faculty Political Practice in Nigeria," 6.

[212] Kofi Annan, "Eradication of poverty and other development issues," 4-7.

[213] See "US Young Nigerian Killed by Soldiers," *The Sun*, (24, Dec., 2006), 5 and "The Police Kills another US-based Nigerian Businessman," *The Sun*,(3rd, Feb., 2007), 1, 8. But why have US-based Nigerians always fallen victims to wimps and caprices of their fellow Nigerians? Why have they been exposed to such degree of insecurity? This is another area one needs to explore.

[214] John Odey, *The Parable of a Wasted Generation*, (Enugu, Nigeria: Snaap Press, 2000), 9.

[215] Efeturi Ojakaninor, *Nigeria's Ghana-Must-Go Republic Happenings*, (Iperu-Remo, Nigeria: Ambassador Publication, 2004), 429-431.

[216] See *The Washington Post,* Nov 9, (1998), A18, in George B.N. Ayittey, *Africa Unchained: The Blueprint for Africa's Future*, (New York: Palgrave Macmillan, 2005), 39.

[217] George B.N. Ayittey, ibid, 40.

[218] Ibid.

[219] Ibid.

[220] John Odey, *The Parable of a Wasted Generation*, 9.

[221] Ayittey, ibid, 41.

[222] Odey, ibid.

[223] Efeturi Ojakaninor, *Nigeria's Ghana-Must-Go Republic Happenings*, 429-431.

[224] Bakasi security outfit hired by the Anambra state government led by Chinwoke Mbadinuju and the Oodua security front often employed by governors in the

Western part of Nigeria to settle scores with political opponents are cases at hand here.

[225] International Confederation of Free Trade Unions, "Labor Standards remain poor in Nigeria," *Afrol News,* 12, Nov, (2006) 3.
[226] Sofo, 50.

[227] Akande Adebowale, "Nigeria Latest," 4.

[228] Cf. *Restoring The Dignity of the Nigerian Women: A pastoral Letter of the Catholic Bishops' Conference of Nigeria,* (Lagos, Nigeria: Catholic secretariat of Nigeria, 2002), 2.

[229] Luke Mbaefo, "The Church Bishop Shanahan Left Behind," *The Nigerian Journal of Theology,* Vol. 8, No. 1, (1994), 34.

[230] Mercy A. Oduyoye would insist that bride prize custom should not be construed as an economic transaction in which a man buys a woman. Instead, it should be understood as a way "to emphasize the worth of women, to provide community participation and social witness to the coming together of the two persons for the religious duty of procreation." See Mercy A. Oduyoye, "Feminist Theology in an African Perspective," in *Paths of African Theology,* 167, in Hans Schwarz, *Theology in a Global Context: The Last Two Hundred Years,* (Michigan: William B. Eerdmans Publishing Co., 2005), 509.

[231] Ibid.

[232] Stan Chu Ilo, *The Face of Africa: Looking Beyond the shadows,* (Bloomington, Indiana: AuthorHouse, 2006), 198.

[233] See Grassroots action for Sustainable Health and Rural Development in Nigeria's report in ibid, 196.

[234] Akande Adebowale, "Nigeria Latest."

[235] See Douglas Oronto, "Shell in Nigeria," and also, US Energy Information Service in Friends of the Earth *Naija Community,* (2006), 23.

[236] *UNEP 2005 Annual Report,* (Produced by UNEP Division of Communication and Public Information, January, 2006), 8.
[237] Godwin Haruna, "Nigeria: Climate Change – Looming Disaster Waiting to Occur," September 24, (2007).

[238] See James Ainsworth, *Island of Spice: Africa's Environment and a Woman's Mission*.

[239] See David Okali, of Nigeria Environmental Study Action Team (NEST), "Nigeria," in Tariq BAnuri, Adil Najam and Nancy Odeh, eds., *Civic Entrepreneurship: A Civil Society Perspective on Sustainable Development*, vol. II: Africa, a UNEP-sponsored project, (Islamabad, Pakistan: Gandhara Academy Press, 2002), 217.

[240] See the series, "Facts on Climate in Nigeria," by the editors, Nigeria Climate Change.

[241] Godwin Haruna, "Nigeria: Climate Change – Looming Disaster Waiting to Occur."

[242] See Bassey Nnimmo, executive director, Environmental Rights Action/Friends of the Earth Nigeria (ERA/FoEN), ibid.

[243] See *Climate Rader*, "Nigeria-Climate Change: 13 Million Citizens at Risk," http://climateradar.wordpress.com/2007/08/01/nigeria-climate-change-13-million-citizens-at-risk.

[244] "Nigeria: Yar'Adua on Climate Change," *Daily Champion*, editorial, 9 October (2007).

[245] See Edwin Kurfi, "Oil Giant Shell has brought Nigeria nothing but Suffering," in *Socialist Worker Online*, 12 Feb., (2005), 19. See also J. Timothy Hunt, *The Politics of Bones: Dr Owens Wiwa and the Struggle for Nigeria's Oil*, (Toronto: McClelland & Stewart Ltd., 2005), 67.

[246] See Akande Adebowale, "Nigeria Latest," 4.

[247] To date, oil accounts for almost 90 percent of the nation's foreign exchange and nearly 80 percent of government revenue. See Efeturi Ojakaminkor, *Nigeria's Ghana-Must-Go Republic Happenings*, 15, 16; Akande Adebowale, "Nigeria Latest." 4.

[248] As Tissa Balasuriya continues, "With the wasteful lifestyle of the rich world over, resource depletion and environmental pollution have become life-threatening to both present and future generation." See Tissa Balasuriya, "Globalization," in Virginia Febella and R.S. Sugirthararjah, eds., *Dictionary of Third World Theologies*, (Maryknoll, New York: Orbis Books, 2000), 93.

249 Ibid. also see Douglas Oronto, "Shell in Nigeria."

250 Refer to our discussion on SAPS and other IFIS policies in chapter one – those inhuman institutional reconstruction policies as a condition for obtaining loans, expertise assistance and full integration into the global economic community that have left many developing countries worse than they met them and has thus been described as the cure that is worse than the disease. Unfortunately, these policies continue to survive in most of its metamorphosed forms, such as Poverty Reduction Strategy (PRS), Fast-Track Initiative (FTI) and National Economic Empowerment Development Strategy (NEEDS). See Stephen Lewis, *Race Against Time*, 61; Stan Ilo, *Faces of Africa*. 221-239.

251 George Ehusani, *The Prophetic Church*, (Ibadan, Nigeria: Intec Printer, 1996), 6.

252 See Tissa, Balasuriya, OMI, "Globalization," in *Dictionary of Third World Theologies*, 92.

253 See Timothy M. Shaw and E. John Inegbedion, *The Marginalization of Africa in the New World (Dis)Oreder,* in Richard Studds and Geoffrey R.D. Underhill, eds., *Political Economy and the Changing Global Order*, (Toronto: McClelland & Stewart Inc., 1994), 391-395.

254 N. I. Ndiokwere, *Search for Greener Pastures: Igbo and African Experience,* (Kearney, NA: Morris Publishing, 1998) 55-63.

255 In a lecture, Okwudiba Nnoli observed that, "the first type of ethnic conflict in Nigeria is the product of the political or administrative policy of divide-and–rule that mobilized and manipulated ethnic consciousness. The first to do so were the colonialists." See Okwudiba Nnoli, *Ethnic violence in Nigeria: A Historical Perspective*, being a lecture given to a group of history students of the University of Jos, June 2003, 2.

256 Raph Uwechue, *Reflection on the Nigerian Civil War: Facing the Future,* (New York: African Publishing Corporation, 1971), xiv. According to Uwechue, the memories of the civil war still haunt Nigeria. It has left the nation with much bitterness, anger and hatred towards one another, as can be seen in the number of renewed fights, revivals and formations of new militant groups calling for peaceful separation.

257 Amy Chua, *World on Fire*, 273.

258 Chesa Chesa, "Polls are rigged, Atiku Admits," in NAIJANET.com August 2005

cited in Joseph Ogbonnaya (2005) 76.

259 John Odey, *After the Madness Called Election 2003*, (Enugu, Nigeria: Snaap Press, 2003), 8. See also Joseph Ogbonnaya (2005), 76.

260 See Clifford Ndujihe, "April Polls Already Rigged, says Nwabueze," *The Guardian*, (Thursday, March 15, 2006), 8.

261 See Olusegun Obasnajo, in *Obasanjo cautions African Leaders against greed, injustice,* in *The Guardian,* (Tuesday, October, 10, 2006), 4.

262 Ayittey, *Africa Unchained: The Blueprint for Africa's Future,* xxv.

263 Patrick Alabi, "Ruminating over the state of our Nation," 4.

264 Ayittey, Ibid.

265 See *New Africa,* (Sept 2000), 9 in Ayittey, ibid.

266 See *The Guardian,* (Nov 13, 1998), 3, in Ayittey, ibid.

267 *Saturday Punch Newspaper,* September 17, 2005.

268 See Festus Owete, "$16bn Power Sector Scam: Hold Obasanjo Responsible" in *Independent Newspaper,* Friday 28, March 2008; Idowu Samuel, "How Obasanjo Spent N22bn on Power Sector in 2 years." In The Nigerian Tribune Newspaper, Friday 28, March 2008.

269 Chinua Achebe, *The Trouble with Nigeria,* (Enugu, Nigeria: Dimension Publishers, 1985), 1.

270 According to John S. Mbiti, "it is religion, more than anything else, which colors their understanding of the universe and their empirical participation in the universe, making life a profoundly religious phenomenon. To be is to be religious in a religious universe." John S. Mbiti, *African Religion and Philosophy,* (London: Heimemann Educational Books, 1969), 262. Also Geoffrey Parrinder argues that "the African [Nigerian] people are deeply religious, so much so that material and the spiritual are intertwined, the former serving as the vehicle for the later. This life and the next are scarcely divided by a narrow stream of death." Geoffrey Parrinder, *African Traditional Religion,* (Connecticut: Greenwood Press, 1976), 27-28.

271 Stan Chu Ilo, *Faces of Africa,* 104

[272] Naomi Chazan, et. al., *Politics and Society in Contemporary Africa,* 2nd edition, (Colorado: Lynne Rienner Publishers Inc., 1992), 106.

[273] See Fredrick Barth, ed., *Ethnic Groups and Boundaries,* (Boston: Little, Brown, 1869), 13-14 in Naomi Chazan, et.al., ibid.

[274] See Aylward Shorter, "The Curse of Ethnocentricism and the African Church," 27-32, in Albert J. Jong, ed., "Ethnicity: Blessing or Curse," *Tangaza Occasional Prayer,* No. 8, (Nairobi: Pauline Publishers, 1999), 29, cited in Joseph Ogbonnaya, (2005), 79.

[275] See "They don't Belong Here: Government Discrimination Against Non-Indigenes," *Human Rights Watch,* (April 2006,), 7-15.

[276] "45 years Later: Is Nigeria at the Throes of Political Disintegration or Economic Revival?" in http:/www.nigeriaworld.com September 2005.

[277] See "Obasanjo cautions African Leaders against greed, injustice", in *The Guardian,* Op. Cit., 4.

[278] One has to acknowledge, based on the African philosophy of life, "I am because I belong," the huge possibilities ethnicity offers. It helps people construct their history and it provides opportunities for fellowships that both protect and develop one. However, recalling the words of Valpy Fitzgerald already cited in chapter one, this particular system of relationship between people can, as it often does, easily create a series of situations which make necessary – and apparently reasonable – that conduct which favors one's own greed or that of one's family or, in this case, one's tribe or ethnicity, at the expense of the life and dignity of many others. Cf. Valpy Fitzgerald in chapter one, also see Stan Ilo, *Faces of Africa,* 104-105.

[279] The *osu* castes system prevalent among the Igbos of Nigeria does not have a single definition. However, it generally describes the practice which categorizes and discriminates against some people as 'untouchables,' 'outcasts.' These are mostly descendants of slaves or *efuluefus* – 'good for nothing people' who on the account of the ill-treatment and discrimination they received from the community flew under the protection of deities. This is like the case in the bible where the children's teeth are set on edge because their fore fathers ate the sour grapes. It is also an institutionalization of injustice against a people and the perpetuation of their miseries. See Stan Ilo, *Faces of Africa,* 207.

[280] Patrick Alabi, "Ruminating over the state of our Nation," 3, in *http:nigeriawprld. com/articles/2006/oct/101.html._*

281 Akande Adebowale, "Nigeria Latest," 6.

282 Ibid.

283 Patrick Alabi, "Ruminating over the state of our Nation," 4.

284 Rose N. Uchem, *Overcoming Women's Subordination: An Igbo African Christian Perspective – Envisioning an Inclusive Theology with Reference to Women*, (Enugu, Nigeria: Snaap Press Ltd, 2001) and Rose N. Uchem MSHR, *Beyond Veiling: A Response to the Issues in Women's Experiences of Subjugation in African Christian Cultures,_* (Enugu, Nigeria: Snaap Press, 2002), 37.

285 Luke Mbaefo., Ibid.

286 Ibid., see also, Rose Uchem, 2002, 37, Ben Okwu Eboh, 133,134.

287 Kwok Pui-lan, as cited in Musa W. Dube, 2000, 32. Some church fathers were associated with anti-women comments which in some ways continue to inform the attitudes and behaviors of many clergy today. Rose Uchem points out some those examples in her work. "Among all savage beasts none is found to be so harmful as woman," – John Chrysostom. "Woman is a sick-ass ... a hideous tapeworm ... the advance post of hell," – John Damascene. Other fathers like Augustine and Thomas Aquinas debated as to whether or not a woman has as soul, and concluded that she might be saved through her attachment to a man in marriage.288

289 P. K. Uchendu as cited in Rose Uchem, 38.

290 Ibid.

291 Uchem, 2001, 60.

292 Ibid., 119.

293 Walligo, 15.

294 Dean Brackley, *Divine Revolution: Salvation and Liberation in Catholic Thought*, (Marykonll, New York: Orbis Books, 1996), 118-119.

295 Robert McAfee Brown, "Towards a Just and Compassionate Society: A Christian View," in *Cross Current, sum*mer (1995), 166.

296 See Gregory Baum, "Critical Theologies in Canada: From Solidarity to

Resistance," Don Schweitzer and Derek Simon, eds., *Intersecting Voices: Critical Theologies in a Land of Diversity*, (Ottawa: Novalis, 2004), 54.

[297] Reuben Abati, "What Young People are Going Through," *The Guardian*, (Sunday October 8, 2006), 8.

[298] I am using church in this context to refer to all Christian denominations, though much emphasis is on the Catholic Church. There is only a slight noticeable variation in the way various Christian denominations in Nigeria react in the face of suffering. So what is said of the Catholic Church holds for most of the other denominations, though in varying degrees and qualifications.

[299] Peter Schineller, Rev., ed., *The Voice of the Voiceless: Pastoral Letters and Communiqués of the Catholic Bishops' Conference of Nigeria 1960-2002*, (Ibadan, Nigeria: Daily Graphics Nigeria Limited, 2002), 1.

[300] Ibid, 51-52.

[301] Ibid, 53-54.

[302] Ibid, 55-56.

[303] Ibid, 58-74.

[304] See Catholic International 6:1 (Jan 1995), 40 as cited in Joseph Ogbonnaya, 71. It is note worthy that up till today Fridays are still days of prayer and fasting in Nigeria for the intentions of the nation.

[305] Allan A. Boesak and Charles Villa-Vicencio, eds., *When Prayer Makes News*, cited in Robert McAfee Brown, *Spirituality and Liberation: Overcoming the Great Fallacy*, (Philadelphia: The Westminster Press, 1988), 15.

[306] See Gregory Baum, "Critical Theologies in Canada: From Solidarity to Resistance," 56.

[307] George Ehusani, *The Prophetic Church*, 109.

[308] Luke Mbaefo, "The Church Bishop Shanahan Left Behind," 34.

[309] Ibid.

[310] See Pope Paul VI, *Octogesima Adveniens*, (May 1971), 1, Richard McCormick

S.J., "The Social Responsibility of the Christian," in *Blueprint for Social Justice,* Vol. LII, No. 3, (November 1998), 1.

[311] Robert McAfee Brown, *Spirituality and Liberation,* (Philadelphia: Westminster Press, 1988), 27.

[312] See Thomas a Kempis cited in Ibid. We can recall that this is a residue of a Middle Age spirituality which was adopted by the early European missionaries which intentionally or otherwise supported the colonialism through which it came. It encouraged the people to despise the world and thus allow their colonial masters to tap the peoples' resources unchallenged. As many Africans would today cry, "When the white man came to our country he had the bible and we had the land. The white man said to us, 'let us pray.' After the prayer, the white man had the land and we had the bible." The author of this saying is anonymous. Sometimes it is alluded to Julius Nyerere of Tanzania, while others say it predates him. Nevertheless, the reality of the meaning of this saying is shared among many Africans. See Dube D. Musa, *Postcolonial Feminist Interpretation of the Bible,* (St. Louis, Mo: Chalice Press, 2006), 6, 9.

[313] See Augustine in *Augustinians in the Church for the World of Today,* Document of the 1998 Intermediate General Chapter of the Order of St. Augustine, (Villanova: July 21-31, 1998), 13.

[314] Richard McCormick S.J., "The Social Responsibility of the Christian," 1-3.

[315] Herbert A. Deane, *The Political and Social Ideas of St. Augustine,* (New York: Columbia University Press, 1963), 11.

[316] Ibid.

[317] One practical example that illustrates this point clearly is the case of benefactors and benefactresses of the church: Consider a situation in which a particular diocese had the launching on a Saturday of its new cathedral project, for which one of the benefactors, a top government official, had donated a huge amount. With next day being Sunday, the same man attended Mass in a church where the priest decided in his homily to address one burning issue of corruption in the state. The benefactor felt insulted, as he thought the priest was directing the preaching to him personally. He went out and called the Bishop of the diocese on the phone. The Bishop summoned the priest to his office the next day. Outrageous, you would say, but things like this do happen. Whatever was the outcome of that meeting does not matter here, but the fact that our voices may and have actually been silenced because of our attachment to materials things is of great concern as we consider our role in society.

Towards a Politics of Compassion

[318] Toyin David-West, 3. The rich are often praised as blessed by God and hardworking leaving the poor to feel responsible for their state and misery.

[319] Reuben Abati, "What the Young People Go Through," 7.

[320] Toyin David-West, 3.

[321] Ibid. This story recalls to memory one of the astonishing captions in *Toronto Star* Sunday March 4, 2007. The article titled, "Holy Profit," highlights, "while 3,000 mostly poor congregants donate as much as 10% of their earnings to the evangelical Prayer Palace, Pastor Paul Melnichuk and his sons drive luxury cars and live in multi-million dollar mansions." A1, A7.

[322] James H. Cone, *God of the Oppressed*, (San Francisco: Harper & Row, Publishers, 1975), 177-183.

[323] Ibid.

[324] See Timothy M. Shaw and E. John Inegbedion, *The Marginalization of Africa in the New World (Dis)Order, Political Economy and the Changing Global Order*, 391-395.

Chapter Four

[325] Gustavo Gutierrez, *A Theology of Liberation,* trans. and ed. Sister Cardidad Inda and John Eagleson, (Maryknoll, New York: Orbis Books, 1973), 63-66.

[326] Ronald Rolheiser, *Against an Infinite Horizon: The Finger of God in our Everyday Lives,* (New York: Crossroad Publishing Co., 2001), 128.

[327] Marcus Borg, *Meeting Jesus Again for the First Time,* (New York: HarperCollins, 1995), 49.

[328] Ronald Rolheiser, *Against an Infinite Horizon,* 124-125.

[329] See the document of 1971 *Justice in the World,* in Milburn J. Thompson, *Justice and Peace: A Christian Primer,* (Maryknoll, New York: Orbis Books, 2003), 195.

[330] Louise Arbour, "Human Rights and Poverty," in *Human Right Day 2006,* (December 10, 2006), 1.

[331] Gregory Baum makes a very remarkable distinction between *preferential option for the poor* and *preferential love for the poor.* He points out that *preferential love for the poor,* is used by some Christian aristocrats to mean, "All people, rich and poor, are entitled to our love, but those whose need is the greatest, namely the poor, have a preferential claim on our love. We must help them first." This idea betrays the intention of the Puebla fathers because it maintains the status quo in favor of the rich and allows the poor 'the Lazaruses,' to eat from the scraps that will fall from Davies', the rich man's table. See Gregory Baum, *Compassion and Solidarity: The Church for Others,* (Toronto: Anansi Press Ltd., 1987), 28-30.

[332] See Bill Ryan SJ, "Some Notes on the Development of Catholic Social teaching," (October, 1999), 2.

[333] See *Gaudium et Spes,* No1, in Austin Flannery, O.P., *Vatican II: Conciliar and Post Conciliar Documents,* (New Delhi, India: St. Pauls, 1975), 794.

[334] I am aware that some people have on this assumption that nothing is more sacred than human beings wantonly violated the earth and other creatures or species. I will take this up in the section on solidarity with the earth. See Feri Betto, *Fidel and Religion,* (Sydney, Australia: Pathfinder Press, 1986), cited in Brown, Robert McAfee, *Spirituality and Liberation,* (Philadelphia: Westminster Press, 1988), 80.

[335] Rebecca S. Chopp, *The Praxis of Suffering: An Interpretation of Liberation and Political Theologies,* (Maryknoll, New York: Orbis Books, 1992), 22-23.

[336] Robert McAfee Brown, *Spirituality and Liberation,* 70.

[337] Chuck Gutenson, "In the Light of Katrina, what would God expect us to do?" 4, in http://www.sojo.net/index.cfm?action=sojomail.display&issue=050...

[338] Chopp, *The Praxis of Suffering,* 23. Richard Cassidy maintains that "although Luke's, Jesus expressed a definite concern for the poor, the infirm, women, and Gentiles, it is also clear that Jesus is not portrayed as unconcerned about those not falling within these groups. Rather 'universalism' is a striking feature of Jesus' social stance. Jesus' position is one of concern and compassion for the people from all works of life, but he does not passively accept values or practices that run counter to his own vision regarding healthy social relationships." Richard J. Cassidy, *Jesus, Politics and Society: A Study of Luke's Gospel,* (Maryknoll, New York: Orbis Books, 1978), 24.

[339] See Wendy McElroy, "Victims Versus Victimhood," Oct. 11 2005, 2 http://lewrockwell.com/mcelroy94.html.

[340] Matthew Fox, *The Spirituality named Compassion: Uniting Mystical Awareness with Social Justice,* (Rochester, Vermont: Inner Traditions Intl., 1999), 220.

[341] See Gandhi in ibid.

[342] Jim Wallis writes that "the listening that leads to compassion is the beginning of understanding. We have not listened very well. Instead, we've been content with easy answers, quick justifications, and rhetorical slogans that make it possible to dismiss the suffering of other people. We satisfy ourselves by arguing that we know about 'them,' what they are like, why they have problems, how most of it is their fault, how dangerous they are." But when we listen they and their sufferings speak vocally and distinctly to us; we then respond by our presence, by being with them, in the real sense going through their sufferings with them. See Jim Wallis, *The Soul of Politics: Beyond "Religious Right" and Secular Left,"* (New York: Harcourt Brace and Company, 1995), 193

[343] See Mary Jo Leddy, "On Naming the Present," Address to Colloqium on *North American Theology,* (San Antonio, Texas: Oblate School of Theology, Oct. 2002), 5.

[344] Sometimes, the Nigerian church leaders are distanced from their parishioners to the extent that it would cost some parishes so much, financially and otherwise

to have their bishops on pastoral visitation. See Emeka Xris Obiezu, OSA, *Who Do They Say I am? Pope John Paul II the Great,* (Jos, Nigeria: Augustinian Publications, 2006), 160-165; Emeka Xris Obiezu OSA, "Gone in Body, not in Spirit," in *The Catholic Register,* (Week of April 16, 2006), 27.

[345] When the poor know that they mean a lot to us they will always appreciate every effort we make to be with them. Just as the youth expressed seeing the frail John Paul II walk down the steps of the plane in Toronto painfully and slowly to see, meet and be with the youth of the world, "He made such an effort to come and see us. We matter to him." See Mary Jo Leddy, "On Naming the Present," 5.

[346] See John Finnis, *Natural Law and Natural Rights,* (Oxford: Clarendon, 1982), 399-402; Lourencino Puntel, "Participation," *Encyclopedia of Theology,* (New York: Seabury, 1975), 478-512 in Edwark, Vacek, S.J., *Love, Human and Divine: The Heart of Christian Ethics,* (Washington D.C.: Washington University Press, 1994), 23.

[347] Vacek, ibid,.

[348] Elizabeth Lynn and Susan Wisely, "Toward a Fourth Philanthropic Response: American Philanthropy and its Public," 1-8, http://civicreflection.org/resource/d/85032/fourth_response.pdf.

[349] Vacek, *Love, Human and Divine,* 23.

[350] Ibid

[351] Daniel Day William, *The Spirit and Forms of Love,* (New York: Harper and Row, 1968), 146, in Vacek, ibid.

[352] Vacek, ibid.

[353] James Gustafson, *Ethics from a Theocentric Perspective,* (Chicago: University of Chicago Press, 1984), 2:13 in Vacek ibid.

[354] Leonardo Boff, *Church: Charism and Power – Liberation Theology and the Institutional Church,* (New York: Crossroad, 1986), 31.

[355] See Paulo Freire, *Pedagogy of the Oppressed,* (Harmondsworth: Penguin, 1972), 75-76 in Duncan B. Forrester, *Theology and Politics,* 155.

[356] Donal Dorr, *The Social Justice Agenda: Justice, Ecology, Power and the Church,* (Maryknoll, New York: Orbis books, 1991), 113-4.

³⁵⁷ Dean Brackley, *The Call to Discernment,* (New York: Crossroad, 2004), 164.

³⁵⁸ Ngugi Wa Thiong'o, in John Okwoeze Odey, *Active Nonviolent Resistance: The moral and Political Power of the Oppressed,* (Enugu, Nigeria: Snaap Press, 1996), 9.

³⁵⁹ Peter Schineller, Rev., ed., *The Voices of the voiceless: Pastoral Letters and Communiqués of the Catholic Bishops' Conference of Nigeria 1960-2002,* (Ibadan, Nigeria: Daily Graphics Nigeria Ltd, 2002), v.

³⁶⁰ Elie Wiesel in Miroslav Volf, *Exclusion and Embrace,* (Nashville: Abingdon Press, 1996), 234.

³⁶¹ Miroslav Volf, ibid.

³⁶² Rosa Luxembourg, in ibid, 235.

³⁶³ Ellon, in Miroslav Volf, *Exclusion and Embrace,* 237.

³⁶⁴ Gregory Baum, "Critical Theologies in Canada: From Solidarity to Resistance," in Don Schweitzer and Derek Simon, eds., *Intersecting Voices: Critical Theologies in a Land of Diversity,* (Ottawa: Novalis, 2004), 59.

³⁶⁵ This murder was suspected to have been masterminded by the military dictator at the time, Gen, Ibrahim Babangida. The allegation is based on the secret of fraud which the editor linked to the dictator and was about to make public. Also there have been rumors linking the death of some clergy to assassination for their speaking out against some vices in the society.

³⁶⁶ Ellon, *op. cit.* 235.

³⁶⁷ Miroslav, Volf, 236.

³⁶⁸ See Michael Kpakala Francis, "The Church in Africa Today," African Faith and Justice, *The African Synod: Documents, Reflections and Perspectives,* (Maryknoll, New York: Orbis Books, 1996), 126.

³⁶⁹ Vatican II Gaudium et Spes No. 4.

³⁷⁰ Dean Brackley, *The Call to Discernment,* 165, 161.

³⁷¹ Karl Barth, *The Epistle to the Romans,* (London: Oxford University Press,

1968/1933), 425, in Dirkie Smit, "Seeing Things Differently: On Prayer and Politics," in Lyn Holness and Ralf K. Wustenberg, eds., *Theology in Dialogue: The Impact of the Arts, Humanities, and Science on Contemporary Religious Thought – Essays in Honor of John W. de Gruchy,* (Grand Rapids, Michigan: William B. Eerdmans Publishing Co., 2002), 280.

[372] I will suggest here that the church include some study of the social sciences in the program of formation of its priests. The church shall as well seek the services of experts in these fields by empowering the laity to rise up to their socio-political responsibilities.

[373] Marcus Borg, *Meeting Jesus for the First time,* (New York: HarperCollins Publishers, 195), 56, 57.

[374] Ibid.

[375] See James F. Cobbles Jr., *The Church and the Powers: A Theology of Church Structure.* (Massachusetts: Hendrickson Publishers, 1988), 81, 101. There might not be a uniform way of achieving this participation. How this is to be done should be open to the discretion and nature of each church.

[376] Charles J. Hay, "The Bible and the Outsider," Inter-Church Coalition for Refugees (ICCR), cf. also: kairoscanada.or/e/refugees/reflection/bible/outsider.

[377] See Martin Marty, *The Public Church,* as quoted in Michael Himes and Kenneth Himes, OFM, *Fullness of Faith: The Public Significance of Theology,* (New Jersey: Paulist Press, 1993), 1-27. The point Martin Marty makes here highlights one of the challenges John Macmurray poses for the Christian church concerning ecumenism. John Costello writes that according to John Macmurray, "ecumenism in the Gospel does not require the relinquishing, let alone the suppression, of distinct cultural traditions in the churches. Genuine union is dependent not on monochromatic sameness but on a shared faith in God through Jesus for the world." See John E. Costello, *John Macmurray: A Biography,* (Edinburgh: Floris Books, 2002), 167.

[378] See John Macmurray, *Persons in Relation,* (New York: Humanity Press, 1999), 118.

[379] Friendship for John Macmurray is the "normative form of personal life – a community unity-pattern. He was aware, according to John Costello, that "'friendship' could easily be seen as a soft and woolly category, one that modern canons of objectivity, so distant from Aristotle's, would not even allow into philosophical discourse." However, "insisting that he is addressing a real mode of

'being,' he maintained friendship as the most adequate term at the time to represent the reality he wants to highlight. In his use of the term he explored friendship within the context of a *logical* inquiry into the structure of personal life and not on the basis of some kind of 'feel good' experience." See John E. Costello, *John Macmurray: A Biography*, 160-161.

380 Ibid, 154-177.

381 Ibid. See also, Macmurray in Frank Kirkpatrick, *Community: A Trinity of Models*, (Washington, D.C.: Georgetown University Press, 1986), 151.

382 See Pius XI, *Qudragesimo anno, On Reconstructing the Social Order*, 1931, 79.

383 See Stephen J. Pope, "Natural Law in Catholic Social Teachings," in Kenneth R. Himes, O.F.M., ed., *Modern Catholic Social Teaching: Commentaries and Interpretations*, (Washington D.C.: Georgetown University Press, 2005), 50.

384 John Paul II, *Sollicitudo Rei Socialis – On Social Concern*, December 30, 1987, n. 38, in Rev. Robert A. Sirico and Rev. Maciej Zieba , O.P., eds., *The Social Agenda: A Collection of Magisterial Texts*, (Vaticano: Libreria Editrice Vaticana, 2000), 66.

385 Charles E. Curran, *Catholic Social Teaching 1891-Present: A Historical, Theological, and Ethical Analysis*, (Washington D.C.: Georgetown University Press, 2002), 36.

386 John Paul II, *World Day of Peace,*1986, n. 5, in Rev. Robert A. Sirico and Rev. Maciej Zieba , O.P., eds., *The Social Agenda*: 66-67.

387 Stephen J. Pope, "Natural Law in Catholic Social Teachings," 63.

388 Ibid.

389 Michael Stoeber, *Reclaiming Theodicy: Reflections on Suffering, Compassion and Spiritual Transformation*, (New York: Palgrave Macmillan, 2005), 42.

390 See William French, "Greening Gaudium et Spes," in William Madges, *Vatican II: Forty Years Later*, (Maryknoll, Orbis Books, 2006), 198.

391 Pope John Paul II, *The Gospel of Life*, (New York, Random House, 1995), cited in Larry Rasmussen, *Earth Community*, see Aruna Gnanadason, "Yes, Creator God, Transform the Earth," in Samuel Kobia, ed., *The Ecumenical Review*, Vol. 57., No. 2, (Geneva: World Council of Churches, 2005), 166.

392 Emefie Ikenga-Metuh, *Comparative Studies of African Traditional Religions*,

(Onitsha, Nigeria: Imico Publishers, 1987), 181.

[393] Some emerging African scholars have described this attitude simply as arrogant superiority and callousness, characteristic of the Christian imperialism of the colonial era that left Africa in what they refer to as *anthropological poverty*. Anthropological poverty, according to Engelbert Mveng, refers to "despoiling human beings not only of what they have, but also of everything that constitutes their being and essence – their identity, history, ethnic roots…" See Engelbert Mveng, "Third World Theology – What Theology? What Third World?: Evaluation by an African Delegate," in Virginia Febella, and S. Torres, eds., *Irruption of Third World: Challenge to Theology*, (Maryknoll, New York: Orbis, 1983), 217.

[394] Michael W. Petty, *A Faith That Loves the Earth: The Ecological Theology of Karl Rahner*, (New York: University Press of America, 1996), 78.

[395] Karl Rahner, "The Man of Today and Religion," *Theological Investigations*, vol. 6, (New York: Crossroad, 1983), 9, in ibid.

[396] Michael Petty, *op. cit.*

[397] This language is borrowed from John Milbank and friends' idea of 'radical orthodoxy' developed in their work, *Radical Orthodoxy*, (New York: Routledge, 1999, reprint 2006).

[398] See D. Sorrell, *St. Francis of Assisi and Nature: Tradition and Innovation in Western Christian Attitudes toward the Environment* (New York and Oxford: Oxford University Press, 1988) and Dawn M. Nothwehr, *Franciscan Theology of the Environment: An Introductory Reader*, (Quincy, Ill.: Franciscan Press, 2002), in French, *Greening Gaudium et Spes*, 198. Adapting this form of relationship, we become aware that the phenomena of the natural world plays an active role in the healing of human spirit as St. Francis of Assisi discovered. For more on this theme, I recommend you to Stoeber's exposition on this in Stoeber, *Reclaiming Theodicy*, 43.

[399] See Augustine, *de trin*. 6, 10, 12; *de gen*. 1, 21, 32; *serm*. 123, 2, 3; *ps*. 81, 2. In light of this Augustine's stance on the relationship with nature, present day Augustinians maintain that "to love nature as God's work is to do theology; to call for respect of it and its enjoyment by all is to practice justice and solidarity" see *Augustinians in the Church for the World of Today: Documents of the 1998 Intermediate General Chapter*, (Rome: Pubblicazioni Agostiniane, 1998), 38.

[400] Aruna Gnanadason uses the concept, *body of God* to refer to the way we see humanity, other creatures and God. Attitudes related to compassion enable us see the whole creation as a community. See Aruna Gnanadason, "Yes, Creator God,

Transform the Earth," in *The Ecumenical Review*, 168.

[401] French, ibid. As a matter of emphasis, to say that theology is "ecological" means that such theology takes the interconnectedness of life seriously. It "works toward an integrative vision in which God, human beings, and the world are seen in their connectedness." However the basis upon which this integration is achieved differs in the case of the models and the emphasis of the theologian. See Michael W. Petty, *A Faith That Loves the Earth*, 172.

[402] See Karl Rahner, *Foundations of Christian Faith*, (New York: Crossroad Publishing Company, 1978, reprint 2007), 190.

[403] See Aquinas, *Summa Theologica* 1a, q. 57, art.2, 1:284 and q. 93, art.6, 1:473, in French, *Greening Gaudium et Spes*, 198.

[404] See Steven Best, Dr., "Compassion and Action," lectures series in drstevenbest,org/ Lectures/CompassionAndActions.php.

[405] See *Patners: Interfaith perspectives on the Environment*, a Greenfaith's Quarterly Newsletter, summer (2007), 2.

[406] See Douglas John Hall, *Professing the Faith: Christian Theology in a North American Context*, 309, in *Earth Community* cited in Aruna Gnanadason, "Yes, Creator God, Transform the Earth," 168.

[407] See Jim Profit, in Michael Swan, , "Morality should trump politics on climate change," *The Catholic Register*, online edition, http://www.catholicregister.org/content/view/1331/856/.

[408] See Ritsuya Kishida, "Extinction is Forever," *Our Planet*, vol. 16, 2(2005), 32.

[409] Michael W. Petty, *A Faith That Loves the Earth*, op. cit.

[410] Duncan B. Forrester, *Theology and Politics*, (New York: Basil Blackwell Inc., 1988), 153.

[411] Gustavo Gutierrez, *A Theology of Liberation*, trans. and eds., Sister Cardidad Inda and John Eagleson, (Maryknoll, New York: Orbis Books, 1973), 63-66.

[412] Herbert A. Deane, *The Political and Social Ideas of St. Augustine*, (New York: Columbia University Press, 1963), 6, 10, 11.

[413] Michael Himes maintains that the word translated in these biblical passages as world is the Greek word, *Kosmos*. According to him the word is of varied meaning in

scripture. It can mean *everything* as the totality of creation referring to the creation account. It can also mean a "designated theatre in which the drama of salvation is played out," as we have in Acts 17:24, "the world and everything in it." Himes maintains that these two nuances have a role in the theology of the New Testament, for when they placed emphasis on divine *agape* as the ground of creation, the "World implies that which is called into being by God's self-gift, as in John 3:16. But when they referred to the eschatological fulfillment of creation by God's loving act, they seem to refer to the world as a theatre which destiny is to be transformed into something else, the Kingdom of God." See Michael Himes, "The Church and the World in Conversation: The City of God an 'Interurban' Dialogue," in *New Theology Review*, Vol. 18, No.1, (February, 2005), 28.

[414] See Augustine in Himes, ibid, 29.

[415] Aquiline Tarimo, "The Relationship Between African Economic Crisis, Cultural Traditions, and Religion," in *African Christian Studies*, Vol. 19, No. 4, (2003), 67.

[416] Emefie Ikenga-Metuh, *op. cit.*

[417] Jonathan P. Slater, *Mindful Jewish Living: Compassionate Practice*, (New York: Aviv Press, 2004), 320-322. Those in italics are mine.

[418] See D. Bonhoeffer, *Ethik*, in Jurgen Moltmann, *Theology of Hope: On the Ground and the Implication of a Christian Eschatology*, (London: SCM Press Ltd., 1965), 198.

[419] See Archbishop Oscar Romero in Robert McAfee Brown, *Spirituality and Liberation: Overcoming the Fallacy*, (Philadelphia: Westminster Press, 1988), 13.

[420] Arturo Paoli, *Freedom to be Free*, tran., Charles Underhill Quinn, (Maryknoll, New York: Orbis Books, 1973), 100.

[421] Gregory Baum, *Amazing Church: A Theologian Remembers a Half-Century of Change*, (Ottawa: Novalis, 2005), 12.

[422] Fellowship for a Christian Social Order (FCSO), as Marilyn Legge reports, was established in Kingston, Ontario, Canada in 1934. It is "an association of Christians whose religious convictions have led them to the belief that the capitalist economic system is fundamentally at variance with Christian principles; and who regard the creation of a new social order to be essential to the realization of the Kingdom of God." See Marilyn Legge, *The Grace of Difference: A Canadian Feminist Theological Ethic*, (Atlanta: Scholar's Press, 1992), 41 cited in Michael Bourgeois, "Historical Anticipations of Critical Theology: Why Social Theory Matters for Theology," in

Don Schweitzer and Derek Simon, *Intersecting Voices: Critical Theologies in a Land of Diversity*, 38.

[423] See Richard Roberts, *The Christian God*, Merrick Lectures, Ohio Wesleyan University, (New York: Macmillan, 1929), 46-60, 78-86 in Michael Bourgeois, ibid, 42.

[424] R.B.Y. Scott & Gregory Vlastos, *Towards the Christian Revolution*, (Chicago: Willett Clark, 1936, reprinted in 1989 Kingston: Ronald P. Frye), 47 in Michael Bourgeois, ibid, 43.

[425] See Katie G. Cannon, "Sin," in Virginia Febella and S.I. Sugirtharajah, eds., *Dictionary of Third World Theologies*, (Maryknoll, New York: Orbis Books, 2000), 185.

[426] Gustavo Gutierrez, *A Theology of Liberation*, trans. and eds., Sister Cardidad Inda and John Eagleson, (Maryknoll, New York: Orbis Books, 1973), 260.

[427] Richard McCormick, "The Social Responsibility of the Christian," in *Blueprint for Social Justice*, Vol. LII, No. 3, (November, 1998), 4.

[428] Michael Himes, "The Church and the World in Conversation: The City of God an 'Interurban' Dialogue," 31.

[429] Ibid.

[430] Gregory Baum, "The Meaning of Hope in Evil Times," *ARC,* Vol. XX, Spring, (1992), 82.

[431] Richard McCormick, "The Social Responsibility of the Christian," 5.

[432] Dean Brackley, *The Call to Discernment*, (New York: Crossroad, 2004), 161.

[433] Peter Schineller, S.J., *The Voice of the Voiceless*, (Ibadan, Nigeria: Daily Graphics Publications, 2002), 394.

[434] Barnabas Chukwudum Okolo, "Liberation Theology: The Nigerian Connections," in Elochukwu E. Uzukwu ed., *Religion and African Culture*, (Enugu, Nigerian: Snaap, 1988), 183, cited in Joseph Ogbonnaya, *The Contemporary Nigerian Church and the Search for Social Justice in Nigeria*, (TST, ThM Thesis, 2005), 75.

[435] Mary Jo Leddy, *Radical Gratitude*, (Maryknoll, New York: Orbis Books, 2002),

127.

[436] Hans Kung, *On Being a Christian*, tran., Edward Quinn, (Garden City, New York: Doubleday & Co., 1976), 252-253.

[437] Frank Kirkpatrick, *Community: A Trinity of Models*, (Washington, D.C.: Georgetown University Press, 1986), 230.

[438] Dean Brackley, *The Call to Discernment*, 168, 169.

[439] Richard R. Gaillardetz, "The Ecclesiological Foundations of Modern Catholic Social Teaching," Kenneth R. Himes, O.F.M., ed., *Modern Catholic Social Teaching: Commentaries and Interpretations*, (Washington D.C.: Georgetown University Press, 2005), 92.

[440] Ibid.

[441] Ibid 93.

[442] Ibid.

[443] John Paul II, *Post-Synodal Apostolic Exhortation: Ecclesia in Africa*, in *The Pope Speaks* [The Church Documents Bimonthly], Vol. 41, No. 2, March/April (1996), 85.

[444] Ibid, 92.

[445] I am strongly suggesting here that it is high time the Nigerian church started admitting religious women and men and laity into our theological colleges. As it is the case, theology is still regarded today as a special and sacred discipline meant for candidates for the priesthood alone. Often it has become a tool of intimidating the religious women and laity in particular by the clergy who by their exclusive knowledge of theology parade themselves as demigods and the only true interpreters of the mind and will of God for the laity. In my own opinion this attitude equals that of the elites in society who make qualitative education and special knowledge a prerogative of the rich which subdues and keeps the poor perpetually on the margin of history.

[446] Richard R. Gaillardetz, "The Ecclesiological Foundations of Modern Catholic Social Teaching," 91.

[447] Ibid.

[448] See John Costello *John Macmurray*, 167.

[449] See Aloysius Pieris, *An Asian Theology of Liberation*, (MaryKnoll, New York: Orbis Books, 1988) in R. S. Sugirtharajah, "Poverty," in Virginia Fabella, M.M., and R.S. Sugirtharajah, eds. *Dictionary of Third World Theologies.* (Maryknoll, New York: Orbis Books, 200), 170-171.

[450] R. S. Sugirtharajah, "Poverty," in Virginia Fabella, M.M., and R.S. Sugirtharajah, eds. *Dictionary of Third World Theologies.* (Maryknoll, New York: Orbis Books, 200).

[451] See Gregory Baum, "Critical Theologies in Canada: From Solidarity to Resistance," Don Schweitzer and Derek Simon, eds., *Intersecting Voices: Critical Theologies in a Land of Diversity*, 56.

[452] Rolheiser, *Against an Infinite Horizon*, 128.

[453] Ibid.

[454] See Rolheiser, *Against an Infinite Horizon*, 130.

[455]; John W. de Gruchy, *Cry Justice*, (London: Collins Liturgical Publications, 1986), 23 in Dirkie Smit, "Seeing Things Differently: On Prayer and Politics," 271.

[456] See Karl Barth, in Robert McAfee Brown, *Spirituality and Liberation: Overcoming the Great Fallacy*, (Philadelphia: Westminster Press, 1988), 13. See also, Laurenti Magesa, *African Religion*, 197-8, in Victor Okumu, OSB, "A Christo-Pastoral Response to Suffering and Evil in Africa: Aylward Shorter's Jesus and Witch Doctors," in *African Christian Studies*, Vol. 21, No. 2, (2005), 5-47.

[457] See John Metz, "Courage to Pray," *Courage to Pray*, Johann Baptist Metz and Karl Rahner, tran. Sarah O, Brien Twohig, (NY: Crossroad, 1981), 13, in Laurenti Magesa, *African Religion*, 197-8, in Victor Okumu, OSB, "A Christo-Pastoral Response to Suffering and Evil in Africa: Aylward Shorter's Jesus and Witch Doctors." Elie Wiesel's *A Prayer for the Days of Awe*, is another good example of this type of prayer. In this prayer Wiesel starts off with a provocative invitation to God to dialogue. He says, "Master of the Universe, let us make up. It is time. How can we go on being angry?" He goes on to bare his mind open to God in the manner an ancient Jew would as we have in the Psalms. He does not pretend nor deny the pains he endured and still harbors as a result of the holocaust. See Elie Wiesel, *A Prayer for the Days of Awe, New York Times*, (October 2, 1997), 2.

[458] Victor Okumu, OSB, "A Christo-Pastoral Response to Suffering and Evil in

Africa: Aylward Shorter's Jesus and Witch Doctors," 5- 47.

[459] Dirkie, Smit, "Seeing Things Differently: On Prayer and Politics," 273-274.

[460] See Douglas J. Hall, *When You Pray: Thinking Your Way into God's World*, (Valley Forge, Pa.: Judson Press, 1987), in ibid, 276.

[461] Smit, ibid, 277.

[462] Nicholas Wolterstorff, "Liturgy, Justice and Holiness," *The Reformed Journal*, (December 1989), 12-20 in ibid. Wolterstorff deriving from his conviction that "in liturgy God's holiness. In lives of justice we reflect God's holiness," concludes that, "when we deal with justice, we are dealing with the sacred. Injustice [therefore] is desecration."

[463] This analysis is derived from the Article 4 in the new Church Order of the United Reformed Church in Southern Africa quoted in Smit's article, "Seeing Things Differently: On Prayer and Politics," *Theology in Dialogue*, 281.

[464] David Cromwell, "A Review," of David Edwards, *The Compassionate Revolution: Radical Politics and Buddhism*, Feb. 7, 2000.

[465] Catherine Philpot, *Intergroup Apologies and Forgiveness*, unpublished PhD thesis,(Brisbane, Australia: University of Queensland, 2006), adopted in *Forgiveness: A Sampling of Research Results*, compiled at the 59th Annual United Nations DPI/NGO Conference by American Psychological Association APA, (United Nations Headquarters, New York: September, 2006), 6.

[466] See Rev. Johnston McMaster, "Towards a Theology of Suffering and Pastoral Healing," in *The Methodist Church in Ireland Council for Social Responsibility*, 3-11.

[467] Gruchy in his work situates this compassionate forgiveness in the South African Apartheid and the reconciliation and restoration of justice that followed after it. See John W. De Gruchy, *Reconciliation: Restoring Justice*, (Minneapolis: Fortress Press, 2002), 171-180; also Michael E. McCullough, et.al., eds., *Forgiveness, Theory, Research, and Practice*, (New York: The Guilford Press, 2000)._

[468] In my article, "Gone in the Body, not in Spirit," in *The Catholic Register* cited earlier in this chapter, I maintain that, to say I am sorry is not cowardice; it is not self-defeatism. It is simply admitting that we don't know it all, that we are not perfect. It is simply being truly human. We find in this, the ability and readiness to say I am sorry, the humility, the power and the determination to remove the remote causes of our bitterness and division.

Conclusion

[469] See Paul Tillich, *Love, Power and Justice,* 1960, 121, cited by Gruchy, ibid.

[470] See *Kairo Document,* (1986), 1, in Duncan B. Forrester, *Theology and Politics,* (New York: Basil Blackwell, 1988), 154.

[471] See Ida Urso, "The New World Order and the Work of the United Nations," a talk given at the World Goodwill Symposium, *Let the Future Stand Revealed: Envisioning the World We Choose,* October 28, (1995), New York City, New York.

[472] Ibid.

[473] Ibid.

[474] Dean Brackley, *The Call for Discernment,* (New York: Crossroad, 2004), 164.

[475] Ibid.

SELECT BIBLIOGRAPHY

Documents and Reference books

American Psychological Association APA. *Forgiveness: A Sampling of Research Results.* Compiled at the 59th Annual United Nations DPI/NGO Conference. New York: September, 2006.

Augustinians in the Church for the World of Today. Document of the 1998 Intermediate Chapter of the Order of St. Augustine, Villanova: July 21-31, 1998.

Augustinians. Document and Decisions of the Ordinary Chapter 2001 of the Order of St. Augustine. Roma: Publicationi Agostiniane, 2001.

Autenrieth, Georg. *Homeric Dictionary.* Tran. Robert Keep. London: Gerald Duckworth & Co. Ltd., 2002.

Barber, Katherine. Ed. *Canadian Oxford Dictionary.* 2nd Edition. Toronto: Oxford University Press, 2004.

Christian Community Bible. Catholic Pastoral Edition. Philippines: St. Paul Publications, 1994.

Flannery, Austin O.P. Ed. *Vatican Council II: The Conciliar and Post Conciliar Documents.* New Delhi, India: St. Paul's, 1975.

Flexner, Stuart Berg Ed. *Random House Unabridged Dictionary.* 2nd Edition. Toronto: Random House Inc., 1983.

John Paul II. *Savifici Doloris: On the Christian Meaning of Human Suffering.* Boston: Pauline Books & Media, 1984.

_____. *Sollicitudo Rei Socialis: Social Concerns.* Sherbrooke, QC: Paulines, 1988.

_____. *Evangelii Vitae: The Gospel of Life.* New York: Random House, 1995.

Paul VI. *Evangelii Nuntiandi: Evangelization in the Modern World.* London: Catholic Truth Society, 1975.

Pius XI. *Qudragesimo Anno: The Reconstruction of Social Order.* 1931.

Pontifical Council for Justice and Peace. *Compendium of the Social Doctrine of the Church.* Ottawa: Canadian Conference of Catholic Bishops, 2005.

Restoring the Dignity of the Nigerian Women: A Pastoral Letter of the Catholic Bishop's Conference of Nigeria. Lagos, Nigeria: Catholic Secretariat of Nigeria, 2002.

The Catholic Encyclopedia for School and Home. Toronto: McGraw-Hill Books Co., 1965.

Traupman, John C. *The New College Latin and English Dictionary.* Revised and Enlarged Edition. New York: Bantam Books, 1995.

Other books

Achebe, Chinua. *The Trouble with Nigeria.* Enugu Nigeria: Dimension Publishers, 1985.

Ayittey, George B.N. *Africa Unchained: The Blueprint for Africa's Future.* New York: Palgrave Macmillan, 2005.

Barth, Fredrick ed. *Ethnic Groups and Boundaries.* Boston: Little, Brown, 1869.

Baum, Gregory. *Amazing Church: A Theologian Remembers a Half-Century of Change.* Ottawa: Novalis, 2005.

_____. *Compassion and Solidarity: The Church for Others.* Toronto: Anansi Press Ltd, 1987.

Barbour, Ian. *Nature, Human Nature, and God.* London: SPCK, 2002.

Bennett, John. *Social Salvation: A Religious Approach to the Problems of Social Change.* New York: Scribners's, 1935.

Betto, Feri. *Fidel and Religion.* Sydney, Australia: Pathfinder Press, 1986.

Blum, Lawrence. *Friendship, Altruism, and Morality.* London: Routledge and Kegan Paul, 1980.

Boff, Leonardo. *Church: Charism and Power.* New York: Crossroad, 1986.

Bonhoeffer, Dietrich. *The Cost of Discipleship.* London SCM, 1982.

Borg, Marcus J. *Meeting Jesus Again for the First Time.* New York: HarperCollins Publishers, 1995.

Bowker, John. *Problems of Suffering in Religions of the World.* Cambridge, UK: Cambridge University Press, 1970.

Brackley, Dean. *The Call to Discernment.* New York: Crossroad, 2004.

_____. *Divine Revolution: Salvation and Liberation in Catholic Thought.* Maryknoll, New York: Orbis Books, 1996.

Brown, Robert McAfee. *Spirituality and Liberation.* Philadelphia: Westminster Press, 1988.

Cassell, Eric. *The Nature of Suffering.* New York: Oxford University Press, 1991.

Cassidy, Richard J. *Jesus, Politics and Society: A Study of Luke's Gospel.* Maryknoll, New York: Orbis Books, 1978.

Chazan, Naomi et. al. *Politics and Society in Contemporary Africa.* 2nd Edition. Colorado: Lynne Rienner Publishers Inc., 1992.

Chesterton, G. K. *Orthodoxy.* Westport, CT.: Greenwood Press, 1974.

Chopp, Rebecca S. *The Praxis of Suffering: An Interpretation of Liberation and Political Theologies.* Maryknoll, New York: Orbis Books, 1992.

Chua, Amy. *World on Fire: How Exporting Free Market Democracy Breeds Ethnic Hatred and Global Instability.* New York: Anchor Books, 2004.

Cobbles, James F. Jr. *The Church and the Powers: A Theology of Church Structure.* Massachusetts: Hendrickson Publishers, 1988.

Coleman, John, A. and William F. Ryan Eds. *Globalization and Catholic Social Thought: Present Crisis, Future Hope.* Ottawa: Novalis, 2005.

Cone, James H. *God of the Oppressed.* San Francisco: Harper & Row, Publishers, 1975.

Costello, E. John. *John Macmurray: A Biography.* Edinburgh: Floris Books, 2002.

Curran, Charles E. *Catholic Social Teaching 1891-Present: A Historical, Theological, and Ethical Analysis.* Washington D.C.: Georgetown University Press, 2002.

Davies, Oliver. *A Theology of Compassion.* Grand Rapids, Michigan: Eerdmans, 2003.

Dean, Herbert A. *The Political and Social Ideas of St. Augustine.* New

York: Columbia University Press, 1963.

De Gruchy, John W. *Cry Justice*. London: Collins Liturgical Publications, 1986.

_____. *Reconciliation: Restoring Justice*. Minneapolis: Fortress Press, 2002.

Dorr, Donal. *The Social Justice Agenda: Justice, Ecology, Power and the Church*. Maryknoll, New York: Orbis Books, 1991.

Douglas, Anne. *The Feminization of American Culture*. New York: Knopf, 1977.

Ehusani, George. *The Prophetic Church*. Ibadan, Nigeria: Intec Printer, 1996.

Elliot, Elisabeth. *A Path Through Suffering: Discovering the Relationship Between God's Mercy and Our Pain*. California: Regal Books, 1990.

Evans, Christopher H. Ed. *Social Gospel Today*. Louisville, Kentucky: Westminster John Knox Press, 2001.

Febella, Virginia and S. Torres. Eds. *Irruption of Third World: Challenge to Theology*. Maryknoll: Orbis Books, 1983.

Febella, Virginia and S.I. Sugirtharajah. Eds. *Dictionary of Third World Theologies*. Maryknoll, New York: Orbis Books, 2000.

Finnis, John. *Natural Law and Natural Rights*. Oxford: Clarendon, 1982.

Frankl, Viktor. *Man's Search for Meaning*. New York: Pocket Books, 1983.

Freire, Paulo. *Pedagogy of the Oppressed*. Harmonsworth: Penguin,

1972.

Forrester, Duncan B. *Theology and Political.* New York: Basil Blackwell Inc., 1988.

Fox, Matthew. *A Spirituality named Compassion: Uniting Mystical Awareness with Social Justice.* Rochester, Vermont: Inner Traditions Intl. 1999.

Gilkey, Langdon. *Maker of Heaven and Earth: The Christian Doctrine of Creation in the Light of Modern Knowledge.* New York: Anchor Books, Doubleday Co., 1965.

Griffin, Donald R. *Animal Minds: Beyond Cognition to Consciousness.* Chicago: University of Chicago Press, 2001.

Gutierrez, Gustavo. *A Theology of Liberation.* Trans. and Eds. Sister Cardidad Inda and John Eagleson. Maryknoll: Orbis Books, 1973.

Hall, Douglas J. *God and Human Suffering: An Exercise in the Theology of the Cross.* Minneapolis: Augsberg Publishing House, 1986.

_____. *When You Pray: Thinking Your Way into God's World.* Valley Forge, Pa.: Judson Press, 1987.

Hamel, Ronald and Kenneth Himes. Eds. Introduction to Christian Ethics. New York: Paulist Press, 1989.

Hauerwas, Stanley. *God, Medicine, and Suffering.* Grand Rapids, Michigan: William B. Eerdmans Publishing Co., 1990.

Hellwig, Monika. *Jesus: The Compassion of God – New Perspectives on the Tradition of Christianity.* Collegeville, Minnesota: The Liturgical Press, 1983.

Hick, John. *Evil and the God of Love.* San Francisco: Harper and Row Publishers, 1966.

Hickey, Raymond, OSA. *Augustinians in Nigeria*. Jos, Nigeria: Augustinian Publications, 1990.

Himes, Michael and Kenneth Himes OFM. *Fullness of Faith: The Public Significance of Theology.* New York: Paulist Press, 1993.

Holness, Lyn and Ralf K. Wustenberg. Eds. *Theology in Dialogue: The Impact of Arts, Humanities, and Science on Contemporary Religious Thought – Essays in Honor of John W. de Gruchy.* Grand Rapids, Michigan: William B. Eerdmans Publishing Co., 2002.

Hunt, J. Timothy. *The Politics of the Bones: Dr. Owens Wiwa and the Struggle for Nigeria's Oil.* Toronto: McClelland & Stwart Inc., 2005.

Ikenga-Metuh, Emefie. *Comparative Studies of African Traditional Religions.* Onithsa, Nigeria: Imico Publishers, 1987.

Ilo, Stan Chu. *Faces of Africa: Looking Beyond the shadows.* Bloomington, Indiana: AuthorHouse, 2006.

Keenan, James F., S.J. *Moral Wisdom: Lesson from the Catholic Church.* New York: Rowman and Littlefield Publishers Inc., 2004.

Kelsey, Morton I. *Healing and Christianity.* New York: Harper and Row, 1973.

Kirkpatrick, Frank. *Community: A Trinity of Models.* Washington, D.C., Georgetown University Press, 1986.

Kitamori, Kazoh. *Theology of the Pain of God.* Vancouver: John Knox Press, 1965.

Kung, Hans. *On Being a Christian.* Tran. Edward Quinn. New York: Doubleday & Co., 1976.

Lamb, Matthew. *Solidarity with Victims: Towards a Theology of Social*

Transformation. New York: Crossroad Publishing Co., 1982.

Lampert, Khlen. *Traditions of Compassion: From Religious Duty to Social Activism.* New York: Palgrave Macmillan, 2005.

Lane, Dermot. *Keeping Hope Alive: Stirrings in Christian Theology.* New York: Paulist Press, 1996.

Leddy, Mary Jo. *Radical Gratitude.* Maryknoll: Orbis Books, 2002.

Legge, Marilyn. *The Grace of Difference: A Canadian Feminist Theological Ethic.* Atlanta: Scholar's Press, 1992.

Lewis, C. S. *The Problem of Pain.* New York: Macmillan & Co., 1994.

Lewis, Stephen. *Race Against Time.* Toronto: Anansi Press Inc., 2005.

Liderbach, Daniel. *Why Do We Suffer? New Ways of Understanding.* New York: Paulist Press, 1992.

Lifton, Robert and Richard Falk. *Indefensible Weapons: The Political and Psychological Case Against Nuclearism.* Toronto: CBC Publication, 1984.

Macmurray, John. *Conditions of Freedom.* Amherst, New York: Humanity Books, 1993.

_____. *Reason and Emotion.* Amherst, New York: Humanity Books, 1999.

_____. *Persons in Relation.* Amherst, New York: Humanity Books, 2000.

Mattson, A.D. *The Social Responsibility of Christians.* Philadelphia: Muhlenberg Press, 1960.

Mbiti, John. *African Religion and Philosophy.* London: Heimemann Educational Books, 1969.

McCullough, Michael E. ET. Al. Eds. *Forgiveness: Theory, Research, and Practice.* New York: The Guilford Press, 2000.

Metz, Johann Baptist and Karl Rahner. *The Courage to Pray.* Tran. Twohig, Sarah O'Brien. New York: Crossroad, 1997.

Milbank, John. *Radical Orthodoxy.* New York: Routledge, 1999, reprint 2006.

Miranda, Jose. *Being and the Messiah.* Maryknoll, New York: 1974.

Mitchell, Donald W. and James, Wiseman O.S.B. *Transforming Suffering: Reflections on Finding Peace in Troubled Times.* Toronto: Doubleday, 2003.

Mitchell, Stephen. *The Book of Job.* New York: Harper Prennial Books, 1972.

Moltmann, Jurgen. *Theology of Hope: On the Ground and Implication of a Christian Eschatology.* London: SCM Press Ltd., 1965.

Musa, Dube D. *Postcolonial Feminist Interpretation of the Bible.* St. Louis, Mo: Chalice Press, 2000.

Myers, Ched. *Binding the Strong Man: A Political Reading of Mark's Story of Jesus.* Maryknoll, New York: Orbis Books, 2005.

Nelson-Pallmeyer, Jack. *The Politics of Compassion.* Maryknoll, New York: Orbis Books, 1986.

Ndiokwere, N.I. *Search for Greener Pastures: Igbo and African Experience.* Nebraska: Morris Publishing, 1998.

Nouwen, Henri J.M. Et.Al. *Compassion: A Reflection on Christian Life.* New York: Doubleday, 1983

Obiezu, Emeka Xris OSA. *Who Do They Say I am? Pope John Paul II the Great.* Jos, Nigeria: Augustinian Publications, 2006.

Odey, John Okwoeze. *Active Nonviolent Resistance: The Moral and Political Power of the Oppressed.* Enugu, Nigeria: Snaap, 1996.

_____. *The Parable of a Wasted Generation.* Enugu, Nigeria: Snaap, 2000.

_____. *After the Madness Called Election 2003.* Enugu, Nigeria: Snaap, 2003.

Ojakaminkor, Efeturi. *Nigeria's Ghana-Must-Go Republic Happenings.* Iperu-Remo, Nigeria: Ambassador Publication, 2004.

Paoli, Arturo. *Freedom to be Free.* Tran. Charles Underhill Quinn. Maryknoll, New York: Orbis Books, 1973.

Parrinder, Geoffery. *African Traditional Religion.* Connecticut: Greenwood Press, 1976.

Petty, Michael W. A Faith That Loves the Earth: The Ecological Theology of Karl Rahner. New York: University Press of America, 1996.

Placher, William C. *Narratives of a Vulnerable God: Christ, Theology, and Scripture.* Louisville: Westminster John Knox Press, 1994.

Plaskow, Judith. *The Coming of Lilith: Essays on Feminism, Judaism, and Sexual Ethics, 1972-2003.* Boston: Beacon Press, 2005.

Rahner, Karl. "The Man of Today and Religion," *Theological Investigations.* vol. 6. New York: Crossroad, 1973.

_____. *Foundations of Christian Faith.* New York: Crossroad Publishing Company, 1978.

Reiser, William. *Jesus in Solidarity with His People: A Theologian Looks* at Mark. Minnesota: The Liturgical Press, 2000.

Roberts, Richard. *The Christian God.* Merrick Lectures, Ohio Wesleyan University. New York: Macmillan, 1929.

Rolheiser, Ronald. *The Holy Longing.* Toronto: Doubleday, 2000.

──────────. *Against an Infinite Horizon: The Finger of God in Our Daily Lives.* Toronto: Doubleday, 2001.

Rowland, Christopher. Ed. *The Cambridge Compassion to Liberation Theology.* Cambridge, UK: Cambridge University Press, 1999.

Saul, John Ralston. *The Collapse of Globalism and the Reinvention of the World.* Toronto: Penguin, 2005.

Scheler, Max. *The Nature of Sympathy.* Hamden, Ct.: Shoestring Press Inc., 1973.

Schreiter, Robert. *The New Catholicity: Theology Between the Global and the Local.* Maryknoll, New York: Orbis Books, 1997.

Schillebeeckx, Edward. *Christ.* New York: Seabury Press, 1980.

Schilling, Paul. *God and Human Anguish.* Nashville: Parthenon Press, 1977.

Schineller, Peter Rev. Ed. *The Voice of the Voiceless: Pastoral Letters and Communiqués of the Catholic Bishops' Conference of Nigeria 1960-2002.* Ibadan, Nigeria: Daily Graphics Nigeria Limited, 2002.

Schopp, Ludwig, Ed. *The Fathers of the Church.* Vol. 5, New York: CIMA Publishing Co., 1948.

Schwarz, Hans. *Theology in a Global Context: The Last Two Hundred Years.* Michigan: William B. Eerdmans Publishing Co., 2005.

Schweitzer, Don and Derek Simon Eds. *Intersecting Voices: Critical*

Theologies in a Land of Diversity. Ottawa: Novalis, 2004.

Scott, R.B.Y. & Gregory Vlastos. *Towards the Christian Revolution.* Chicago: Willett Clark, 1936, reprinted in 1989 Kingston: Ronald P. Frye.

Shannan, William H. Ed. *The Hidden Ground of Love: Letters,* New York: Farrar, 1985.

Sharma, Arvind. Ed. *Women in World Religions.* New York: State University of New York Press, 1987.

Sirico, Robert A. Rev. and Rev. Maciej Zieba, O.P. Eds. *The Social Agenda: A Collection of Magisterial Texts.* Vaticano: Libreria Editrice Vaticana. 2000.

Slater, Jonathan P. *Mindful Jewish Living: Compassionate Practice.* New York: Aviv Press, 2004.

Smith, Garry, S.J. *Radical Compassion: Finding Christ in the Heart of the Poor.* Chicago: Loyola Press, 2002.

Sobrino, Jon and Juan Hernandez Pico. *Theology of Christian Solidarity.* Maryknoll, New York: Orbis Books, 1985.

Soelle, Dorothee. *Suffering.* Tran. Everett R. Kalin. Philadelphia: Fortress Press, 1975.

Song, C. S. *The Compassionate God.* Maryknoll, New York: Orbis Books, 1982.

Stoeber, Michael. *Reclaiming Theodicy: Reflection on suffering, Compassion and Spiritual Transformation.* New York: Palgrave Macmillan, 2005.

Stuuds, Richard and Geoffrey R.D. Underhill. Eds. *Political Economy and the Changing Global Order.* Toronto: McClelland & Stewart Inc., 1994.

Taylor, Charles. *Sources of the Self.* San Francisco: Harper, 1991.

Thompson, J. Milburn. *Justice and Peace: A Christian Primer.* Maryknoll, New York: Orbis Books, 2003.

Topel, John L. *Children of a Compassionate God: A Theological Exegesis of Luke 6: 20-49.* Minnesota: The Liturgical Press, 2001.

Uchem, Rose N. *Overcoming Women's Subordination: An Igbo African Christian Perspective – Envisioning an Inclusive Theology with Reference to Women.* Enugu, Nigeria: Snaap Press, 2001.

_____. *Beyond Veiling: A Response to the Issues in Women's Experiences of Subjugation in African Christian Cultures.* Enugu, Nigeria: Snaap Press, 2002.

Uwechue, Raph. *Reflection on the Nigerian Civil War: Facing the Future.* New York: African Publishing Corporation, 1971.

Vacek, Edward. *Love, Human and Divine: The Heart of Christian Ethics.* Washington D.C.: Georgetown University Press, 1994.

Volf, Miroslaw, *Exclusion and Embrace.* Nashville: Abingdon Press, 1996.

Wallis, Jim. *The Soul of Politics: Beyond "Religious Right" and "Secular."* New York: Harcourt Brace and Company, 1995.

William, Daniel Day. *The Spirit and Forms of Love.* New York: Harper and Row, 1968.

Articles

Abati, Ruben. "What Young People are Going Through." *The Guardian.* Sunday, October 8, 2006, 7.

Aderinokun, Kunle. "UN Report is Compass to End Extreme Poverty." *This Day Newspaper.* Sept. 8. 2005, 15.

Ainsworth, James. *Island of Spice: Africa's Environment and a*

Woman's Mission.

Akande, Adebowale. "Nigeria Latest." *One World.Net*. Nov. 12, 2006, 1-7. http://pneworld.net/guides/nigeria/development.

Akin, Wale. "Faulty Political Practices in Nigeria." Tell. July 7, 2006, 6.

Alabi, Patrick. "Ruminating over the state of our Nation." *Nigeria World*. (2006): 1-4. http://nigeriaworld.com/articles/2006/oct/101.html.

Arbour, Louise. "Human Rights and Poverty." *Human Right Day 2006*. (December 10, 2006): 1-5.

Aruna, Gnanadason. "Yes, Creator God, Transform the Earth." *The Ecumenical Review*. Vol. 57, No. 2 (2005): 159-170.

Azcuy, Virginia. "Theology in light of Challenges of Poor Women." *Theology Digest*. Vol.52 No.1 (2005): 19-26.

Baum, Gregory. "Critical Theologies in Canada: From Solidarity to Resistance." *Intersecting Voices: Critical Theologies in a Land of Diversity*. Ottawa: Novalis, 2004.

Berry, Wendell. "The Idea of Local Economy." *Orion Magazine*. (Nov/Dec 2004): 1-11.

Blair, David. "Nigeria's Dictators Squandered $500Billion." *National Post*. Sat. June 25, 2004, 21, 6.

Bourgeois, Michael. "Historical Anticipations of Critical Theology: Why Theories Matter for Theology." *Intersecting Voices: Critical Theologies in a Land of Diversity*. Ottawa: Novalis, 2004.

Brown Robert McAfee, "Towards a Just and Compassionate Society: A Christian View." Cross Currents. Vol. 45, No. 2 (summer,

1995): 164-174.

Carrol, Daniel M. R. "Considering the case for 'Prophetic Ethics': Surveying Options and Recognizing Obstacles." *Ashland Theological Journal.* Vol. 34 (2004): 5-15.

Caselman, Randall. "Hope in Times of Crisis." http://www.churchofchristusa.com/archives/old%20bulletin%20articles/Hope%2020In%20Time%20Of%Crisishtm.

Chesa, Chesa. "Polls are Rigged, Atiku Admits." NAIJANET.com. August 2005, 5.

Climate Rader. "Nigeria-Climate Change: 13 Million Citizens at Risk" http://climateradar.wordpress.com/2007/08/01/nigeria-climate-change-13-million- citizens-at-risk.

Cromwell, David. "A Review," of Edwards, David. *The Compassionate Revolution: Radical Politics and Buddhism.* Feb. 7, 2000.

David-West, Toye. "Death of Nigeria's First Lady, Stella Obasanjo: A Lesson for Life and Death." *ThisDay online.* Wednesday, October 26, 2005, 23.

_____. "Our Dollar Pastor$." *This Day.* Online Edition. November 10, 2005, 3.

De Klerk, B.J. "Worship, Prayers and Poverty." *The Ecumenical Review.* Vol.57, No. 3 (2005): 343-357.

Drengson, Alan. "Compassion and Transcendence of Duty and Inclination." *Philosophy Today.* 25(Spring 1981): 39

Editorial. "Nigeria: Yar'Adua on Climate Change." *Daily Champion,* 9 October (2007).

Ekeke, Kingston C. Rev. "Nigeria still Crawling at 45: The Urgency for

National Core Values." *Nigeria News.* October 2005, 4-6. http://www.nigerianews.com.

Ekwunife, Anthony. "The Image of the Priest in Contemporary Africa: The Nigerian Connection." in *The Clergy in Nigeria Today.* (1994): 21-32.

Elliot, Larry. "A Cure that is Worse than the Disease." *Guardian Weekly.* Jan. 24-30 2002, 14.

"Facts on Climate in Nigeria." by the editors, Nigeria Climate Change. www.nestinteractive.org/climate_change_docs/factsheet2.pdf.

Falt, Eric. *UNEP 2005 Annual Report.* UNEP, (2006): 7-21.

Federman, Joel. "The Politics of Universal Compassion." *The Search for Common Value.* http://www.topia.net/common_understanding.html

Ferguson, Wayne. "Beyond the Problem of Evil." (2005): 1-14 http://ccat.sas.upenn.edu/jod/augustine/ferg.htm.

Francis, Michael Kpakala. "The Church in Africa Today." African Faith and Justice. *The African Synod: Documents, Reflections and Perspectives.* Maryknoll, New York: Orbis Books, 1996.

French, William. "Greening Gaudium et Spes." William Madges. Ed. *Vatican II: Forty Years Later.* Maryknoll, Orbis Books, 2006. 196-207.

Gaillardetz, Richard R. "The Ecclesiological Foundations of Modern Catholic Social Teaching." Kenneth R. Himes. Ed. *Modern Catholic Social Teaching: Commentaries and Interpretations.* Washington D.C.: Georgetown University Press, 2005. 72-98.

Garba, Chris. "12 Million Nigerian Children out of School, says

Report." *Nigerian Guardian Newspaper.* Wed. Oct. 27, 2004, 4-6.

Goetz, Jennifer. "Annotated Bibliography." *Peace Center.* (2005) http://peacecenter.berkley.edu/research_compassion.html.

Gutenson, Chuck. "In the light of Katrina, What would God Expect us to do? *Sojourners.* (2005): 15.http://www.sojo.net/index.cfm?action=sojomail.display&issue=050.

Haruna, Godwin. "Nigeria: Climate Change – Looming Disaster Waiting to Occur." September 24 (2007).

Hay, Charles J. "The Bible and the Outsider." *Kairos: Canadian Ecumenical Justice Initiatives.* (September 1996): 1-10. http://Kairoscanada.or/e/refugees/reflection/bible/outsider.

Hehir, Bryan J. Rev. "Leadership and Hope in a Time of Crisis and Conflict." Sept. 6 2002. http://www.catholicchartiesusa.org/news/opinion/content_display.cfm?fuseaction=display_document&210location=16

Himes, Michael J. "The Church and the World in Conversation: The City of God and 'Interurban' Dialogue." *New Theology Review.* Vol. 18, No. 1 (Feb. 2005): 27-35.

Houreld, Katherine. "269 Dead after Nigerian Pipeline Explodes while Scavengers were Collecting Fuel." *Toronto Star.* Wednesday, December 27, 2006, A7.

Hug, Jim. "Catholic Social Teaching and Trade." *Center Focus.* (Nov. 1999): 4-23.

International Confederation of Free Trade Unions. "Labor Standards Remain Poor in Nigeria." *Afrol News.* Nov. 12, 2006, 1-3.

Jong, Albert J. ed. "Ethnicity: Blessing or Curse." *Tangaza Occasional Prayer,* No. 8. (1999):29

Keenan, James, S.J. "Suffering and the Christian Tradition." *The Journal of Humanities in Medicine.* (2003): 25-30. http://info.med.yale.edu/intmed/jjhm/spirit2003/suffering/jkeenan.1.htm.

Kishida, Ritsuya. Extinction is Forever." *Our Planet.* Vol. 16, No. 2 (2005): 32.

Kurfi, Edwin. "Oil Giant Shell has Brought Nigeria Nothing but Suffering." *Socialist Worker online.* Feb. 12, 2005, 19.

Mbaefo, Luke. "The Church Bishop Shanahan Left Behind." *The Nigerian Journal of Theology.* Vol. 8, No. 1, (1994): 34.

McCormick, Richard, A. SJ. "The Social Responsibility of the Christian." *Blueprint for Social Justice.* Vol. LII, No. 3 (Nov. 1998): 1-7.

McMaster, Johnston. "Towards a Theology of Pastoral Healing." *The Methodist Church in Ireland Council for Social Responsibility.* www.irishmethodist.org/serve/csr/documents/TowardsaTheologyofSufferingandPastoralHealing2.doc.

Mveng, Engelbert. "Third World Theology – What Theology? What Third World?: Evaluation by an African Delegate." Virginia Febella, and S. Torres, Eds. *Irruption of Third World: Challenge to Theology.* Maryknoll, New York: Orbis, 1983.

Ndujihe, Clifford. "April Polls Already Rigged, says Nwabueze." *The Guardian.* Thursday, March 15, 2006, 8.

Newell, Kara and Dueck, Judith, "Responses." *Conrad Grebel Reviews.* Vol. 13, No. 3 (1995): 233-241.

Netter, Thomas. Ed. "Forced Labor Today." *World of Work.* No. 54 (August, 2005): 4-11.

Nnamani, Amaluche Greg. "The Dialectics of Poverty and Oppression – from an African and Theological Perspective. *Bulletin of Ecumenical Theology.* Vol. 12 (2000): 10-15.

Nussbaum, Martha. "Compassion: The Basic Social Emotion." *Social Philosophy and Policy.* Vol.13 (1996): 27-58.

Nweke, Nkechi. "Open Letter to the Nigerian President." *Youth Action Net: Connecting Youths to Create Change.* (June 2005): 1. http://YouthActionNet.org/resources/essaycontest/employability/nkechi.cfm.

"Obasanjo Cautions African Leaders Against Greed, Injustice." *The Guardian.* Tuesday, October 10, 2006, 4.

Obasanjo, Olusegun. "Time to reject Pseudo Leaders." *Nigerian Guardian.* Online edition. Sunday, October 1st 2006, 15.

Obiezu, Emeka Xris OSA. "Gone in Body, not in Spirit." *The Catholic Register.* Week of April 16, 2006, 27.

Okali, David. Nigeria Environmental Study Action Team (NEST), "Nigeria." Tariq BAnuri, Adil Najam and Nancy Odeh, eds., *Civic Entrepreneurship: A Civil Society Perspective on Sustainable Development,* vol. II: Africa. A UNEP-sponsored project. Islamabad, Pakistan: Gandhara Academy Press, 2002. 198-250.

Okolo, Barnabas Chukwudum. "Liberation Theology: The Nigerian Connections." *Religion and African Culture.* (1988): 180-190.

Okumu, Victor, "A Christo-Pastoral Response to Suffering and Evil in Africa: Aylward Shorter's 'Jesus and the Witch Doctor.'" *African Christian Studies.* Vol. 21, No.2 (2005): 5-46.

Oloja, Martins. "Nigeria's Population now 140 Million," *The Guardian.*

Saturday, December 30, 2006, 1.

Oronto, Douglas. "Shell in Nigeria." *Naija Community.* (2006): 7.

Overberg, Kenneth. "The Mystery of Suffering: How Should I Suffer?" *American Catholic Newsletter.* http://americancatholic.org/Newsletters/CU/ac0702.asp.

Patners: Interfaith perspectives on the Environment. A Greenfaith's Quarterly Newsletter. summer (2007):1-4.

Peters, Rebecca Todd. "The Future of Globalization: Seeking Pathways of Transformation." *Journal of the Society of Christian Ethics.* Vol. 24, No. 1 (2004): 105-133.

Pope, Stephen J. "Natural Law in Catholic Social Teaching." Kenneth R. Himes. Ed. *Modern Catholic Social Teaching: Commentaries and Interpretations.* 41- 71.

Puntel, Lourencino. "Participation." *Encyclopedia of Theology.* New York: Seabury,1975.

Radcliffe, Dana. "Compassion and Commanded Love," *Faith and Philosophy.* Vol. 11, No. 2 (April 1988): 50-71.

Smith, Steven R. "Keeping Our Distance in Compassion-Based Social Relations," *Journal of Moral Philosophy.* Vol. 2, No. 1 (2005): 69-87.

Star Wire Service, "655,000 Iraqi Deaths: Study," *Toronto Star,* Thursday, October 12, 2006, A7.

Stoeber, Michael. "Book Review." of Davies. Oliver, *A Theology of Compassion: Metaphysics of Difference and the Renewal of Tradition. Toronto Journal of Theology.* Vol. 22, No. 1 (2006).

Swan, Michael. "Morality should trump politics on climate change." *The*

Catholic Register. online edition. http://www.catholicregister.org/content/view/1331/856/.

Tarimo, Aquiline. He Relationship Between African Economic Crisis, Cultural Traditions, and Religion," *African Christian Studies.* Vol. 19, No. 4(2003): 55-70.

Wiesel, Elie. "A Prayer for the Days of Awe." *New York Times.* October 2, 1997, 14.

Wolterstorff, Nicholas. "Liturgy, Justice and Holiness." *The Reformed Journal.* (December 1989): 12-20.

Others references

Annan, Kofi. "Eradication of Poverty and other Development Issues: Implementation of the First United Nations Decade for the Eradication of Poverty (1997-2006) Observance of the International Day for the Eradication." Delivered at the United Nations 61 General Assembly, 5, September 2006, 1-20.

Best, Steven. "Compassion and Action." http://drstevebest.org/Lectures/CompassionAndactions.php.

Brandt, Deborah. "Naming the Moment: Political Analysis for Action." Toronto: Jesuit Centre, 1989.

Hurley, Elisa A. and Matthew, Burstein. "Blunted Affect: The Flattening of Emotion in Nussbaum's Upheavals of Thought." 1-13. http://philosophy.georgetown.edu/news_events/grad_papers/HurleyBurstein10.7.doc.

Leddy, Mary Jo. "On Naming the Present," Address to Colloquium on North American Context Theology." San Antonio, Texas: Oblate School of Theology. October 2002.

Lowi, Miriam S. "A Politics of Compassion as the Humanistic Response to the Crisis." prepared for the Forum on the Sept. 11 Crisis.

Lynn, Elizabeth and Wisely, Susan. "Toward a Fourth Philanthropic Response: American Philanthropy and its Public."

McElroy, Wendy. "Victims versus Victimhood." Oct. 11 2005.

Ogbonnaya, Joseph. *The Contemporary Nigerian Church and the Search for Social Justice in Nigeria.* TST, ThM Thesis. Toronto: University of St. Michael, 2005.

Philpot, Catherine. <u>Intergroup *Apologies and Forgiveness.*</u> Unpublished PhD Thesis. Brisbane, Australia: University of Queensland, 2006.

Ryan, Bill SJ. "Some Notes on the Development of Catholic social teaching." October, 1999.

Szura, John. "Theological Interpretation of the new Augustinian Venture at the United Nations." Workshop on Justice and Peace and OSA UN/NGO in Augustinian Formation. Racine: September 18th-22nd, 2006.

INDEX

A

Abacha, Sani 50, 62, 71, 73
Abati, Ruben 146, 183
Abubakar, Abdusalam 63
Abubakar, Atiku 61
Achebe, Chinua 63, 151, 172
Adaka, Isaac 50
Adebowale, Akande 54, 145, 148, 149, 153
Advocacy x
Al-Khalifa, Rashed Haya 55
Amina, Alhaja 66
Anamnesia 119
Androcentrism 95
Annan, Kofi 191
Anthropological poverty 8, 132, 163
Apartheid 72, 123
Apathy: political apathy 15
Arrogant superiority 99, 100, 163
Articulated Christianity 76
Association for Better Nigeria (ABN) xv, 63
Ayittey, B. N 62, 147, 151, 172
a Kempis, Thomas 75

B

Balasuriya, Tissa 8, 59, 132, 149
Barth, Fredrick 64, 152, 172
Baum, Gregory 73, 93, 111, 116, 153, 154, 157, 160, 165, 166, 168, 172, 184
Bennett, John 6, 130, 173
Best, Stephen xx, 103
Boff, Leonardo 89, 173
Bonhoeffer, Dietrich 108, 173
Borg, Marcus xxi, 33, 95, 127, 137, 141, 157, 161, 173
Brackley, Dean 6, 30, 69, 92, 94, 111, 117, 124, 130, 139, 153, 160, 166, 167, 170

C

Callousness 99, 100, 163
Cannon, G. Katie 110, 166
Cassidy, Richard 33, 35, 141, 158, 174
Catholic Bishops Conference of Nigeria (CBCN) xv, 76, 111
Catholic Charismatic Renewal Movement (CCRM) xv, 73
Catholic social teaching 29, 97, 98, 131, 192
Charity, private charity 22, 23, 84, 85, 124
Chazan, Naomi 64, 152, 174
Chesterton, G. K. 40, 174
Chua, Amy 61, 130, 150, 174
Clericalism 77
Cobbles, James F. 96, 161, 174
Commission (EFCC) ix, xiv, xv, xvi, 47, 73, 74, 146
Committed action 86, 87, 88
Common good 2, 7, 41, 97, 98
Communal prayer xxiv, 117, 118
Compassion: compassionate, biblical compassion, critics of compassion viii, xx, xxi, xxii, xxiv, 11, 18, 19, 22, 24, 25, 27, 28, 30, 31, 32, 33, 34, 35, , 37, 106, 120, 124, 103, 140, 143, 169, xi, 140, 41, 84, 85, 86, 93, 95, 98, 102
Cone, James 79, 174
Conformism 111
Conscientization 88, 90, 91, 92, 94
Contemporary samaritanism 110
Conversion 6, 9, 37, 107, 109, 111, 112, 116, 117,
Corruption ix, xv, 19, 58, 60, 61, 62, 63, 80, 111, 116, 155
Cum patior 20

D

Dariye, Joshua 63
David-West, Toyin 78, 156
Deane, Herbert A. 76, 155, 164
Deforestation 6, 54, 55, 56, 99, 100
Democracy 49, 61, 130, 174
Department of Program and Information/Non-Governmental Organizations(DPI/NGO) xv, 129, 169, 171
Deuteronomic theology 15
de Gruchy, W. 117, 141, 161, 168, 177
Dialogue x, xxii, 13, 94, 106, 110, 168
Dokubo-Asari, Mujahid Alhaji 51
Dominance 8, 60, 77, 111
Drengson, Alan 21, 137, 185
Due good 2

E

Ecclesia in Africa 114, 167
Ecology: ecological destruction x
Economic and Financial Crimes xv, 146
Egalitarian praxis 95
Ehusani, George 59, 73, 150, 154, 175
Eleos 21
Elitism 95
Emotion, emotionalism 22, 136, 143, 178, 189, 191
Empathy 20, 24, 31, 42
Employment, unemployment 8, 47, 50, 59, 65, 71, 131, 145
Empowerment Development Strategy xvi, 150
Environmental destruction, distortion, devastation x, xix, xxi, 2, 3, 8, 13, 45, 46, 51, 52, 54, 57, 59, 101, 121, 124
Ethics xi, 42, 83, 121
Ethnic, ethnicism, ethnicity 52, 64, 65, 66, 116, 130, 150, 152, 163, 172, 174, 188
Evangelii Nutiandi – (Evangelization in the modern world) xv
Evil: structural, natural, moral 1
Explicit or tacit agreement 97

F

Fast-Track Initiative (FTI) 150
Favoritism 116
Fellowship for Christian Social Order xv
Fields, Leslie 55
Fitzgerald, Valpy 6, 9, 131, 152
Forgiveness, Fox, Matthew viii, xxii, xxiv, 19, 20, 87, 93, 117, 120, 121, 122, 136, 158, 169, 171, 179, 192

G

Gaillardetz, Richard R 113, 167
Gaillardetz, Richard R. 186
Gandhi 88, 158
Gaudiium et Spes xv
Gilkey, Langdon 129, 176
Giwa, Dele 93
Gladden, Washington 26, 138
Globalization 128, 131, 132, 145, 149, 150, 174, 190
Global economy 64
Good Samaritan 28, 31, 35, 38, 140
(GASHRUD) Grassroots Action for Sustainable Health and Rural Development (GS) xv, 54
(GDP) Gross Domestic Product xv, 58
Gustafson, James 89, 159
Gutenson, Chuck 87, 158
Gutierrez, Gustavo 80, 110, 157, 164, 166, 176

H

Hall, Douglas John 119, 134
Hausa-fulani 64

Hesed 21
Hick, John 2, 12, 129, 176
Himes, Kenneth 27, 135, 139, 161, 176, 177
Himes, Michael 110, 139, 161, 164, 165, 166, 177, 187
Holy, holiness xxii, 22, 27, 33, 34, 96, 113, 119, 137, 139, 141, 156, 169, 181, 191
Humanization 90
(HDR) Human Development Report xv, 5, 130
(HIV/AIDS) Human Immunodeficiency xvi

I

Igboland 73
Ijaw, Ijawland, Ijaw people 49, 50, 51, 59
Ikenga-Metuh, Emefie 100, 108, 162, 165, 177
Imitatio deis 33
Immanuel 28, 30
Immunodeficiency Syndrome Hypocrisy xvi
Inclusive community xxiii, 86, 95, 112
Indirect rule, divide and rule 60
Individual, Individuality, individualism x, xix, xx, 6, 12, 23, 29, 32, 33, 39, 41, 42, 58, 69, 74, 76, 77, 85, 87, 90, 97, 98, 103, 107, 109, 110, 112, 116, 128, 131, 138
Injustice: structural injustice, 36
Institutions xix, 6, 7, 33, 37, 42, 48, 58, 64, 65, 66, 67, 69, 73, 80, 84, 92, 98, 116
(ICFTU) International Confederation of Free Trade Unions xvi, 52, 148, 187
(ILO) International Labor Organization xvi, 47, 131
(IMF) International Monetary Fund xvi, 9

Interpersonal: Inter-personalism 25
Interrelatedness 102
Intrinsic and instrumental value 3, 21, 41, 77, 106

J

Jangedi, Mallam 66
John Paul II 1, 31, 100, 114, 127, 128, 129, 130, 139, 140, 159, 162, 167, 171, 180
Juridicism 112
(JDPC) Justice, Peace and Development Commission xvi
Justice: distributive justice, social justice, justice-making,
Justice and Peace Commission x, xi, xiv, xvi, xix, xxii, xxiii, 6, 11, 13, 15, 17, 21, 22, 26, 27, 29, 34, 37, 38, 42, 49, 50, 69, 71, 72, 73, 76, 80, 83, 84, 85, 86, 87, 91, 92, 94, 98, 101, 102, 104, 107, 110, 111, 112, 113, 115, 117, 119, 120, 122, 124, 125, 139, 163, 169
Justice and Peace Commission xiv
(JM) Justitia in Mundo – Justice in the xvi

K

kaiama declaration 50
Kairos, crisis 51, 65, 123
Katrina hurricane 4
Kishida, Ritsuya 105, 164, 188
Kuka, Hasan 145
Kung, Hans 112, 167, 177

L

Leddy, Mary Jo 88, 158, 159, 166, 178, 191
Liberation: liberator 110
Liderbach, Daniel 9, 132, 178
Liturgicism 112
Lived Christianity 76

Luxembourg, Rosa 92, 160

M

Macmurray, John xxii, 21, 32, 40, 97, 116, 127, 136, 140, 143, 161, 162, 168, 174, 178
Majoritarianism 113
Marginalized xix, xxi, 33, 37, 73, 78, 112, 118, 122
Marty, Martin 96, 161
Masochism 25, 75
Masterson, Reginald 2, 128
Mattson, A.D. 178
Mbaefo, Luke 53, 67, 148, 153, 154, 188
McAfee, Richard 130
McCormick, Richard 26, 76, 110, 154, 155, 166, 188
McElroy, Wendy 87, 158, 192
Mercy 20, 21, 24, 27, 30, 32, 60, 69, 72, 89, 110, 139
Metz, John Baptist 118
Misericodia 137
Misogyny 3, 36, 66
Mispat 21
Morality: private, social 143, 164, 173, 190
(MOSOP) Movement for the Survival of the Ogoni People xvi, 50
Multinational corporations 8, 58, 59, 61
Multmann, Jurgen 108
Myers, Ched 179
Mystical 136, 158, 176
Mystical body of Christ 105

N

(NEEDS) National Economic xvi, 150
(NGO) Non-governmental Organization Nouwen, Henry xvi
(NPC) National Population Commission Newell, Kara xvi, 146

Ndujihe, Clifford 61, 151, 188
Nelson-Pallmeyer, Jack Niger Delta 140
Nicholas, Wolterstorff 34, 141, 169
Nigeria: Nigerian(s), Nigerian Churches, Nigerian Christian, Nigerian situation, Nigerian context xi, xxiii, 45, 73, 113
Nigeria: Nigerian(s), Nigerian Churches, Nigerian Christian, Nigerian situation, Nigeria context x, xxi, 42, 43, 57, 58, 67, 70, 73, 76, 83, 96, 101, 104, 107, 116, 122
(NLC) Nigerian Labor Congress xvi
Niger Delta xvi, 49, 50, 51, 54, 55, 59, 63
(NDVF) Niger Delta Volunteer Force xvi, 50
Nnimmo, Bassey 56, 149
Nussbaum, Martha 40, 136, 143, 189
Nwabueze, Ben 61
Nzeribe, Arthur 63

O

Obasanjo, Olusegun 51, 146, 189
Odey, John 61, 146, 147, 151, 180
Odi military massacre 49, 51
Okadigbo, Chuba 63
Omnibenevolence 14
Omnibenevolent 14
Omnipotence 14
Onayikan, John 92
Oppression: oppressed, oppress, oppressor ix, x, xix, xxi, xxii, 15, 33, 36, 37, 57, 62, 72, 76, 80, 87, 91, 112, 120, 121, 122, 124, 141
(OPEC) Organization of the Petroleum Exporting Countries xvi
Orthodoxy 14, 163
Osu 65, 66, 73, 152

P

Pain: emotional and physical xix
Palliative measures xx
Paradigm: new paradigm, social paradigm, Christ's paradigm, paradigm shift xi, xxi, xxii, xxiii, 26, 33, 34, 38, 73, 83, 84, 85, 87, 95, 97, 107, 110, 113, 124, 142
Participation: Christian participation in the political process and economy x
Partner, partnership xxiv, 96, 97
Paternalism 77
Pathological 13
Patriarchy 35, 36, 77, 95
Paul VI xxi, 74, 127, 154, 172
Philanthropism, philanthropy 127, 159, 192
Pietas 20
Plaskow, Judith 36, 142, 180
Pluralism 111
Political action xi, xix, 22, 23, 39, 83, 107, 117
Politics of Compassion 84, 85, 107, 117, 140, 179, 191, , iii, vii, viii
Poor, option for the poor xxiii, 86, 88, 89, 95, 105, 157,
Pope, J. Stephen 98, 162
(PRS) Poverty Reduction Strategy Profit, Jim xvi, 150
Poverty, material, evangelical and voluntary xxii, 3, 5, 8, 14, 22, 23, 25, 29, 32, 46, 48, 54, 55, 65, 70, 73, 77, 78, 84, 85, 95, 102, 109, 112, 116, 122, 124, 132, 138, 145, 147, 151, 156, 163
Psychic numbing 15
Public church 96
Pui-lan, Kwok 67, 153

R

Racism 3
Radical Christianity 109
Rahamim 137

Rahner, Karl 103, 163, 164, 168, 179, 180
Rationality 40, 42
Reconciliation xxii, 93, 121, 169
Renuminization 103
Response: Christian responses to suffering , iii
Ritualism 112
Road block 49
Roberts, Robert C. 40
Robot, robotization 131
Rolheiser, Ronald 83, 84, 116, 137, 157, 181

S

Sacramentalism 112
Saro-Wiwa, Ken Beeson 50
Scheler, Max 12, 133, 181
Schillbeeckx, Edward 17, 135
Secrecy 93
Self-aggrandizement 110
Self-centeredness, 112
Self-consciousness 110
Self-preoccupation, 112
Self-preservation 112
Self-sufficiency 124
Sentient beings, non-sentient life xix, 3
Sentiment: sentimental, sentimentality, sentimentalism xx, 16, 20, 21, 22, 27, 33, 40, 84, 121, 139
Sexism 36, 77, 97
Shar'ia 66
Signs of time 94
Sin: sinfulness, sinlessness xx, xxi, 5, 6, 9, 14, 17, 30, 46, 58, 68, 69, 75, 76, 77, 86, 92, 95, 107, 109, 110, 135
Smit, Dirkie 119, 141, 161, 168
Sobrino, Jon 29, 139, 182
Socially dormant conscience 24
Socio-political, socio-moral, socio-economic viii, ix, x, xi, xxii, xxiii, 9, 19, 23, 24, 26, 29, 32, 33, 35, 37, 39, 40, 43, 70, 73,

45, 38, 39, 75, 124, 77, 87, 95, 131, 76, 83, viii, 84, 87, 90, 105, 106, 107, 84, 114, 115, 120, 122, 161, 107, , 75

Solidarity, solidarity with the poor, solidarity with the earth viii, x, xxii, xxiii, 1, 5, 12, 16, 18, 20, 29, 30, 38, 43, 70, 74, 86, 87, 88, 90, 92, 97, 98, 99, 100, 102, 103, 104, 105, 109, 111, 112, 118, 140, 157, 163

Spiritual: spirituality xi, xxiii, 16, 17, 42, 68, 75, 76, 77, , 80, 83, 100, 101, 102, 108, 111, 117, 122, 124, 155

Status quo xxi, 68, 73, 87, 124, 157

Stoeber, Michael xiv, 2, 127, 128, 129, 144, 162, 182, 190

(SAPs) Structural Adjustment Programs xvi, 9

Subjugation 35, 67, 68, 115

Subordinate, subordination 7, 21, 68, 77, 115, 142

Subsidarity, subsidium 97

Suffering: destructive, transformative, redemptive, suffering humanity, ecological suffering, suffering God vii, ix, x, xi, xix, xx, xxi, xxii, xxiii, 1, 2, 3, 4, 7, 9, 10, 11, 12, 13, 14, 15, 16, 17, 18, 19, 20, 22, 23, 24, 25, 26, 27, 28, 30, 31, 38, 41, 43, 45, 46, 47, 48, 54, 57, 58, 59, 60, 62, 64, 65, 70, 74, 75, 76, 79, 80, 84, 86, 87, 88, 92, 93, 95, 104, 105, 106, 107, 109, 110, 118, 121, 122, 124, 128, 129, 132, 133, 134, 135, 139, 140, 143, 154, 158, 182, 188

Syndrome or Acquired xvi

T

Taylor, Charles 40, 143, 182

Theodicy: theoretical, classical vii, 4, 13, 14, 15, 18, 134, x, xxi, xxii, xxiii, 13, 14, 15, 18, 38, 43, 134

Theological geography Trans-species 25, 37, 103

Therapeutic individualism 98

Thiong'o, Ngugi Wa 92, 160

Transformation: socially transformative way, social transformation Tribalism xix, xxi, 10, 11, 13, 30, 37, 38, 60, 65, 77, 85, 91, 97, 114, 116, 117, 118, 124, 134

(TNCs) Transnational Corporations that make up the WTO xvii

U

Uchem, Rose 67, 68, 153, 183

Uchendu, P.K. 67, 153

Umuada 68

(UN/ISDR) United Nations' International Strategy for Disaster Reduction Organization xvii

(UNEP) United Nations Environmental Program xvii

(UNFCCC) United Nations Framework Convention on Climate Change xvii

Unjust social structure, unjust system, xxi

Urso, Ida 123, 170

US-based 49, 147

V

Vacek, Edward 40, 88, 89, 137, 143, 183

Via negativa 20

Victim, victimization, victimizer, victimhood xx, 5, 11, 13, 15, 16, 19, 49, 54, 120, 121, 131, 140, 158, 192

Virus/Acquired Immune Deficiencycy xvi

Vita Christiana 108

Vocation x, xx, 17, 23, 43, 80, 105, 115, 142

Volf, Miroslav 92, 160

W

(WB) World Bank xv, xvii, 9, 47, 146
Wei-chi 123
William, Daniel Day 89, 159, 183
Womb, wombish 21, 22, 137
World xv, xvi, xvii, 7, 8, 9, 38, 47, 59,
 63, 75, 85, 86, 105, 127, 130,
 131, 132, 142, 145, 146, 149,
 150, 155, 156, 157, 162, 163,
 165, 166, 168, 169, 170, 171,
 172, 173, 174, 175, 176, 181,
 182, 184, 187, 188
(WTC) World Trade Center xvii, 130
(WTO) World Trade Organization
 Yar'dua, Musa xvii, 7

Z

Zaki-Biam blood spill 49

Printed in the United States
123848LV00004B/151-177/P